THE IMPROVEMENT OF THE MIND

THE IMPROVEMENT OF THE MIND

ISAAC WATTS
JOSEPH EMERSON

Published by

Isha Books
B-63, Ist Floor
New Gupta Colony
Near DDA Market
Delhi - 110009

Distribution Network
gyanbooks.com
India, USA, Canada, UK, Australia

ISBN: 978-93-3314-030-0 (HB)

First Published, 1855

2nd Impression 2025

Printed at: Gyan Press, Delhi.

THE IMPROVEMENT OF THE MIND
Author: ISAAC WATTS, JOSEPH EMERSON

THE

IMPROVEMENT OF THE MIND.

BY ISAAC WATTS, D. D.

WITH

CORRECTIONS, QUESTIONS AND SUPPLEMENT.

BY JOSEPH EMERSON,

Principal of the Female Seminary, Wethersfield, Ct.,

Author of the Evangelical Primer, Lectures on the Millennium, &c.

Revised Stereotype Edition.

BOSTON:

PUBLISHED BY JAMES LORING, 132 WASHINGTON ST.

☞ The Editor indulges the belief, that this volume contains all the instructions upon education, of much importance, ever written by the excellent WATTS. The circumstances, under which the original work was composed and published, may account for its numerous inaccuracies. These, however, may be regarded as minute spots upon the face of a glorious luminary. That these should be wiped away, must be the desire of every friend to the great author. This has been attempted by one, who begs to be considered among the most ardent and devoted. The corrections relate principally to grammar, punctuation, orthography and superfluous words.

TO TEACHERS.

Beloved Fellow-Laborers,

Permit me to assure you, that I have found no other human text-book, that appears nearly equal to this treatise of Watts, for interest and utility. Having taught it to sixteen classes, it has appeared brighter and brighter, like the finest gold. May you have occasion to estimate its solid worth still more and more.

To teach in the best manner, you must have your own plan. If in any measure, you adopt that of another, you must approve and use it as wholly your own. It must become, as it were, a part of your very selves, like your daily bread. I shall rejoice, if any of you can derive assistance from the following

HINTS FOR TEACHING WATTS ON THE MIND.

1. Assign for a lesson from 3 to 8 pages.
2. Mention any printed questions, which you would omit.
3. Direct your pupils to read the lesson once, chiefly with a view to understand it.
4. Let them read it again, to judge, whether the sentiments are true; to perceive their connection, and fix in the mind the leading thoughts.
5. They may read it once more, ascertaining and committing to memory the answers to the questions.
6. Fill your own mind and heart with the contents and spirit of the lesson.
7. Ask your pupils the printed questions, keeping a record of their performances.
8. Go over the lesson again, without record, with much lecturing, questioning and plain talk.
9. Make the utmost efforts to impress their minds with the truths and duties inculcated.
10. Encourage them to state with freedom their inquiries and objections.
11. Give them questions to be answered in writing or otherwise, at a future recitation.
12. Let their compositions be upon the subjects of their lessons.
13. Let every 5th or 6th lesson be a review of the preceding 4 or 5, the pupils first reciting to each other, with mutual certificates, to be recorded.

Form of Certificate. Miss A—B— has promptly and correctly recited to me — answers, in the last review.

[Date] C——D.

14. Let them review the whole, and be faithfully examined at the close of each quarter.
15. Inquire from time to time, their manner of studying.
16. After two or three years, let them go through the course again, inquiring particularly, how far they have practised the directions of Watts, and with what advantage.

J. E.

EDITOR'S

INTRODUCTION.

1. *Popularity of Watts on the Mind.* Probably no other work, upon the same subject, has been so highly and so justly approved, as this little treatise of Watts—no other, upon which the hours of the reader and student have been so pleasantly and so usefully employed. And of all literary subjects, this seems to be the most important.

2. *Object of this work.* The grand object, which the author keeps continually in view, and continually presses upon the reader's attention, is to improve and enrich the mind; "to teach the young idea how to shoot;" to unfold and invigorate the faculties; to store the mind with the most useful knowledge; to nip the buds of prejudice; to counteract its poison; to stay the tide of passion; to emancipate the mind enthralled; to expand, to elevate and liberalize the views; to form the habits; to subject every power, thought and pursuit, to the empire of reason; to subordinate all to the service of God—in short, to prepare the mortal and immortal part of our nature, for the greatest possible usefulness and enjoyment both here and forever.

3. *Usefulness of this work.* Of all human compositions, then, this is probably the most useful for the young, as soon as they can understand it. Such a conclusion might be warranted, though we considered merely its immediate effect upon the

---

Grand object of Watts of this treatise? What would he unfold and invigorate?

With what would he store the mind?

What poison would he counteract?

What would he subject to the empire of reason?

To whose service, should every thing be subordinate?

For what, would he prepare the whole of our nature?

What human composition seems to be most useful to the young?

How early should they attend to it?

mind. Much more must it appear just, when we consider, that the chief advantages of an acquaintance with this work, arise from its more remote influence. It lays a foundation to pursue every other study, and to employ every other means of knowledge and improvement, in the best manner.

The unhesitating voice, of every examiner, seems to have been, "The work is excellent." It is, doubtless, the most approved and admired, of all the prose works of the great, the good, the candid, the liberal, the useful man, whose name it bears. It is not the growth of a day; but the worthy product of twenty years—a product, from the choicest seed, in the richest soil, with the finest culture, beneath the most genial suns, and refreshing showers.

4. *Johnson's Encomium.* "Few books," says Dr. Johnson, in his Life of Watts, "have been perused by me, with greater pleasure, than his Improvement of the Mind; of which the radical principles may indeed be found in Locke's Conduct of the Understanding; but they are so ramified by Watts, as to confer on him, the merit of a work, in the highest degree useful and pleasing. Whoever has the care of instructing others, may be charged with deficiency in his duty, if this book is not recommended."

5. *This work, considered as a Logic.* Considered as a treatise of Logic, it is probably superior to any work, bearing the name—better suited to answer the great and noble end of logic. The author, indeed, seems to have regarded this work as some thing very much like a logic. Having some years before, published a treatise of logic, that had been well received, he thought "the learned world might possibly admit this as a second part or supplement to that treatise."

But though the author considers it scarcely worthy to be called a treatise, yet to me, it appears greatly superior to the elder work, and in point of merit, much better entitled to be considered the first or principal part. There is another reason, why it should be considered the first part, at least, in the order of time, or in the arrangement of studies. It is much more easily understood.

If, as it is generally and most justly acknowledged, logic is the art of investigating and communicating truth this little work, which the author was willing should pass for a mere Supplement, is perhaps better entitled to be called A Logic, than any other, that has yet appeared. Surely no other human

---

For what, does an acquaintance with this work lay a foundation?
What is the most approved of all the prose works of Watts?
What great critic has given a high encomium of this work?
Meaning of *encomium*?
Character of this work, considered as a treatise of logic?
What is logic?

production is suited to afford such a clear, steady, safe, brilliant light, to direct, animate, and encourage us, in the path of knowledge. Its unrivalled simplicity and perspicuity of style, notwithstanding some minor faults, its lively and touching illustrations, its plain, sound and useful maxims and precepts, can hardly fail to recommend it to the understanding and heart of every lover of truth.

6. *Its Grand Characteristic.* Its grand characteristic is, that it is so practical. While it is far enough from being an assemblage of dry maxims, a mere compend of dogmas—while the author most fully, clearly, and delightfully states his reasons, he is continually informing us, how to think, how to feel, how to converse, how to act, in order to grow wiser and better—"and better thence again, and better still, in infinite progression."

7. *It most happily combines theory and practice.* Probably in no other work of man, are excellent theory, practical direction and illustration more happily combined. We are addressed, as being at once capable of the most noble speculation, and the most useful practice; and each of these is made to reflect the most brilliant lustre, from the effulgence of the other. Perhaps it is not venturing too much to say, that probably this little volume contains a greater number and weight of useful directions, to aid us in the most important business of life, than are to be found in all the great works of Locke, Reid, Stewart and Brown.

8. *Should be faithfully studied.* A work, so enriched with instructions—instructions, so excellent, so momentous—instructions, which are continually needful, to regulate our conduct, and rouse our energies—instructions, that should be most familiarly fixed in the mind, and seem to make a part of our very identity—a work, replete with such instructions should be *studied; faithfully and laboriously studied.* One or two hasty, or even thorough perusals of such a work, are by no means sufficient.

9. *Yet one reading may be useful.* Not that in such a case, indeed, the time would be lost. One reading, and that a very rapid one, may prove of real utility to a vigorous youth, who pants for improvement. Though he may be able to retain scarcely a maxim or an idea, for a single year, yet his mind receives impressions, that can hardly fail to be salutary. He is induced to form a higher estimate of knowledge and mental improvement, and his heart beats higher and more effectually

---

Grand characteristic of this work? What information is the author continually giving us? What does this work most happily combine?—Meaning of *theory*?

In what manner, should it be studied? Of what, may one reading of this work induce a person to form a higher estimate?

for their attainment. Pride, egotism, prejudice, dogmatism, prating, reviling, &c. are here most powerfully assailed; and though he gains but very faint and obscure views of these evils, yet he sees something of their odious deformities, and receives an impulse, to hate, avoid and shun them; while on the other hand, he gains a glimpse of the beauty and loveliness of candor, docility, meekness, kindness, affability, liberality of feeling, and independence of thought, which urges him to assume and wear these more than earthly ornaments. An impression is thus made upon his feelings and habits, which tends to give a turn to his future pursuits, and to render him greater and better. It must be confessed, however, that in such a case, such happy results, would be very likely to be in a great measure, prevented by untoward circumstances.

There is probably no other book, that will more richly reward the labor of ten or fifteen hours' cursory application. The style is so luminous, the thoughts so weighty, the illustrations so striking, that it seems hardly possible to read a page of it, without some advantage.

10. *Watts a Pellucido.* Perhaps no writer is more like the picture of his own favorite Pellucido, which he has so finely drawn, than Watts himself. "Sometimes," says he, "you will find a person, who in his conversion or his writings, delivers his thoughts in so plain, so easy, so familiar and perspicuous a manner, that you both understand and assent to every thing he says, as fast, as you read or hear it. Hereupon, some have been ready to conclude in haste, "Surely, this man says none but common things. I knew as much before, or, I could have said all this myself." This is a frequent mistake. Pellucido was a very great genius. When he spoke in the senate, he was wont to convey his ideas in so simple and happy a manner, as to instruct and convince every hearer, and to enforce the conviction through the whole illustrious assembly; and that with so much evidence, that you would have been ready to wonder, that every one, who had spoke, had not said the same things. But Pellucido was the only man, that could do it."

11. *Danger from this excellence.* One evil, however, may result from this incomparable excellence of Watts. As we do not give him credit for half the instructions we receive from him, we are not so likely to ponder them, to fix them in our minds, and make special efforts to apply them in practice, as though they were more difficult, and had more of the charm of novelty. Doubtless, many might have derived much more advantage from this work, if it had not appeared so easy and

---

Why is it hardly possible to read a page of it, without advantage?

For what, are we not likely to give the author full credit?

familiar—so much like an old acquaintance and friend. Having read it once or twice through, and perhaps reviewed some parts of it, they seemed to know almost the whole of it, while in fact, their practical acquaintance was almost nothing. They afterwards continued to talk at random, to dispute at random, to read at random, to think at random, &c. very much as they had done before. The admired maxims of Watts were not sufficiently known, to prove of any considerable advantage; at least their utility was almost nothing, compared with what it might have been. Hence it appears exceedingly desirable, that this work should be *studied*, faithfully, laboriously and abundantly studied, and often reviewed and pondered.

12. *The knowledge of this work a great attainment.* To become thoroughly acquainted with this work, to gain a familiar knowledge of all its practical instructions, to apply them continually to the great business of thought, feeling and action, is a task far greater, than any person, at first, can easily imagine. I have been grieved and distressed, to find after the tenth perusal—nay, after teaching its contents more than ten times—after lecturing and conversing much upon the various topics, I have been grieved and distressed, to find how many of its admirable precepts, I had but imperfectly learned, and more imperfectly practised. Yet I cannot but indulge a hope, that this work has been of some advantage to me—that every hour, that I have spent in studying, pondering, teaching or recommending its contents, has conduced to aid me in the regulation of my thoughts, feelings and pursuits—has conduced to render my practice less defective, than it otherwise would have been. Had I regularly and thoroughly studied it in my childhood and youth—had I been cheered and animated, by affectionate and ardent classmates, and aided by a kind, able and faithful teacher, there is no doubt, that the advantage might have been incomparably superior. O that it had been the appointed text book of my youth, instead of the immortal work of Locke.

13. *Should be taught to millions.* It is my heart's desire and prayer to God, that millions of youthful students, of the present, and of future ages, may derive from this work, all the advantages, that I have realized—all that I might have gained, and much more. For such an object, I would gladly do something more, than to wish and pray. Something more than this, I have indeed already done. For fourteen years, it has been my most delightful task, season after season, to instruct a class in Watts. No other literary branch, that I have taught, has been so gratifying to myself, and probably no other so interesting, or so profitable, to successive pupils. Under no other instructions, have I witnessed such manifest improvement of mind.

14. *Different methods of teaching it.* With different classes, I have pursued methods somewhat different, hoping, however, that I have been enabled to make some improvement from year to year, and certainly finding my task more and more delightful. So far from fading—so far from growing old and dry, this tree of intellectual life has appeared more green and more fragrant every year.

15. *Written Questions.* For some years, I have used written questions. Notwithstanding the labor of transcribing, the advantage of these has been manifest. The questions are doubtless much better, than I could suggest extemporaneously. They direct the pupils' attention to the most important points of instruction; and are suited to rouse their attention to a particular consideration of those points. But perhaps the most important advantage is, by asking the same questions over and over, and especially by using them at examinations, forever to rivet the most important ideas in the mind. There is not the least reason to think, that this could be nearly so well effected in any other way. If the whole book were committed to memory verbatim, it is doubtful, whether the knowledge acquired, would be so much, or so permanent. Or if the pupil should learn all the ideas, so as to be able to answer every minute question, he would not be likely to distinguish between the more important and the less important; and would be in danger of much sooner forgetting the whole together.

16. *It is an advantage of fixed questions, that they aid and encourage the pupils to question each other.* It is most deeply to be regretted, that some distinguished teachers are disposed to object to the use of fixed questions, written or printed. Surely their objections will not stand the test of judicious, faithful experiment, and sound philosophy. If questions already extant, are not good, let them make and publish better. The method of using fixed questions, is undoubtedly the greatest improvement, that has been extensively adopted by teachers of the present age. Some extemporaneous questions, however, should be interspered with these, to ensure the pupil's attention to his whole lesson; not that he may become equally acquainted with every minute particular, but that he may have a clear view of the connection, and fully understand the most important parts.

Which questions are likely to be best, written or extemporaneous?

To what, do written questions direct the pupil's attention?

Most important advantage of written questions?

Meaning of *verbatim*?

What if the pupil commits to memory every idea, even the most minute?

What is probably the greatest improvement, that has recently been adopted in teaching?

Why should extemporaneous questions be interspersed?

17. *Printed Questions.* Though some special advantages may result from using questions in manuscript, and from the pupil's transcribing them, it seems much better, on the whole, that they should be printed. (It saves the great labor of transcribing.) This is more especially the case, when important additional questions, with answers, are thrown in among them. Such are a great number of the following questions; at least, it is hoped, that they will be found valuable. These, with the answers, are to be considered a part of the Supplement.

18. *A Supplement to this work desirable.* It seems peculiarly desirable, that this supplement, in a concise and cheap form, should be added to this work of Watts. The whole work of Watts on the Improvement of the Mind, may be considered, as consisting of three parts. But the volume, bearing this title, so extensively circulated, and so much admired, contains only the first of these parts. This first part is longer, and unquestionably very much better, than the other two. Some parts of these two, however, are much more valuable, than some parts of the first, and may well constitute a part of the Supplement. Still more important parts may be drawn from his Logic. And here it is important to be considered, that the author seems to take it for granted, that those, who attend to his work on the Improvement of the Mind, are already acquainted with his Logic. In consequence of this, no doubt, the former work is considerably different, from what it otherwise would have been. It seems, then, of peculiar importance, that some parts, at least, some ideas, should be taken from the Logic, to supply intentional omissions in the other work. Such supplement is here attempted.

19. *Definition-Questions.* It is earnestly desired, that no one may be displeased with the questions, requiring definitions for answers. In proportion to the ground they occupy, these may be found the most useful of all the questions.

20. *Importance of defining words.* There is, probably, no other branch of literary education of equal importance, that is so neglected, or imperfectly taught, as defining—no other, that has now such demands upon the attention of teachers. It is often astonishing and grievous to see, how grossly ignorant are children and youth, and even men and women, of the meaning of important words and phrases—an ignorance, which in general, they are very far from feeling or mistrusting. (They cannot express their thoughts, for the want of words; and often they express thoughts, very different from what they intend, because they do not understand the words they employ.) And

---

Advantage of having the questions printed, rather than in manuscript?

Why are many unable to express their thoughts?

Why do many express thoughts

very frequently from the same cause, they take no idea, or wrong ideas, from what they read and hear. Probably, more than three fourths of the disputes, that have troubled the world, have arisen from the ignorance or misapprehension of words. No doubt, one of the greatest reasons, why so little good is effected by preaching, is, that the language of the preacher is but very imperfectly understood by most of the hearers. Said a venerable and pious lady to her little grandchild, just recovering from sickness, "Now, you must be thankful." But the poor little child did not know — could not guess, the meaning of *thankful*; and was afraid to ask. So her excellent instruction was lost upon the child, at least for years, till he ascertained the meaning of the word. So it is, no doubt, with a great part of the instructions, that parents and teachers, as well as ministers, give to those under their care.

A remedy for these various and abounding evils, is devoutly to be wished and sought. What is it? Proper attention to the exercise of defining, is doubtless one of the remedies, and perhaps the best of all. And it would be easy to show, that all other methods must be ineffectual to gain an accurate knowledge of words, at least of many words, without this.

But the exercise of defining, may not only prevent much evil, but effect much positive good. When properly attended to, it is one of the best of exercises for improving at once the memory and the judgement, and storing the mind with useful knowledge. And when a good acquaintance with language, I mean the vernacular language, is once acquired, this knowledge is one of the best aids, ever devised by human ingenuity, to assist the reasoning faculty in the search of truth. We make much use of words in thinking, especially in close thinking; and it is perhaps impossible to pursue a train of thought, to any considerable length, without their aid. But how often do we impose upon ourselves, and draw wrong conclusions, by imperfectly understanding the words, we silently and perhaps insensibly use, or by using them in different senses. And how often do we think in words, of which we have no definite understanding, flattering ourselves, that we are nobly investigating thoughts and things, while in reality, we are only making progress in pride and darkness. As words are only the signs of thoughts and things and the relations of things, so it is very important, in order to improve our acquaintance with thoughts, things and relations, that we should have a very clear and correct knowledge of the meanings of words, or the ob-

---

different from what they intend?

What has caused a great part of the disputes, that have troubled the world?

What reason is mentioned, why so little good is done by preaching?

What is mentioned as one of the best remedies for ignorance of words?

jects, which they represent. This cannot be gained by attending to the manner and connection, in which words are used, whether written, printed or spoken. This will often leave the sense very vague and indeterminate, or positively wrong.

21. *An acquaintance with other languages will not give us a correct knowledge of English words.* For, in the first place, all the English words derived from these three languages, do not constitute one fifth part of our language.

In the second place, there is scarcely an instance, in which a knowledge of the original word can give us any precise idea of the meaning of its derivative. The fact is, that the meaning of almost every word, includes several ideas; and when we borrow a word from another language, we scarcely ever use it, to signify just the same ideas, denoted by its original. For example, our words *cap*, *captain*, *caption*, *capital*, *capitol*, *capitation*, *decapitate*, are all derived from *caput*—a head. But they all differ in signification from caput, as well as from one another. There is, indeed, some resemblance among the significations of all. This makes it a little easier to learn and to retain their meanings; but an acquaintance with these various meanings cannot be gained, but from other sources. The same might be shown by multitudes of other examples. Hence it has come to pass, that *use* and not derivation, is the law of language; and hence our word *virtue* has by no means, the same signification, as its original *virtus*. Hence too, it has come to pass, that a knowledge of the original word has often led the unwary youth to misunderstand and misuse its derivative of different meaning.

It is the grand object of the dictionary to tell us the sense or senses, in which our words are used by good writers and speakers. Derivation is but of secondary, and comparatively very little importance. It seems to be a matter, rather curious, than useful. Or perhaps it is useful, rather, because it is curious—because it tends to awaken in the mind, such a fondness for that noble and all-important science, philology, which has such an intimate and important connection with every literary and scientific pursuit.

To learn the meaning of words, then, must constitute a capital part of a good education. It should be begun, as soon as the child can distinguish between one word and another, and continued, as long as sight or hearing continue. The chief study in this pursuit, is that of defining, principally in the use of a dictionary. The best way of pursuing this study, is doubtless in connection with other studies — to learn and fix in the

---

What is the law of language?
What is the grand object of a dictionary?
How soon should a child begin to learn the meaning of words?

mind, the definitions of the most important words, as they occur. The instructions of the lessons will greatly assist to fix in the mind, the definitions, and the definitions, to fix the instructions. To promote this exercise, it is thought needful to have a large number of questions, to be answered by definitions. But the pupil should not content himself merely with learning these. He should consult his dictionary for the meaning of every word, that he does not clearly understand. Let him also consider the connection, and endeavor to gain the exact import, not only of each word, but also of each phrase and sentence, as he proceeds. In this way, though his progress from page to page, will be slow, especially at first, yet it will be sure, and exceedingly conducive to mental improvement, and the acquisition of knowledge.

22. *Cursory reading of this work.* It may be well, however, in the first place, if the pupil is sufficiently improved to find it interesting, for him to devote two or three days to read through this work on the Mind, in rather a cursory manner, without stopping to look out words in a dictionary, or to commit ideas to memory. In this way, he may gain some general acquaintance with the subject, and also with the author's manner of thinking and writing, and thus become prepared more readily to perceive the meaning and feel the force of any particular passage.

23. *Webster's Dictionaries.* It is deeply to be regretted, that dictionaries in common use are so exceedingly imperfect, as it respects the grand object. Many important words are omitted, phrases are omitted, and most of the definitions are by no means what they should be. If the pupil can have the use of Webster's great dictionary in two volumes, he will find it a treasure of treasures. It is admirable indeed for the fulness of its vocabulary of words and phrases defined, for the excellence of its definitions, for its philological instructions, for its historical elucidations, and for its interesting and instructive examples of the various uses of words. In all these respects, except the last, it is vastly superior to Johnson's great work. If one of these could be in each of our schools, for the use of teachers and pupils, it would be of unspeakable advantage to our country. Next to this, the abridgement of the same work in one volume, is probably the best of all English dictionaries.

In what respects, are most dictionaries imperfect?

What dictionary is here recommended?

What are some of the excellences of this dictionary?

WATTS'S

PREFACE.

In the last page of the Treatise of Logic, which I published many years ago, it is observed, that there are several other things, which might assist the cultivation of the mind, and its improvement in knowledge, which are not usually represented among the principles or precepts of that art or science. These are the subjects, which compose this book. These are the sentiments and rules, many of which I had then in view, and which I now venture into public light.

The present treatise, if it may assume the honor of that name, is made up of a variety of remarks and directions for the improvement of the mind in useful knowledge. It was collected from the observations, which I had made on my own studies, and on the temper and sentiments, the humor and conduct of other men in their pursuit of learning or in the affairs of life; and it has been considerably augmented by occasional collections in the course of my reading, from many authors,

---

Of what, is this treatise made up?

Meaning of *treatise*?

From what sources, was this treatise collected? Experience, observation and reading.

Difference between *experience* and *observation*?

What opportunity had Watts for experience? He was a close student for almost 70 years.

What opportunity had he for observation? He was early a teacher; and had afterwards much intercourse with the best society.

Where was he born? At Southampton in England.

Which way is Southampton, from London?

In what year, was Watts born? In 1674.

How old would Watts have been, if he had lived till the declaration of our independence?—till this time?

What was his profession? He was a minister of the gospel.

Where was he settled? In London.

Character of his piety? He is generally considered, as one of the most pious men, that ever lived.

Character of his scholarship? He was ranked among the greatest scholars of his age.

General state of his health? Very feeble.

His most distinguished work? His Psalms and Hymns.

Advantage of knowing something of an author? His works are rendered more intelligible, and much more interesting.

and on different subjects. I confess, in far the greatest part I stand bound to answer for the weaknesses or defects, that will be found in these papers, not being able to point to other writers, whence the twentieth part of them is derived.

The work was composed at different times, and by slow degrees. Now and then, indeed, it spread itself into branches and leaves, like a plant in April, and advanced seven or eight pages in a week; and sometimes it lay by without growth, like a vegetable in the winter, and did not increase half so much in the revolution of a year.

As these thoughts occurred to me in reading or meditation, or in my notices of the various appearances of things among mankind, they were thrown under those heads, which make the present titles of the chapters, and were by degrees, reduced to something like a method, such as the subject would admit.

On these accounts, it is not to be expected, that the same accurate order should be observed, either in the whole book, or in the particular chapters, which is necessary in the system of any science, whose scheme is projected at once. A book, which has been twenty years in writing, may be indulged in some variety of style and manner, though I hope, there will not be found any great difference of sentiment; for wherein I had improved in later years, beyond what I had first written, a few dashes and alterations have corrected the mistakes. And if the candor of the reader will but allow what is defective in one place, to be supplied by additions from another, I hope, there will be found a sufficient reconciliation of what might seem at first to be scarcely consistent.

The language and dress of these sentiments is such, as the present temper of mind dictated, whether it were grave or pleasant, severe or smiling. If there has been any thing expressed with too much severity, I suspect it will be found to fall upon those sneering or daring writers of the age against religion, and against the Christian scheme, who seemed to have left reason or decency or both behind them, in some of their writings.

The same apology of the length of years in composing this book, may serve also to excuse a repetition of the same sentiments, which may happen to be found in different places, without the author's design; but in other pages, it was intended; so that those rules for the conduct of the understanding, which are most necessary, should be set in several lights, that they might with more frequency and more force, impress the soul. I shall be sufficiently satisfied with the good humor and

---

Who, does he say, must answer for the imperfections of this work on the Mind?

How long was he in composing this treatise?

lenity of my readers, if they will please to regard these papers as parcels of imperfect sketches, which were designed by a sudden pencil, and in a thousand leisure moments, to be one day collected into landskips of some little prospects in the regions of learning, and in the world of common life, pointing out the fairest and most fruitful spots, as well as the rocks and wildernesses and faithless morasses of the country. But I feel age advancing upon me, and my health is insufficient to perfect what I had designed, to increase and amplify these remarks, to confirm and improve these rules, and to illuminate the several pages with a richer and more beautiful variety of examples. The subject is almost endless, and new writers in the present and in following ages may still find sufficient follies, weaknesses and dangers among mankind, to be represented in such a manner, as to guard youth against them.

These hints, such as they are, I hope may be rendered some way useful to persons in younger years, who will favor them with a perusal, and who would seek the cultivation of their own understandings in the early days of life. Perhaps they may find something here, which may awake a latent genius, and direct the studies of a willing mind. Perhaps it may point out to a student now and then, what may employ the most useful labors of his thoughts, and accelerate his diligence in the most momentous inquiries. Perhaps a sprightly youth may here meet with something to guard or warn him against mistakes, and withhold him at other times from those pursuits which are likely to be fruitless and disappointing.

Let it be observed also, that in our age, several of the ladies pursue science with success; and others of them are desirous of improving their reason even in the common affairs of life, as well as the men; yet the characters which are here drawn occasionally, are almost universally applied to one sex; but if any of the other shall find a character which suits them, they may, by a small change of the termination, apply and assume it to themselves, and accept the instruction, the admonition, or the applause which is designed in it.

I. W.

In what manner, composed? Often by very short and hasty sketches.

Consequence of this manner? Imperfections of style, and some repetions.

What prevented the author from improving this work, as he intended?—*Meaning of amplify?*

For whom, is this work more particularly designed?

What is it calculated to awaken?

Meaning of *latent*?—of *genius*?

What were several ladies then pursuing with success?

Meaning of *science*?

In what were others desirous of improving their reason?

Meaning of *lenity*?—of *morasses*?—of *accelerate*?—of *momentous*?

CONTENTS.

Page.

Editor's Introduction, ... 3
Author's Preface, ... 13
Importance of knowledge and mental improvement, . . 17
Sixteen general rules for gaining knowledge and improvement, ... 20
Observation, reading, instruction by lectures, conversation and study, compared, ... 37
Rules relating to observation, ... 51
Of reading and books, ... 59
Judgment of books, ... 74
Of living instructions and lectures—of teachers and learners, ... 86
Of inquiring into the sense and meaning of any writer or speaker, and especially the sense of the sacred writings, ... 91
Rules of improvement by conversation, ... 97
Of disputes, ... 113
The Socratic way of disputation, ... 125
Of study, or meditation, ... 129
Of fixing the attention, ... 141
Of enlarging the capacity of the mind, ... 144
Of improving the memory, ... 163
Of determinining a question, ... 185
Of inquiring into causes and effects, ... 202
Of the sciences, and their use in particular professions, 206

INTRODUCTION.

IMPORTANCE OF KNOWLEDGE AND MENTAL IMPROVEMENT.

No man is obliged to learn and know every thing. This can neither be sought nor required; for it is utterly impossible. Yet all persons are under some obligation to improve their own understanding. Otherwise, it will be a barren desert, or a forest overgrown with weeds and brambles. Universal ignorance or infinite errors will overspread the mind, which is utterly neglected, and lies without any cultivation.

Skill in the sciences is indeed the business and profession but of a small part of mankind. But there are many others, placed in such an exalted rank in the world, as allows them much leisure and large opportunities to cultivate their reason, and to beautify and enrich their minds with various knowledge. Even the lower orders of men have particular callings in life, wherein they ought to acquire a just degree of skill; and this is not to be done well, without thinking and reasoning about them.

Subject of the introduction?

Difference between knowledge and mental improvement? Knowledge is the store of information, which the mind possesses. Mental improvement is the progress of the mental faculties.

Meaning of *progress*?

What is a mental faculty? The mind itself, considered as capable of acting, feeling or existing, in a certain manner or state.

How is this definition illustrated in the case of perception, attention, memory, judgment and sensibility? Perception is the mind, considered as capable of perceiving; attention is the mind, considered as capable of attending, &c.

Why is no man obliged to learn every thing?

What evil will be likely to result from attempting to learn too many things? Nothing will be learnt well; and the faculties will be injured by distraction.

Meaning of *distraction*?

Who ought to improve their minds?

What will be the mind, if unimproved?

In what, should the lower orders of men acquire skill?

What mental effort is necessary for this?

2*

The common duties and benefits of society, which belong to every man living, as we are social creatures, and even our native and necessary relations to a family, a neighborhood, or a government oblige all persons whatever to use their reasoning powers upon a thousand occasions. Every hour of life calls for some regular exercise of our judgment as to times and things, persons and actions. Without a prudent and discreet determination in matters before us, we shall be plunged into perpetual errors in our conduct. Now, that which should always be practised, must at some time, be learnt.

Besides, every son and daughter of Adam has a most important concern in the affairs of a life to come; and therefore, it is a matter of the highest moment for every one to understand, to judge, and to reason right about the things of religion. It is in vain for any to say, We have no leisure or time for it. The daily intervals of time, and vacancies from necessary labor, together with the one day in seven in the Christian world, allow sufficient time for this. If men would but apply themselves to it with half as much zeal and diligence, as they do to the trifles and amusements of this life, and it would turn to infinitely better account.

Thus it appears to be the necessary duty and the interest of every person living to improve his understanding, to inform his judgment, to treasure up useful knowledge, and to acquire the skill of good reasoning, as far as his station, capacity and circumstances furnish him with proper means. Our mistakes in judgment may plunge us into much folly and guilt in practice. By acting without thought or reason, we dishonor the God that made us reasonable creatures, we often become injurious to our neighbors, kindred or friends; and we bring sin and misery upon ourselves. For we are accountable to God our judge for every part of our irregular and mistaken conduct, where he has given us sufficient advantages to guard against those mistakes.

About what subjects, is it most important, that we should reason correctly?

Why is it in vain for any one to say, that he has no time to attend to religion?

What if men were as zealous for religious knowledge, as they are for trifles?

What mental skill is it peculiarly desirable, that all should acquire?

Into what, may our mistakes in judgment plunge us?

Whom do we dishonor, by acting without reason?—Why?

When are we accountable to God, for our mistakes?

What is Logic? The art of investigating and communicating truth?

Meaning of *investigate*?

It is the design of Logic to give this improvement to the mind, and to teach us the right use of reason in the acquirement and communication of all useful knowledge; though the greatest part of writers on that subject, have turned it into a composition of hard words, trifles and subtilties, for the mere use of the schools, and that only to amuse the minds and the ears of men with empty sounds, which flatter their vanity, and puff up their pride, with a pompous and glittering show of false learning; and thus they have perverted the great and valuable design of that science.

A few modern writers have endeavored to recover the honor of Logic, since that excellent author of the Art of Thinking led the way. Among the rest, I have presumed to make an attempt of the same kind, in a treatise published several years ago, wherein it was my constant aim to assist the reasoning powers of every rank and order of men, as well as to keep an eye to the best interest of the schools, and the candidates for true learning. There I have endeavored to show the mistakes, we are exposed to, in our conception, judgment and reasoning; and pointed out the various springs of them. I have also laid down many general and particular rules, how to escape error, and attain truth in matters of civil and religious life, as well as in the sciences.

But there are several other observations, very pertinent to this purpose, which have not fallen so directly under any of those heads of discourse; or at least, they would have swelled that treatise to an improper size; and therefore, I have made a distinct collection of them here, from various authors, as well as from my own observation, and set them down under the following heads.

The learned world, who has done so much unmerited honor to that logical treatise, as to receive it into our two

---

Of what, does Logic teach us the right use?

What is reason? The faculty, by which we compare ideas, and draw inferences.

Meaning of *inference*? A truth or proposition, drawn from others.

Technical name of the propositions, from which inferences are drawn? Premises.

Meaning of *technical*?

Another name for inference? Conclusion.

More appropriate name of the reasoning faculty? Judgment.

More exact definition of judgment? The faculty, by which we perceive relations.

Into what, has Logic been turned by many writers?

What would Watts have us consider this book, in relation to his treatise of Logic?

Why have some thought, that it should rather be considered the first part? Because it is more easily understood, and more interesting.

flourishing universities, may possibly admit this as a second part or supplement to that treatise. And I may venture to persuade myself, that if the common and the busy ranks of mankind, as well as the scholar and the gentleman, would but transcribe such rules into their understanding, and practise them upon all occasions, there would be much more truth and knowledge found among men; and it is reasonable to hope, that justice, virtue and goodness would attend as the happy consequences.

CHAPTER I.

SIXTEEN GENERAL RULES FOR GAINING KNOWLEDGE AND IMPROVEMENT.

I. DEEPLY possess your mind with the vast importance of a good judgment, and the rich and inestimable advantage of right reasoning. Review the instances of your own misconduct in life. Think seriously with yourselves, how many follies and sorrows you had escaped, and how much guilt and misery you had prevented, if from your early years, you had but taken due pains to judge aright concerning persons, times and things. This will awaken in you a lively vigor to address yourselves to the work of improving your reasoning powers, and seizing every opportunity and advantage for that end.

II. Consider the weaknesses, frailties and mistakes of human nature in general, which arise from the very constitution of a soul united to an animal body, and by this, subjected to many inconveniences. Consider the many additional weaknesses, mistakes and frailties, which are derived from our original apostasy from a state of innocence; how much our powers of understanding are yet more darkened, enfeebled and imposed upon, by our senses, our fancies, our unruly passions, &c. Consider the depth and difficulty of many truths, and the flattering appearances of

---

Of what, does the first chapter consist?

Substance of the first rule? We should realize the importance of good judgment and logic.

Whose misconduct should we review, in order to realize this?

Causes of this misconduct? The imperfection of the human faculties, the difficulty of many truths, and human depravity.

How does it appear, that the depravity of the soul, does not necessarily result from its connection with the body?—or that it does?

falsehood; whence arise an infinite variety of dangers, to which we are exposed in our judgment of things. Read with eagerness, those authors, that treat of the doctrine of prejudices, prepossessions, and springs of error, on purpose to make your soul watchful on all sides, that it suffer not itself to be imposed upon by any of them. See more on this subject, Logic, Part II. Chap. 3. and Part III. Chap. 3.

III. A slight view of things so momentous, is not sufficient. You should, therefore, contrive and practise some proper methods, to acquaint yourself with your own ignorance, and to impress your mind with a deep and painful sense of the low and imperfect degrees of your present knowledge, that you may be incited with labor and activity, to pursue after greater measures. Among others, you may find some such methods as these successful.

1. Take a wide survey, now and then, of the vast and unlimited regions of learning. Let your meditations run over the names of all the sciences, with their numerous branchings, and innumerable particular themes of knowledge; and then reflect, how few of them you are acquainted with, in any tolerable degree. The most learned of mortals will never find occasion to act over again what is fabled of Alexander the Great, that when he had conquered what was called the Eastern World, he wept for more worlds to conquer. The worlds of science are immense and endless.

What works should we read most eagerly, in order to correct our judgment?

Meaning of *prejudice*? A judgment without evidence, or a state of mind, that tends to such judgment.

Literal meaning of *prejudice*? Prejudging.

Are our prejudices in favor of persons and things, or against them?

Which prejudices are most numerous, those in favor of objects, or those against them? Perhaps about equal.

At what age of life, are persons influenced by prejudice?

When do persons most easily imbibe prejudice?

When are prejudices strongest?

Principal causes of prejudice? Indolence, wrong feelings and bad logic.

How does indolence produce prejudice? By preventing proper examination.

How does wrong feeling produce prejudice? Principally, by keeping the attention upon one side of the question.

How does bad logic produce prejudice? By using bad rules of reasoning, or abusing good ones.

To what interests, is prejudice injurious? To all—temporal, spiritual and eternal.

How shall we cure our present prejudices, and guard against imbibing more? By faithfully attending to logic, by studying the scriptures, by conversing with the wise and good, by watchfulness and prayer, and by the faithfulness of judicious friends.

Whose ignorance should we most deeply feel and deplore?

Meaning of *deplore*?

Mention some of the methods, that may lead us to feel our ignorance?

Meaning of *immense*?—of *theorem*?—of *demonstration*?—of *bewilder*?—of *vacuum*?—of *incredible*?

2. Think, what a numberless variety of questions and difficulties there are, belonging even to that particular science, in which you have made the greatest progress, and how few of them there are, in which you have arrived at a final and undoubted certainty; excepting only those questions in the pure and simple mathematics, whose theorems are demonstrable, and leave scarcely any doubt. And yet even in the pursuit of some few of these, mankind have been strangely bewildered.

3. Spend a few thoughts sometimes on the puzzling inquiries concerning vacuums and atoms, the doctrine of infinites, indivisibles and incommensurables in geometry, wherein there appear some insolvable difficulties. Do this, on purpose to give you a more sensible impression of the poverty of your understanding, and the imperfection of your knowledge. This will teach you, what a vain thing it is to fancy, that you know all things; and will instruct you to think modestly of your present attainments, when every dust of the earth, and every inch of empty space surmounts your understanding, and triumphs over your presumption. Arithmo had been bred up to accounts all his life, and thought himself a complete master of numbers. But when he was pushed hard to give the square root of the number 2, he tried at it, and labored long in millesimal fractions, until he confessed there was no end of the inquiry; and yet he learnt so much modesty by this perplexing question, that he was afraid to say, it was an impossible thing. It is some good degree of improvement, when we are afraid to be positive.

4. Read the accounts of those vast treasures of knowledge, which some of the dead have possessed, and some of the living do possess. Read, and be astonished at the almost incredible advances, which have been made in science. Acquaint yourselves with some persons of great learning, that by converse among them, and comparing yourselves with them, you may acquire a mean opinion of your own attainments, and may be thereby animated with new zeal to equal them, as far as possible, or to exceed. Thus let your diligence be quickened by a generous and

---

What does it indicate, when we are afraid to be positive?

What is said of the fool in Prov. 14: 16?

What conclusion may we draw, concerning a man, who appears outrageously confident? That he is probably in the wrong.

What, does the author say, should animate us with zeal to increase our attainments?

What is emulation? A desire to surpass others.

When is emulation wrong? When

laudable emulation. If Vanillus had never met with Scitorio and Polydes, he had never imagined himself a mere novice in Philosophy, nor ever set himself to study in good earnest. Remember this, that if upon some few superficial acquirements, you exalt and swell yourself, as though you were a man of learning already, you are thereby building a most unpassable barrier against all improvement; you will lie down and indulge idleness, and rest yourself contented in the midst of deep and shameful ignorance. *Multi ad scientiam pervenissent, si se illuc pervenisse non putassent.*

IV. Presume not too much upon a bright genius, a ready wit and good parts; for this, without labor and study, will never make a man of knowledge and wisdom. This has been an unhappy temptation to persons of a vigorous and gay fancy, to despise learning and study. They have been acknowledged to shine in an assembly, and sparkle in discourse upon common topics; and thence they took it into their heads to abandon reading and labor, and grow old in ignorance. But when they had lost the vivacities of animal nature and youth, they became stupid and sottish, even to contempt and ridicule. Lucidas and Scintillo are young men of this stamp: they shine in conversation; they spread their native riches before the ignorant; they pride themselves in their own lively images of fancy, and imagine themselves wise and learned. But they had best avoid the presence of the skilful and the test of reasoning; and I would advise them, once a day, to think forward a little, what a contemptible figure they will make in age.

The witty men sometimes have sense enough to know their own foible, and therefore, they craftily shun the at-

---

we desire to excel, merely for the sake of excelling.

When is it right? When we desire to excel, for the sake of doing good.

How will good emulation make us feel in relation to the improvements of others? To rejoice.

Effect of bad emulation in such a case? To make us grieve.

Should emulation be encouraged or not? Good emulation should be encouraged, and bad emulation opposed.

Why is it, that some good men profess to be opposed to all emulation? Probably, by mistaking the meaning of the word.

If we exalt ourselves upon some superficial attainment, what effect, will it be likely to have upon our future progress?

Meaning of the Latin sentence, *Multi ad scientiam*, &c.? Many might become learned, did they not fancy themselves such already.

What is said under the fourth rule, respecting genius?

What, besides genius, is necessary to make a person truly wise? Study and the blessing of God.

If persons neglect study in youth, what is likely to be the character of their elder life? Contemptible.

Why do witty men sometimes pretend to despise argument? Because they cannot reason.

tacks of argument, or boldly pretend to despise and renounce them; because they are conscious of their own ignorance, and inwardly confess their want of acquaintance with the skill of reasoning.

V. As you are not to fancy yourself a learned man, because you are blessed with a ready wit, so neither must you imagine, that large and laborious reading, and a strong memory, can denominate you truly wise.

It is meditation and studious thought, it is the exercise of your own reason and judgment upon all you read, that gives good sense even to the best genius, and affords your understanding the truest improvement. A boy of strong memory may repeat a whole book of Euclid, yet be no geometer; for he may not be able perhaps to demonstrate one single theorem. Memorino has learnt half the Bible by heart, and is become a living concordance, and a speaking index to theological folios, and yet he understands little of divinity.

A well furnished library and a capacious memory are indeed of singular use toward the improvement of the mind. But if all your learning be nothing else but a mere amassment of what others have written, without a due penetration into their meaning, and without a judicious choice and determination of your own sentiments, I do not see, what title your head has to true learning, above your shelves. Though you have read Philosophy and Theology, Morals and Metaphysics in abundance, and every other art and science, yet if your memory is the only faculty employed, you can justly claim no higher character than that of a good historian of the sciences.

Here note, Many of the foregoing advices are more peculiarly proper for those, who are conceited of their abilities, and are ready to entertain a high opinion of themselves. But a modest, humble youth of a good genius, should not suffer himself to be discouraged by any of these considerations. They are designed only as a spur to diligence, and a guard against vanity and pride.

VI. Be not so weak, as to imagine, that a life of learning is a life of laziness and ease. Dare not give up yourself to any of the learned professions, unless you are resolved to

---

What of reading, under the fifth rule?

What should we exercise upon all we read?

What will this give to genius?

What of Memorino?

Meaning of *concordance*?

What if a person has read much, and scarcely employed any faculty but memory?

What caution is given in the sixth rule, respecting a life of learning?

labor hard at study, and can make it your delight and the joy of your life, according to the motto of our late Lord Chancellor King, *Labor ipse voluptas.*

It is no idle thing to be a scholar indeed. A man, much addicted to luxury and pleasure, recreation and pastime, should never pretend to devote himself entirely to the sciences, unless his soul be so refined, that he can taste all these entertainments eminently in his closet, among his books and papers. Sobrino is a temperate man and a philosopher, and he feeds upon partridge and pheasant, venison and ragoos and every delicacy, in a growing understanding, and a serene and healthy soul, though he dines on a dish of sprouts or turnips. Languinos loved his ease, and therefore, chose to be brought up a scholar; he had much indolence in his temper, and as he never cared for study, he falls under universal contempt in his profession, because he has nothing but the gown and the name.

VII. Let the hope of new discoveries, as well as the satisfaction and pleasure of known truths, animate your daily industry. Do not think learning in general has arrived at its perfection, or that the knowledge of any particular subject in any science cannot be improved, merely because it has lain five hundred or a thousand years, without improvement. The present age, by the blessing of God on the ingenuity and diligence of men, has brought to light, such truths in natural philosophy, and such discoveries in the heavens and the earth, as seemed to be beyond the reach of man. But may not there be Sir Isaac Newtons in every science? You should never despair, therefore, of finding out, that which has never yet been found, unless you see something in the nature of it, which renders it unsearchable, and above the reach of our faculties.

Nor should a student in divinity imagine, that our age has arrived at a full understanding of every thing, which can be known by the scriptures. Every age since the Reformation, has thrown some further light on difficult

---

Meaning of the Latin phrase, *Labor ipse voluptas*? Labor itself is pleasure.

Why did Languinos choose to be brought up a scholar?

How was he regarded in his profession?

To what, should the hope of new discoveries animate us?

In what cases, should we not despair of making discoveries?

Meaning of *unsearchable*?

Upon what, has light been thrown, in every age, since the Reformation?

What reformation is here meant? The great reformation from Popery, begun by Martin Luther.— When? In 1517.

Why is it called *the Reformation*? By way of eminence, because it was so great and important.

texts and paragraphs of the Bible, which had been long obscured by the early rise of Antichrist; and since there are at present many difficulties and darknesses hanging about certain truths of the Christian Religion, and since several of these relate to important doctrines, such as the Origin of Sin, the Fall of Adam, the Person of Christ, the blessed Trinity, the Decrees of God, &c. which do still embarrass the minds of honest and inquiring readers, and which make work for noisy controversy; it is certain there are several things in the Bible yet unknown, and not sufficiently explained; and it is certain, that there is some way to solve these difficulties, and to reconcile these seeming contradictions. And why may not a sincere teacher of truth in the present age, by labor, diligence, study and prayer, with the best use of his reasoning powers, find out the proper solution of those knots and perplexities which have hitherto been unsolved, and which have afforded matter for angry quarrelling? Happy is every man, who shall be favored of Heaven to give a helping hand toward that introduction of the blessed age of light and love.

VIII. Do not hover always on the surface of things, nor take up suddenly with mere appearances; but penetrate into the depth of matters, as far as your time and circumstances allow, especially in those things, which relate to your own profession. Do not indulge yourselves to judge of things by the first glimpse, or a short and superficial view of them; for this will fill the mind with errors and prejudices, and give it a wrong turn and ill habit of thinking, and make much work for retraction. Subito is carried away with title pages, so that he ventures to pronounce upon a large octavo at once, and to recommend it wonderfully when he had read half the Preface. Another volume of controversies of equal size, was discarded by him at once, because it pretended to treat of the Trinity; and yet he could neither find the word *essence* nor *subsistencies*, in the

---

By what, had those passages been obscured?—Literal meaning of *Antichrist*? An adversary of Christ.—Meaning of *adversary*?

To what does Antichrist here refer? The Papal power.

Meaning of *Papal*?

What age, is it very desirable, that we should aid in introducing?

What is that age generally called? The Millennium.

Meaning of *Millennium*?

State of mankind during that age? Peculiarly holy and happy. See Isaiah 2:

Meaning of *obscure*?—of *embarrass*?—of *solve*?

If we judge of things by the first glimpse, with what, will it fill the mind?

What four things are generally necessary for thorough investigation? Time, attention, patience and perseverance.

12 first pages. But Subito changes his opinions of men and books and things so often, that nobody regards him.

As for those sciences, or those parts of knowledge, which either your profession, your leisure, your inclination or your incapacity, forbid you to pursue with much application, or to search far into them, you must be contented with an historical and superficial knowledge of them, and not pretend to form many judgments of your own on those subjects, which you understand very imperfectly.

IX. Once a day, especially in the early years of life and study, Call yourselves to an account, and consider what new ideas, what new proposition or truth you have gained, what further confirmation of known truths, and what advances you have made in any part of knowledge; and if possible, let no day pass away without some intellectual gain. Such a course well pursued, must certainly advance us in useful knowledge. It is a wise proverb among the learned, borrowed from the lips and practice of a celebrated painter, *Nulla dies sine linea;* let no day pass without one line at least; and it was a sacred rule among the Pythagoreans, that they should every evening thrice run over the actions and affairs of the day, and examine, what their conduct had been, what they had done, or what they had neglected; and they assured their pupils, that by this method, they would make a noble progress in the path of virtue.

Nor let soft slumber close your eyes,
Before you've recollected thrice
The train of actions thro' the day.
Where have my feet chose out the way?
What have I learnt, where'er I've been,
From all I've heard, from all I've seen?
What know I more, that's worth the knowing?
What have I done, that's worth the doing?
What have I sought, that I should shun?
What duty have I left undone?
Or into what new follies, run?
These self-inquiries are the road,
That leads to virtue and to God.

Why does no one regard the opinion of Subito?

Upon what subjects, should we form scarcely any opinion?

How often should we inquire, what new ideas we have gained?

What gain should we endeavor to acquire every day?

How many times did the Pythagoreans review the affairs of each day?

Who were the Pythagoreans? The followers of Pythagoras.

Who was Pythagoras? One of the greatest of the Grecian philosophers.

What great Hebrew prophets were cotemporary with Pythagoras? Jeremiah, Ezekiel and Daniel.

Meaning of *cotemporary*?

I would be glad among a nation of Christians to find young men heartily engaged in the practice of what this heathen writer teaches.

X. Maintain a constant watch, at all times, against a dogmatic spirit. Fix not your assent to any proposition in a firm and unalterable manner, till you have some firm and unalterable ground for it, nor till you have arrived at some clear and sure evidence; till you have turned the proposition on all sides, and searched the matter through and through, so that you cannot be mistaken. And even where you may think you have full grounds of assurance, be not too early nor too frequent in expressing this assurance, in too peremptory and positive a manner, remembering, that human nature is always liable to mistake in this corrupt and feeble state. A dogmatic spirit has many inconveniences attending it: as,

1. It stops the ear against all further reasoning upon that subject, and shuts up the mind from all further improvements of knowledge. If you have resolutely fixed your opinion, though it be upon too slight and insufficient grounds, yet you will stand determined to renounce the strongest reason, brought for the contrary opinion, and grow obstinate against the force of the clearest argument. Positivo is a man of this character, and has often pronounced his assurance of the Cartesian vortexes. Last year, some further light broke in upon his understanding, with uncontrollable force, by reading something of mathematical philosophy. Yet having asserted his former opinions in a most confident manner, he is tempted now to wink a little against the truth, or to prevaricate in his discourse upon that subject, lest by admitting conviction, he should expose himself to the necessity of confessing his former folly and mistake; and he has not humility enough for that.

2. A dogmatic spirit naturally leads us to arrogance, and gives a man some airs in conversation, which are too haughty and assuming. Audens is a man of learning, and very good company, but his infallible assurance renders his carriage sometimes insupportable.

Against what spirit, does the tenth rule require us continually to watch?

Meaning of *dogmatic*?

When may we be firmly decided in opinion? After faithful examination with clear evidence.

Against what, does dogmatism stop the ear?

Why is Positivo unwilling to confess his errors?

Meaning of *prevaricate*?

What airs does dogmatism give to conversation?

What sometimes renders the manners of Audens insupportable?

3. A dogmatic spirit inclines a man to be censorious. Every one of his opinions appears to him written as it were with sun-beams, and he grows angry that his neighbor does not see it in the same light. He is tempted to disdain his correspondents, as men of low and dark understanding; because they will not believe what he does. Furio goes farther in this wild track, and charges those, who refuse his notions, with wilful obstinacy and vile hypocrisy. He tells them boldly, that they resist the truth, and sin against their consciences.

These are the men, that when they deal in controversy, delight in reproaches. They abound in tossing about absurdity and stupidity among their brethren. They cast the imputation of heresy and nonsense plentifully upon their antagonists; and in matters of sacred importance, they deal out their anathemas in abundance upon Christians better than themselves. They denounce damnation upon their neighbors, without either justice or mercy, and when they pronounce sentences of divine wrath against supposed heretics, they add their own human fire and indignation. A dogmatist in religion is not a great way off from a bigot, and is in high danger of growing up to be a bloody persecutor.

XI. Though caution and slow assent will guard you against frequent mistakes and retractions, yet you should get humility and courage enough to retract any mistake, and confess an error. Frequent changes are tokens of levity in our first determinations. Yet you should never be too proud to change your opinion, nor frighted at the name of changling. Learn to scorn those vulgar bugbears, which confirm foolish man in his own mistakes, for fear of being charged with inconstancy. I confess, it is better not to judge, than to judge falsely; and it is wiser to withhold our assent, till we see complete evidence. But if we have too suddenly given our assent, as the wisest man does sometimes, if we have professed what we find afterwards to be false, we should never be ashamed nor afraid to renounce

---

With what, does Furio charge those, who refuse his notions?

Against what, does he say, they sin?

When such men deal in controversy, in what do they delight?

Meaning of *controversy*?

Meaning of *antagonist*? of *heresy*?—of *anathema*?—of *bigot*?

What is a dogmatist in danger of becoming?

Can you now mention three or four great evils of dogmatism?

What should we be willing to retract?—to confess?

Meaning of *retract*?

Which is worst, to judge falsely, or not to judge?

a mistake. That is a noble essay, that is found among the Occasional Papers, to encourage the world to practise retractions; and I would recommend it to the perusal of every scholar and every Christian.

XII. He, that would raise his judgments above the vulgar rank of mankind, and learn to pass a just sentence on persons and things, must take heed of a fanciful temper of mind, and a humorous conduct in his affairs. Fancy and humor, early and constantly indulged, may expect an old age over-run with follies.

A humorist is one that is greatly pleased or greatly displeased with little things; who sets his heart much upon matters of very small importance; who has his will determined every day by trifles, his actions seldom directed by the reason and nature of things, and his passions frequently raised by things of little moment. Where this practice is allowed, it will insensibly warp the judgment to pronounce little things great, and tempt you to lay a great weight upon them. In short, this temper will incline you to pass an unjust value on almost every thing that occurs; and every step, that you take in this path, is just so far out of the way to wisdom.

XIII. For the same reason, have a care of trifling with things important and momentous, or of sporting with things awful and sacred. Do not indulge a spirit of ridicule, as some witty men do on all occasions and subjects. This will as unhappily bias the judgment on the other side, and incline you to pass a low esteem on the most valuable objects. Whatsoever evil habit we indulge in practice, it will insensibly obtain a power over our understanding, and betray us into many errors. Jocander is ready with his jest, to answer every thing that he hears. He reads books in the same jovial humor, and has got the art of turning every thought and sentence into merriment. How many aukward and irregular judgments does this man pass upon solemn subjects, even when he designs to be grave and in earnest? His mirth and laughing humor is formed into

---

Meaning of *humorist*?

Upon what, will this temper incline us to place an undue value?

With what things, should we not trifle?

With what subjects, is it peculiarly criminal to sport? Religious subjects.

Should we mention passages of Scripture, or relate serious anecdotes, for mere amusement? Never for mere amusement, though we may sometimes relate such, as are amusing.

With what, is Jocander ready to answer every thing, that he hears?

Into what, does he turn every thought and sentence?

habit and temper, and leads his understanding shamefully astray. You will see him wandering in pursuit of a gay flying feather, and he is drawn by a sort of *ignis fatuus* into bogs and mire, almost every day of his life.

XIV. Ever maintain a virtuous and pious frame of spirit; for an indulgence of vicious inclinations debases the understanding, and perverts the judgment. Whoredom and wine and new wine, take away the heart and soul and reason of a man. Sensuality ruins the better faculties of the mind. An indulgence of appetite and passion enfeebles the powers of reason; it makes the judgment weak and susceptive of every falsehood, and especially of such mistakes, as have a tendency towards the gratification of the animal; and it warps the soul aside strangely from that stedfast honesty and integrity, that necessarily belongs to the pursuit of truth. It is the virtuous man, who is in a fair way to wisdom. "God gives to those, that are good in his sight, wisdom and knowledge and joy." Ec. 2:26.

Piety toward God, as well as sobriety and virtue, are necessary qualifications to make a truly wise and judicious man. He, that abandons religion, must act in such a contradiction to his own conscience and best judgment, that he abuses and spoils the faculty itself. It is thus in the nature of things; and it is thus by the righteous judgment of God. Even the pretended sages among the Heathens, "who did not like to retain God in their knowledge, were given up to a reprobate mind;" an undistinguishing or injudicious mind, so that they judged inconsistently, and practised mere asburdities. Rom. 1:28.

And it is the character of the slaves of Antichrist, 2 Thes.

What effect upon his understanding, has Jocander's laughing humor? How? By diverting his attention from the merits of the subject.

Meaning of *ignis fatuus*? A meteor or light, that appears in the night over marshy grounds.

What is it vulgarly called? Will with the wisp, or Jack with a lantern.

Figurative meaning of *ignis fatuus*? That which dazzles, to lead astray.

What frame of spirit should we maintain, in order to advance in knowledge and mental improvement?

What influence upon the mind, has vicious indulgence?

What does God give to those, who are good in his sight?

What is implied in being good in the sight of God? A good life, and a good heart.

How does it appear, that a good heart is implied? Because God looks at the heart.

What is implied in having a good heart? That we obey the law of God from the heart.

Two great commandments of the law of God? Mat. 22: 37, 39.

Tendency of acting contrary to conscience and judgment?

Whom were the Heathen sages unwilling to retain in their knowledge?

To what, did God give them up?

Meaning of *reprobate mind*?—of *sage*?—of *transubstantiation*?

2: 10, &c. that those "who receive not the love of the truth," were exposed to the power of diabolical sleights and lying wonders. When divine revelation shines and blazes in the face of men with glorious evidence, and they wink their eyes against it, the God of this world is suffered to blind them, even in the most obvious, common and sensible things. The great God of heaven, for this cause, "sends them strong delusions, that they should believe a lie;" and the nonsense of transubstantiation in the popish world, is a most glaring accomplishment of this prophecy, beyond ever what could have been thought of or expected among creatures who pretend to reason.

XV. Watch against the pride of your own reason, and a vain conceit of your intellectual powers, with the neglect of divine aid and blessing. Presume not upon great attainments in knowledge by your own self-sufficiency. Those, who trust to their own understanding entirely, are pronounced fools in the word of God: and it is the wisest of men, who gives them this character. "He, that trusteth in his own heart, is a fool," Prov. 28: 26. And the same divine writer advises us to "trust in the Lord with all our heart, and not to lean to our own understandings, nor to be wise in our own eyes," Chap. 3: 5, 7.

Those, who with a neglect of religion, and of dependence on God, apply themselves to search out every article in the things of God, by the mere dint of their own reason, have been suffered to run into wild excesses of foolery, and strange extravagance of opinions. Every one, who pursues this vain course, and will not ask for the conduct of God in the study of religion, has just reason to fear he shall be left of God, and given up a prey to a thousand prejudices; that he shall be consigned over to the follies of his own heart, and pursue his own temporal and eternal ruin. And even in common studies, we should by humility and dependence, engage the God of truth on our side.

XVI. Offer up, therefore, your daily requests to God, the Father of lights, that he would bless all your attempts and labors in reading, study and conversation. Think with

---

Against what form of pride, should we be peculiarly watchful?

What does the Scripture call him, who trusts in his own heart?

What is there reason to fear, we shall be left to pursue, if we do not seek the divine aid in the investigation of truth?

How often should we pray for a divine blessing upon our intellectual labors?

Meaning of *clue*?—of *intricate*?—of *labyrinth*?—of *implore*?

Meaning of a Latin phrase under rule 16? God is the source or beginning.

yourself, how easily and how insensibly, by one turn of thought, he can lead you into a large scene of useful ideas. He can teach you to lay hold on a clue, which may guide your thoughts with safety and ease, through all the difficulties of an intricate subject. Think, how easily the Author of your being can direct your motions, by his providence, so that the glance of an eye, or a word striking the ear, or a sudden turn of the fancy, shall conduct you to a train of happy sentiments. By this secret and supreme method of government, he can draw you to read such a treatise, or to converse with such a person, who may give you more light into some deep subject in an hour, than you could obtain by a month of your own solitary labor.

Think with yourself, with how much ease the God of spirits can cast into your mind, some useful suggestion, and give a happy turn to your own thoughts, or the thoughts of those, with whom you converse, whence you may derive unspeakable light and satisfaction in a matter, that has long puzzled and entangled you. He can show you a path, "which the vulture's eye has not seen," and lead you by some unknown gate or portal, out of a wilderness and labyrinth of difficulties, wherein you have been long wandering.

Implore constantly his divine grace, to point your inclination to proper studies, and to fix your heart there. He can keep off temptations on the right hand and on the left, both by the course of his providence, and by the secret and insensible intimations of his Spirit. He can guard your understanding from every evil influence of error, and secure you from the danger of evil books and men, which might otherwise have a fatal effect, and lead you into pernicious mistakes.

Nor let this sort of advice fall under the censure of the godless and profane, as a mere piece of bigotry or enthusiasm, derived from faith and the bible; for the reasons, which I have given to support this pious practice of invoking the blessing of God on our studies, are derived from the light of nature as well as revelation. He, that made our souls, and is the Father of spirits, shall he not be supposed to have a most friendly influence toward the instruction and government of them? The Author of our rational powers can involve them in darkness, when he pleases, by a sudden distemper, or he can abandon them, to wander into dark and foolish opinions, when they are filled with a vain conceit of their own light. He expects to be acknowledged in the common affairs of life, and he does as certainly expect it in the superior operations of the mind, and in the search of knowledge and truth. The Latins were taught to say, *A Jove principium musæ.* In the works of learning, they thought it necessary to begin with God. Even the poets call upon the muse as a goddess, to assist them in their compositions.

The first lines of Homer in his Iliad and Odyssey, the first line of Museus in his song of Hero and Leander, the beginning of Hesiod in his poem of Works and Days, and several others, furnish us with sufficient examples of this kind. Nor does Ovid leave out this piece of devotion, as he begins his stories of the Metamorphosis. Christianity so much the more obliges us by the precepts of Scripture, to invoke the assistance of the true God in all our labors of the mind, for the improvement of ourselves and others. Bishop Saunderson says, that *study without prayer is atheism,* as well as, that *prayer without study is presumption.* And we are still more abundantly encouraged by the testimony of those who have acknowledged from their own experience, that sincere prayer was no hinderance to their studies. They have gotten more knowledge sometimes upon their knees, than by their labor in perusing a variety of authors; and they have left this observation for such as follow, *Bene orasse est bene studuisse.* Praying is the best studying.

To conclude, let industry and devotion join together; and you need not doubt the happy success, Prov. 2: 1—6. "My son, if thou wilt receive my words, and hide my commandments within thee; so that thou incline thine ear unto wisdom, and apply thine heart to understanding; yea, if thou criest after knowledge, and liftest up thy voice for understanding; if thou seekest her as silver, and searchest for her as for hid treasures; then shalt thou understand the fear of the Lord, and find the knowledge of God. For the Lord giveth wisdom: out of his mouth cometh knowledge and understanding."

NOTE I, BY THE EDITOR.

[*Prayer for instruction.*—It is earnestly desired, that these excellent remarks of Watts upon prayer in connection with study, may not be lost upon a single pupil. May he attend to them closely, ponder them deeply, and improve them

---

According to Bishop Saunderson, what is study without prayer?—prayer without study?

What desire is expressed in the beginning of Note I.?

faithfully. Perhaps there is no other subject, which in proportion to its importance, has been so little regarded in the pursuit of literature as prayer. If we would gain knowledge, we should seek it from the Father of lights. If we would have a wise and understanding heart, we should seek it from Him, whose understanding is infinite; not in the way of sloth and idleness, but in the assiduous use of the appointed means. We must dig for knowledge, as well as cry for it. Here the pupil is advised, to turn to that admirable passage in Prov. 2: 1—9, and study these verses, till he can almost or quite repeat them; and endeavor to understand and feel and relish the weighty thoughts. He is also advised, not only to offer his daily prayer for divine instruction, but to put up two or three short petitions, as he commences the study of each lesson. They may be purely extemporaneous or not; they may be composed by himself or others; they may be read or repeated. These circumstances are of no importance, provided the prayer is breathed forth, from a contrite and fervent heart. Perhaps some of the following forms may be helpful to those, who have had little or no experience in crying to God after knowledge, and lifting up their voice for understanding.

Form of Prayer for a Student.—O thou Father of lights and God of grace, I beseech thee, to pardon my unworthiness, to enlighten my mind, to invigorate my faculties, to quicken my attention, to deliver me from prejudice, and enable me to pursue my study with great success, that I may be prepared for usefulness and glory, for the Redeemer's sake.

Another.—O thou Sun of righteousness, thou Light of the world, I entreat thee to enlighten my soul. Shine upon the pages before me. May I understand them. May I be enabled to distinguish between the precious and the vile. If they contain any thing, not true, may I be enabled to

---

On what special occasions, should we pray, that God would aid us in gaining knowledge?

Should we pray extemporaneously, or otherwise? How must we pray, in order that our prayers may avail?

How can prayer conduce to furnish our minds with knowledge? It tends to make us love it more ardently, to seek it more vigorously, patiently and candidly, and to procure the special blessing of God upon our efforts.

What use may we make of the following forms of prayer?

Should we confine ourselves to these? By no means.

What if we do not need them? It will be better to pray without them.

What if students were as much engaged in seeking knowledge from God as from books?

perceive and reject it; and whatever is true and important, may I hide in my heart, and improve it to thy glory, and the good of mankind, for Christ's sake.

Another.—O thou gracious Giver of every good gift, I desire to bless and praise thee, that there is a spirit in man, and thy inspiration gives him understanding; that thou hast thus exalted him above the beasts of the field and the fowls of heaven. I beseech thee to increase my understanding, that every faculty may be greatly improved and invigorated; that every lesson may add to the precious stock of knowledge, and that it may conduce to the good of mankind, and my own immortal benefit, through Jesus Christ the Redeemer, to whom be glory everlasting. Amen.

Another.—Most great and gracious God, I desire forever to bless and praise thee, for the noble faculties of my soul. I have reason to blush and to be ashamed, that I have made so little effort for their improvement. O Lord, how have I hated instruction, and despised reproof. I beseech thee to forgive my great transgression, and all my other transgressions, and enable me hereafter most vigorously and devoutly to improve all my means of knowledge and understanding, and prepare for life eternal, for the Redeemer's sake.

Form of Prayer for the use of one who is studying the Scriptures.—O God of nature and of grace; Father of angels and of saints, I bless thee for the light of sun, moon and stars. But more especially would I praise thee, for the light of redemption; the light that beams forth from the face of Jesus, that glows on the pages of thy holy word. To this holy word, may I ever take heed, as to a light, shining in a dark place. O Lord, I beseech thee to show me thy glory; teach me wondrous things out of thy law; open my understanding, that I may understand the Scriptures; quicken my memory, to retain thy truth; and my heart, to obey it; that by thy word and Spirit, I may be trained for everlasting life, through Jesus Christ, to whom be honor, praise, dominion and glory forever. Amen.

Another.—Father of lights, and Fountain of knowledge, I thank thee for the Bible—that all Scripture is given by thy inspiration, and that it is profitable for doctrine, for reproof, for correction, for instruction in righteousness. May it be thus profitable to me. May I read it with close and devout attention, with understanding, with love. May it be the joy and rejoicing of my soul, and may it nourish me up into everlasting life, for Christ's sake. Amen.

Another.—O Lord, I entreat thee, to assist me in reading thy word. May I receive it into a good and honest heart. May it conduce to make me perfect, to furnish me for every good, and to prepare me for heaven, for Christ's sake. Amen.

If students, were as much engaged to seek knowledge from God, as they are to gain information from books, no doubt it would have a most happy influence to hasten the blessed day, when the watchmen shall see eye to eye, and the earth be filled with the knowledge and salvation of the Lord.]

CHAPTER II.

OBSERVATION, READING, INSTRUCTION BY LECTURES, CONVERSATION AND STUDY, COMPARED.

THERE are five eminent means or methods, whereby the mind is improved in the knowledge of things, and these are observation, reading, instruction by lectures, conversation and meditation; which last in a most peculiar manner, is called study.

Let us survey the general definitions or descriptions of them all.

I. Observation is the notice, that we take of all occurrences in human life, whether they are sensible or intellectual, whether relating to persons or things, to ourselves or others. It is this, that furnishes us, even from our infancy, with a rich variety of ideas and propositions, words and phrases. It is by this, we know, that fire will burn, that the sun gives light, that a horse eats grass, that an acorn produces an oak, that man is a being capable of reasoning and discourse, that our judgment is weak, that our mistakes are many, that our sorrows are great, that our bodies die, and are carried to the grave, and that one generation succeeds another. All those things, which we see, which we hear or feel, which we perceive by sense or con-

---

Subject of the second chapter? General view of the Five Methods of gaining instruction.

What are the five methods of instruction?

What is the best arrangement of these?

Why should observation be placed first—conversation next?

What is observation? The notice we take of objects.

Where are those objects in relation to ourselves? Some of them are within us, and some, without us.

What objects can we observe within us?

sciousness, or which we know in a direct manner, with scarcely any exercise of our reflecting faculties, or our reasoning powers, may be included under the general name of observation.

When this observation relates to any thing, that immediately concerns ourselves, and of which we are conscious, it may be called experience. So I am said to know or experience, that I have in myself a power of thinking, fearing, loving, &c. that I have appetites and passions, working in me, and that many personal occurrences have attended me in this life.

Observation therefore includes all that Mr. Locke means by sensation and reflection.

When we are searching out the nature or properties of any being, by various methods of trial; or when we apply some active powers, or set some causes at work, to observe, what effects they would produce, this sort of observation is called experiment. So, when I throw a bullet into water, I find it sinks; and when I throw the same bullet into quicksilver, I see it swims; but if I beat out this bullet into a thin, hollow shape, like a dish, then it will swim in the water too. So, when I strike two flints together, I find they produce fire; when I throw a seed into the earth, it grows up into a plant.

All these belong to the first method of knowledge, which I call observation.

II. Reading is that means or method of knowledge, whereby we acquaint ourselves with what other men have published to the world, in their writings. These arts of reading and writing are of infinite advantage; for by them, we are made partakers of the sentiments, observations, reasonings and improvements of all the learned world, in the most remote nations, and in former ages, almost from the begining of mankind.

Name of this inward observation? More technical name? Consciousness.

General meaning of *observation*? Notice of external objects.

By how many senses, do we observe externals?—What are they?

When we employ causes, in order to witness their effects, what is the operation called?

Mention some experiments.

Can we make experiments upon minds?

How? By using methods of instruction, and presenting motives.

Meaning of *motive*?

Two grand distinctions in reading? Silent and audible.

Meaning of *audible*?

Design of silent reading?—of audible?

Which kind of reading does the author here mean?

Of what, may we be made partakers by means of reading?

III. Public or private lectures are such verbal instructions, as are given by a teacher, while the learners attend in silence. This is the way of learning religion from the pulpit, or philosophy or theology from the professor's chair, or mathematics, by a teacher, showing us various theorems or problems, that is, speculations or practices, by demonstration and operation, with all the instruments of art necessary to those operations.

IV. Conversation is another method of improving our minds, wherein by mutual discourse and inquiry, we learn the sentiments of others, as well as communicate our sentiments to them, in the same manner. Sometimes indeed, though both parties speak by turns, yet the advantage is only on one side; as when a teacher and a learner meet and discourse together; but frequently the profit is mutual. Under this head of conversation, we may also rank disputes of various kinds.

V. Meditation or study includes all those exercises of mind, whereby we render all the former methods useful for our increase in true knowledge and wisdom. It is by meditation, we come to confirm our memory of things, that pass through our thoughts in the occurrences of life, in our own experiences, and in the observations we make. It is by meditation, that we draw various inferences, and establish in our minds general principles of knowledge. It is by meditation, that we compare the various ideas, which we derive from our senses, or from the operations of our souls, and join them in propositions. It is by meditation, that we fix in our memory, whatsoever we learn, and form our own judgment of the truth or falsehood, the strength or weakness, of what others speak or write. It is meditation, or

---

What are lectures?

What common religious exercise may be considered lecturing?

What is conversation? Mutual discourse.—Meaning of *mutual*?

Meaning of *conversation*, as used in Scripture?

Which of the five methods is peculiarly fitted to render the others useful?

What word does Watts here use as synonymous with *meditation*?

Meaning of *synonymous*?

By what exercise, do we generally fix ideas in the memory?—draw inferences?—join our ideas, so as to form propositions?

What is a proposition? An assertion, in which one thing is declared respecting another.

Grand excellence or defect of every proposition? Every proposition is either true or false.

What does every truth become, when expressed? A true proposition.

What does every falsehood become, when expressed? A false proposition.

What is a proposition, existing merely in the mind, without being expressed? A mental proposition.

What is the grand business of logic? To ascertain, whether pro-

study, that draws out long chains of argument, and searches and finds deep and difficult truths, which before lay concealed in darkness.

It would be a needless thing to prove, that our own solitary meditations, together with the few observations, that the most part of mankind are capable of making, are not sufficient of themselves, to lead us into the attainment of any considerable proportion of knowledge, at least in an age so much improved as ours, without the assistance of conversation and reading, and other proper instructions, that are to be attained in our days. Yet each of these five methods has its peculiar advantages, whereby they assist each other; and its peculiar defects, which need to be supplied by the others' assistance. Let us trace over some of the particular advantages of each.

I. One method of improving the mind is observation; and the advantages of it are these.

1. It is owing to observation, that our mind is furnished with the first, simple and complex ideas. It is this, lays the foundation of all knowledge; and makes us capable of using the other methods for improving the mind. For, if we did not attain a variety of sensible and intellectual ideas, by the perception of outward objects, by the consciousness of our own appetites and passions, pleasures and pains, and by inward experience of the actings of our own spirits, it would be impossible either for men or books to teach us any thing. It is observation, that must give us our first ideas of things, as it includes sense and consciousness.

2. All our knowledge, derived from observation, whether it be of single ideas or of propositions, is knowledge gotten at first hand. Hereby, we see and know things, as they are, or as they appear to us; we take the impressions of them on our minds, from the original objects themselves; which give a clearer and stronger conception of things. These ideas are more lively; and the propositions, at least in many cases, are much more evident. Whereas, what

---

positions are true or false.

What may we infer from this? That the subject of propositions is exceedingly important, as it is a subject, with which all truth is intimately connected.

Which of the 5 methods has its peculiar excellences and defects?

How many are the chief excellences of observation?

What are they? From observation, we receive our first ideas—ideas at first hand—ideas more clear and lively—foundation of all other ideas—gain continually.

From what, do we take impressions of things, by observation?

knowledge we derive from lectures, reading and conversation, is but the copy of other men's ideas; that is, the picture of a picture; and is one remove further from the original.

3. Another advantage of observation is, that we may gain knowledge all the day long, and every moment of our lives; and every moment of our existence, we may be adding something to our intellectual treasures, except only while we are asleep; and even then, the remembrance of our dreamings will teach us some truths, and lay the foundation for a better acquaintance with human nature, both in its powers and frailties.

II. The next way of improving the mind is by reading; and the advantages are such as these.

1. By reading, we acquaint ourselves, in a very extensive manner, with the affairs, actions and thoughts of the living and the dead, in the most remote nations, and in most distant ages; and that with as much ease, as though they lived in our own age and nation. By reading, we may learn something from all parts of mankind. Whereas by observation, we learn all from ourselves, and only what comes within our own direct cognizance. By conversation, we can only enjoy the assistance of a very few persons, namely, those who are near us, and live at the same time. But our knowledge is much more narrowed still, if we confine ourselves merely to our own solitary reasonings, without much observation or reading; for then, all our improvement must arise only from our own inward powers and meditations.

2. By reading, we learn not only the actions and the sentiments of distant nations and ages, but we transfer to ourselves, the knowledge and improvements of the most learned men, the wisest and the best of mankind, when or wheresoever they lived. For though many books have been written by weak and injudicious persons, yet the most of those books, which have obtained great reputation in the world, are the products of great and wise men in their

---

Of what, are the ideas derived from lectures, reading and conversation, the copies?

With what, may we gain some acquaintance, by means of dreams?

Chief advantages of reading? By reading, we may converse with the remotest ages and nations—with the wisest and best of men — learn their best thoughts — review what we learn — consult dictionaries—choose our companions — dismiss them at pleasure.

To what objects, are we limited in observation?

To what sources of knowledge, are we confined in conversation? Principally to cotemporaries and neighbors.

several ages and nations; whereas we can obtain the conversation and instruction of those only, who are within the reach of our dwelling, or our acquaintance, whether they are wise or unwise; and sometimes that narrow sphere scarcely affords any person of great eminence in wisdom or learning, unless our instructor happens to have this character. And as for our own study and meditations, even when we arrive at some good degrees of learning, our advantage for further improvement in knowledge by them, is still far more contracted, than what we may derive from reading.

3. When we read good authors, we learn the best sentiments, even of those wise and learned men. For they studied hard, and committed to writing, their maturest thoughts, and the result of their long study and experience. Whereas, by conversation, and in some lectures, we obtain, many times, only the present thoughts of our tutors or friends, which, though they may be bright and useful, yet, at first perhaps, may be sudden and indigested, and are mere hints, which have risen to no maturity.

4. It is another advantage of reading, that we may review what we read; we may consult the page again and again, and meditate on it, at successive seasons, in our serenest and retired hours, having the book always at hand. But what we obtain by conversation and lectures, is oftentimes lost, as soon as the company breaks up, or at least, when the day vanishes; unless we happen to have the talent of a good memory, or quickly retire, and note down, what remarkables we have found in these discourses. And for the same reason, and for want of retiring and writing, many a learned man has lost several useful meditations of his own, and could never recal them.

III. The advantages of verbal instructions by public or private lectures, are these.

1. There is something more sprightly, more delightful and entertaining in the living discourse of a wise, learned and well qualified teacher, than in silent reading. The very turn of voice, the good pronunciation, and the polite and alluring manner, which some teachers have attained, will engage the attention, keep the soul fixed, and insinuate

---

What kind of thoughts, do we generally gain in conversation?

Advantages of lectures? Lectures are generally more intelligible than reading, more interesting — may be illustrated by experiments—may admit of questions.

What may conduce to render lecturing peculiarly interesting? Eloquence.

What other method is lecturing most like?

Meaning of *compendium?—intelligible?—similitude?*

into the mind, the ideas of things in a more lively and forcible way, than the mere reading of books in the silence and retirement of the closet.

2. A tutor or instructor, when he paraphrases and explains other authors, can mark out the precise point of difficulty or controversy, and unfold it. He can shew you, which paragraphs are of greatest importance, and which are of less moment. He can teach his hearers, what authors, or what parts of an author, are best worth reading, on any particular subject; and thus save his disciples much time and pains, by shortening the labors of their closet and private studies. He can shew you, what were the doctrines of the ancients in a compendium, which perhaps would cost much labor. He can inform you, what new doctrines or sentiments are rising in the world, before they come to be public, as well as acquaint you with his own private thoughts, and his own experiments and observations; which never were, and perhaps never will be, published to the world; and yet may be very valuable and useful.

3. A living instructor can convey to our senses, those notions, with which he would furnish our minds, when he teaches us natural philosophy, or most parts of mathematical learning. He can make the experiments before our eyes. He can describe figures and diagrams, point to the lines and angles, and make out the demonstration in a more intelligible manner, by sensible means, which cannot be done so well by mere reading, even though we should have the same figures lying in a book before our eyes. A living teacher, therefore, is a most necessary help in these studies.

I might add also, that even where the subject of discourse is moral, logical or rhetorical, &c. and which does not directly come under the notice of our senses, a tutor may explain his ideas by such familiar examples, and plain similitudes, as seldom find place in books.

4. When an instructor in his lectures delivers any matter of difficulty, or expresses himself in such a manner, as seems obscure, so that you do not take his ideas clearly or fully, you have opportunity, at least when the lecture is finished, or at other proper seasons, to inquire, how such a sentence should be understood, or how such a difficulty may be explained and removed.

If there be permission given to free converse with the tutor, either in the midst of the lecture, or rather at the end, concerning any doubts or difficulties, that occur to the hearer, this brings it very near to conversation or discourse.

IV. Conversation is the next method of improvement; and it is attended with the following advantages.

1. When we converse familiarly with a learned friend, we have his own help at hand, to explain to us every word and sentiment, that seems obscure in his discourse, and to inform us of his whole meaning; so that we are in much less danger of mistaking his sense; whereas in books, whatsoever is really obscure, may also abide always obscure, since the author is not at hand, that we may inquire his sense.

If we mistake the meaning of our friend in conversation, we may be quickly set at right again. But in reading, we many times go on in the same mistake; and are not capable of recovering ourselves from it. Thence it comes to pass, that we have so many contests, in all ages, about the meaning of ancient authors, and especially the sacred writers. Happy should we be, could we but converse with Moses, Isaiah and Paul, and consult the prophets and apostles, when we meet with a difficult text! But that glorious conversation is reserved for the ages of future blessedness.

2. When we are discoursing upon any theme with a friend, we may propose our doubts and objections against his sentiments, and have them solved and answered at once. The difficulties, that arise in our minds, may be removed by one enlightening word. Whereas in reading, if a difficulty or question arises in our thoughts, which the author has not happened to mention, we must be content without a present answer or solution. Books cannot speak.

3. Not only the doubts, which arise in the mind upon any subject of discourse, are easily proposed and solved in conversation, but the very difficulties we meet with in books and in our private studies, may find a relief by friendly conference. We may pore upon a knotty point in solitary meditation many months, without a solution; because perhaps we have gotten into a wrong tract of thought; and our labor is not only useless and unsuccessful, but it leads us perhaps into a train of error, for want of being corrected in the first step. But if we note down this difficulty, when we read it, we may propose it to an ingenious correspond-

---

Advantages of conversation? It affords opportunity for explanation—for proposing objections—for selecting a subject. It peculiarly stimulates the faculties—allows criticism, without public exposure—shows us human nature—exhilarates the mind—improves friendship—improves the manners.

ent, when we see him; we may be relieved in a moment. He beholds the object perhaps in a different view, sets it before us in quite another light, and leads us at once into evidence and truth, and that, with a delightful surprise.

4. Conversation calls out into light, what has been lodged in the recesses and secret chambers of the soul. By occasional hints and incidents, it brings old useful notions into remembrance. It unfolds and displays the hidden treasures of knowledge, with which reading, observation and study, had before furnished the mind. By mutual discourse, the soul is awakened, and allured to bring forth its hoards of knowledge; and it learns, how to render them most useful to mankind. A man of vast reading, without conversation, is like a miser, who lives only to himself.

5. In free and friendly conversation, our intellectual powers are more animated, and our spirits act with a superior vigor in quest of unknown truths. There is a sharpness and sagacity of truth, that attends conversation, beyond what we find, while we are shut up, reading and musing in our retirements. Our souls may be serene in solitude, but not sparkling, though perhaps we are employed in reading the works of the brightest writers. Often has it happened in free discourse, that new thoughts are strangely struck out, and the seeds of truth sparkle and blaze through the company, which in calm and silent reading, would never have been excited. By conversation, you will both give and receive this benefit; as flints, when put into motion and striking against each other, produce living fire on both sides, which would never have risen from the same hard materials in a state of rest.

6. In generous conversation, among ingenious and learned men, we have a great advantage of proposing our opinions and of bringing our own sentiments to the test, and of learning in a more compendious and a safer way, what the world will judge of them, how mankind will receive them, what objections may be raised against them, what defects there are in our scheme, and how to correct our own mistakes; which advantages are not so easy to be obtained by our own private meditations. For the pleasure we take in our own notions, and the passion of self-love, as well as the narrowness of our own views, tempt us to pass too favourable an opinion on our own schemes; whereas the variety

---

To what, does Watts compare a man of vast reading, without conversation? — Meaning of *miser*?

of genius in our several associates, will give happy notices, how our opinion will stand in the view of mankind.

7. It is also another considerable advantage of conversation, that it furnishes the student with the knowledge of men and the affairs of life, as reading furnishes him with book-learning. A man, who dwells all his days among books, may have amassed together a vast heap of notions; but he may be a mere scholar, which is a contemptible sort of character in the world. A hermit, who has been shut up in his cell in a college, has contracted a sort of mould and rust upon his soul, and all his airs of behavior have a certain aukwardness in them. But these aukward airs are worn away by degrees in company. The rust and the mould are filed and brushed off by polite conversation. The scholar now becomes a citizen or a gentleman, a neighbor and a friend; he learns how to dress his sentiments in the fairest colors, as well as to set them in the strongest light. Thus, he brings out his notions with honor; he makes some use of them in the world; and improves the theory by the practice.

But before we proceed too far in finishing a bright character by conversation, we should consider, that something else is necessary, besides an acquaintance with men and books; and therefore I add,

V. Mere lecture, reading and conversation, without thinking, are not sufficient to make a man of knowledge and wisdom. It is our own thought and reflection, study and meditation, which must attend all the other methods of improvement, and perfect them. It carries these advantages with it.

1. Though observation and instruction, reading and con-

How is a mere scholar generally regarded by the world?

What is a college student in danger of contracting?

How should students endeavor to avoid this? By treating each other more politely.

Which method of instruction must attend all the rest, in order to perfect them?

Advantages of meditation? It forms our judgment of things—makes the sentiments of others our own—improves hints otherwise acquired.

How shall we learn facts, that we do not witness? Principally by testimony.

Meaning of *testimony*?

How shall we determine, what credit to give to testimony? By considering its credibility.

Meaning of *credit*?

Six principal circumstances, that render testimony credible? Probability of the fact; veracity of the witness; his power to judge; his opportunity to judge; his freedom from bias, and the consistency of his testimony.

Of what, is a person in danger, who confines himself principally to meditation? Self-conceit, despising others, and falling into great errors.

versation may furnish us with many ideas of men and things, yet it is our own meditation, and the labor of our own thoughts, that must form our judgment of things. Our own thoughts should join or disjoin these ideas in a proposition for ourselves. It is our own mind, that must judge for ourselves, concerning the agreement or disagreement of ideas, and form propositions of truth out of them. Reading and conversation may acquaint us with many truths, and with many arguments to support them. But it is our own study and reasoning, that must determine, whether these propositions are true, and whether these arguments are just and solid.

It is confessed, there are a thousand things, which our eyes have not seen, and which would never come within the reach of our observation, because of the distance of times and places. These must be known by consulting other persons; and that is done, either in their writings, or in their discourses. But after all, let this be a fixed point with us, that it is our own reflection and judgment, which must determine, how far we should receive that which books or men inform us of, and how far they are worthy of our assent and credit.

2. It is meditation, that conveys the notions and sentiments of others to ourselves, so as to make them properly our own. It is our own judgment upon them, as well as our memory of them, that makes them become our own property. It does, as it were, concoct our intellectual food, and turns it into a part of ourselves; just as a man may call his limbs and his flesh his own, whether he borrowed the materials from the ox or the sheep, from the lark or the lobster; whether he derived it from corn or milk, the fruits of the trees, or the herbs and roots of the earth. It has all now become one substance with himself; and he wields and manages those muscles and limbs, for his own proper purposes, which once were the substance of other animals or vegetables; that very substance, which last week was grazing in the field, or swimming in the sea, waving in the milk-pail, or growing in the garden, has now become part of the man.

3. By meditation, we improve the hints, that we have acquired by observation, conversation and reading; we take more time in thinking; and by the labor of the mind, we penetrate deeper into themes of knowledge, and carry our thoughts sometimes much farther on many subjects, than we ever met with either in the books of the dead, or dis-

courses of the living. It is our own reasoning, that draws out one truth from another, and forms a whole scheme of science, from a few hints, which we borrowed elsewhere.

By a survey of these things, we may justly conclude, that he, who spends all his time in hearing lectures, or poring upon books, without observation, meditation or converse, will have but a mere historical knowledge of learning, and be able only to tell, what others have known or said on the subject. He, that lets all his time flow away in conversation, without due observation, reading or study, will gain but a slight or superficial knowledge; which will be in danger of vanishing with the voice of the speaker; and he, that confines himself merely to his closet, and his own narrow observation of things, and is taught only by his own solitary thoughts, without instruction by lectures, reading or free conversation, will be in danger of a narrow spirit, a vain conceit of himself, and an unreasonable contempt of others; and after all, he will obtain but a very limited and imperfect view and knowledge of things, and he will seldom learn, how to make that knowledge useful.

These five methods of improvement should be pursued jointly, and go hand in hand, where our circumstances are so happy, as to find opportunity and conveniency to enjoy them all; though I must give my opinion, that two of them, reading and meditation, should employ much more of our time, than public lectures or conversation. As for observation, we may be always acquiring knowledge that way, whether we are alone or in company.

But it will be for our further improvement, if we go over all these five methods of obtaining knowledge more distinctly, and more at large, and see, what special advances in useful science we may draw from them all.

Note II, by the Editor.

[Here it is earnestly recommended, that the learner review the preceding pages—that he carefully consider and weigh every sentiment and fact, and endeavor to fix it in his mind forever. Here is a rich treasure, vastly superior to

---

Which of these 5 methods should be pursued jointly?

Meaning of *jointly*?

From what verb, does *jointly* appear to be derived?

To which of these 5 methods, should most time be devoted?

How early in life, should children be taught to read? As soon, as they can understand what they read.

Should they be encouraged to read much, that they do not understand?

Why is it desirable, that children should understand what they read?

what he has yet imagined. Let him faithfully examine every sentence, endeavor to ascertain its exact meaning, to feel its force, and perceive its connection, that it may become, as it were, a part of his very soul. It is often much easier to gain, than to keep, especially ideas. He may have faithfully learnt and recited every answer. But he is in danger of soon losing the greater part. One of the best methods of preventing this, is a regular and thorough review. It may be in one lesson or more, according to the judgment of the teacher. One hour thus spent may conduce more to fix the answers in the memory, than three in common study. Nor is this all. It will peculiarly tend to improve the faculty, so that the pupil will more easily learn, and better retain his future lessons.

But so imperfect is the human memory, that we are by no means to suppose, that merely once learning and reviewing will permanently fix in the mind so many particulars. Other methods must be pursued. Among the best, no doubt, is the method by miscellaneous questions. This goes over the same ground, as the regular lessons; but the arrangement is altogether miscellaneous, and most of the questions different. A great part of them are reversed questions, in which the questions and answers substantially change places. The following may serve as a specimen. *How long was Watts in composing his treatise on the Mind? What work was Watts 20 years in composing?*

Those, who have well understood and committed the preceding lessons, will find it an easy task to learn the miscellaneous questions. But this easy task, in proportion to the time it costs, will probably be found the most useful of all methods for increasing the intellectual stores.

The miscellaneous arrangement is of inestimable value. Nothing else perhaps so completely subjects our knowledge to our control and management, whenever we have occasion to use it.]

Miscellaneous Questions, No. 1.

What work of Watts has been the most distinguished?

Into what, may we be plunged by our mistakes in judgment?

Of what, does the first chapter consist?

What is emulation?

If we judge of things by the first glimpse, with what will it fill the mind?

Which chapter contains 16 general rules for gaining knowledge and improvement?

From what do we take impressions of objects by observation?

What are some of the chief advantages of conversation?

Advantage of knowing something of an author?

Whom do we dishonor by acting without reason?

When are we accountable to God for mistakes?

Whose misconduct should we chiefly consider, in order to feel the importance of good judgment?

When is emulation right?

How often should we inquire, what new ideas we have gained?

What is logic?

What works should we read most eagerly, to correct our judgment?

When is emulation wrong?

Meaning of *dogmatic*?

Benefit of dreams?

Which of the five methods most improves the manners?

Occasion of imperfect style and repetitions in this book?

What is a judgment without evidence?

What besides genius, is necessary to make a person truly wise?

Against what, does dogmatism stop the ears?

When did the Reformation begin?

How many rules does the first chapter contain, for gaining knowledge and mental improvement?

How many methods of gaining instruction, does Watts mention?

In what manner, was this work composed?

Why do witty men sometimes pretend to despise argument?

Why is Positivo unwilling to confess his errors?

What distinguished the year 1517?

Some of the chief advantages of reading?

Some special advantages of conversation?

Which of the 5 methods gives us ideas, the most clear and lively?

Which of the 5 methods should attend all the rest?

For whom is this work more particularly designed?

What name is given to that state of mind, which tends to make a person judge without evidence?

What should we exercise upon all we read?

What sometimes renders the manners of Audens insupportable?

With what, is Jocander ready to answer every thing he hears?

Meaning of *prejudice*?

Most interesting of the 5 methods?

By which of these, do we form our judgment of things?

What prevented Watts's improving this work, as he intended?

Who by his infallible assurance, sometimes rendered his manners insupportable?

Who is ready to turn every thought into a joke?

What are the 5 principal methods of instruction?

Which of the 5 methods are most convenient for experiments?

By which of the 5 methods, do we gain our fundamental ideas?

Which of the 5 methods makes the sentiments of others our own?

What is the art of investigating and communicating truth?

When are prejudices most easily imbibed?

To what, should the hope of new discoveries animate us?

Which of the 5 methods is most convenient for questions?

By which, do we draw inferences?

Why are we accountable for some mistakes?

Of what, does logic teach us the right use?

At what period of life, are prejudices strongest?

What is said of the fool in Prov. 14: 16?

Who exceedingly impairs his understanding, by his laughing humor?

By which of the 5 methods, do we join our ideas into propositions?

What is false induction?

Evil of attempting to learn too many things?

Meaning of *premises*?

How does bad feeling produce prejudice?

With whose ignorance, are we most deeply concerned?

Meaning of *Millennium*?

What character is in peculiar danger of becoming a bloody persecutor?

What influence upon the mind, has vicious indulgence?

Meaning of *consciousness*?

When we employ causes to witness effects, what is it called?

What opportunity had Watts enjoyed, for observation?

Why is no man obliged to learn every thing?

What will be the state of the world during the Millennium?

What should we be willing to retract?

What does God give to those, who are good in his sight?

Which of the 5 methods affords us the best opportunity for conversing with the wisest and best of men?

If we attempt to learn too many things, how will it be likely to injure the faculties?

In what period of the world, will all men be holy and happy?

What should we be willing to confess?

To whom, does God give wisdom and knowledge and joy?

Which of the 5 methods affords us the best opportunity of choosing companions?

When was Watts born?

Who ought to improve their minds?

Why does no one regard the opinion of Subito?

What is it to be good in the sight of God?

Scripture sense of *conversation*?

Profession of Watts?

What will the mind be, if unimproved?

To what interests is prejudice injurious?

What great reformation did Martin Luther begin?

Tendency of acting contrary to judgment and conscience?

To what objects, are we limited in observation?

Which of the 5 methods may be most aided by eloquence?

Where was Watts born?

To which of the 5 methods should most time be devoted?

Where was Watts settled?

Upon what subjects, is it most important, that we reason correctly?

Who began the great reformation from Popery?

Which of the 5 methods is peculiarly important to the rest?

Which is most favorable for explanation?

Character of Watts's piety?

What time has every one to attend to religion?

What have many turned into a composition of hard words, trifles and subtilties?

Whose ignorance should we most deeply deplore?

What is prayer without study?

What does every truth become, when expressed in words?

By which of the 5 methods, do we gain ideas at first hand?—Which most exhilarates the mind?

What is a proposition?

Which of the 5 methods is most limited to its objects?

Why should children understand what they read?

General state of Watts's health?

What is study without prayer?

What mental skill is very desirable for all?

Into what, have many turned logic?

Why should we most deeply deplore our own ignorance?

Which of the 5 methods has its peculiar excellences and defects?

Some of the chief advantages of meditation?

CHAPTER III.

RULES RELATING TO OBSERVATION.

THOUGH observation in the strict sense of the word, and as it is distinguished from meditation and study, is the first means of our improvement, and in its strictest sense, does not include in it any reasonings of the mind upon the things which we observe, or inferences drawn from them; yet the motions of the mind are so exceedingly swift, that it is hardly possible for a thinking man to gain experience or observation, without making some secret and short reflections upon them; and therefore, in giving a few directions concerning this method of improvement, I shall not so narrowly confine myself to the first mere impressions of objects on the mind, by observation; but include also some hints, which relate to the first, most easy, and obvious reflections or reasonings, which arise from them.

I. Let the enlargement of your knowledge be one constant view and design in life; since there is no time or place, no transactions, occurrences or engagements in life, which exclude us from this method of improving the mind. When we are alone, even in darkness and silence, we may converse with our own hearts, observe the working of our own spirits, and reflect upon the inward motions of our own passions in some of the latest occurrences in life; we may acquaint ourselves with the powers and properties, the tendencies and inclinations both of body and spirit, and gain a more intimate knowledge of ourselves. When we are in company, we may discover something more of human nature, of human passions and follies, and of human affairs, vices and virtues, by conversing with mankind, and observing their conduct. Nor is there any thing more valuable, than the knowledge of ourselves and the knowledge of men, except it be the knowledge of God who made us, and our relation to him as our governor.

When we are in the house or the city, wherever we turn our eyes, we see the works of men. When we are abroad in the country, we behold more of the works of God. The skies and the ground above and beneath us, and the animal and vegetable world around about us, may entertain our observation with ten thousand varieties.

Endeavor, therefore, to derive some instruction or improvement of mind from every thing which you see or hear,

---

Subject of the third chapter?

Of what other exercise, is observation considered as including a small degree?

When should we keep in view the enlargement of our knowledge?

When should we be engaged for the improvement of our mental faculties? Constantly.

How can we continually pursue both these objects? Probably to acquire useful knowledge, in the best manner, is the best way to improve the faculties.

With what, can we converse, alone, in darkness?

What nature have we peculiar opportunities to learn in company?

With what creatures, is it most important for us to be acquainted?

What knowledge is not less important, than that of mankind?

Whose works may we principally see in the city?—in the country?

From what, should we endeavor to derive instruction?

from every thing, which occurs in human life, from every thing within you or without you.

Fetch down some knowledge from the clouds, the stars, the sun, the moon, and the revolution of all the planets. Dig and draw up some valuable meditations from the depths of the earth; and search them through the vast oceans of water. Extract some intellectual improvements from the minerals and metals, from the wonders of nature among the vegetables, the herbs, trees and flowers. Learn some lessons from the birds, and the beasts and the meanest insect. Read the wisdom of God, and his admirable contrivance in them all. Read his almighty power, his rich and various goodness, in all the works of his hands.

From the day and the night, the hours and the flying minutes, learn a wise improvement of time; and be watchful to seize every opportunity to increase in knowledge.

From the vicissitudes and revolutions of nations and families, and from the various occurrences of the world, learn the instability of mortal affairs, the uncertainty of life, the certainty of death. From a coffin and a funeral, learn to meditate upon your own departure.

From the vices and follies of others, observe what is hateful in them. Consider how such a practice looks in another person; and remember, that it looks as ill or worse in yourself. From the virtues of others, learn something worthy of your imitation.

From the deformity, the distress or calamity of others, derive lessons of thankfulness to God, and hymns of grateful praise to your Creator, Governor and Benefactor, who has formed you in a better mould, and guarded you from those evils. Learn also the sacred lesson of contentment in your own estate, and compassion to your neighbor under his miseries.

From your natural powers, sensations, judgment, memory, hands, feet, &c. make this inference, that they were not given you for nothing, but for some useful employment, to the honor of your Maker, and for the good of your fellow-creatures, as well as for your own best interests and final happiness.

From what, should we fetch down knowledge?

What may we learn from the vicissitudes and revolutions of nations and families?

What may we learn from the vices and follies of others?—from the virtues of others?—from the calamities of others?

For what, were our natural powers and members given us?

From the sorrows, the pains, the sicknesses and sufferings, that attend you, learn the evil of sin, and the imperfection of your present state. From your own sins and follies, learn the patience of God toward you, and the practice of humility toward God and man.

Thus, from every appearance in nature, from every occurrence of life, you may derive natural, moral and religious observations, to entertain your minds, as well as rules of conduct in the affairs relating to this life, and that which is to come.

II. In order to furnish the mind with a rich variety of ideas, the laudable curiosity of young people should be indulged and gratified, rather than discouraged. It is a very hopeful sign in young persons, to see them curious in observing, and inquisitive in searching into the greatest part of things that occur; nor should such an inquiring temper be frowned into silence, nor be rigorously restrained, but should rather be satisfied by proper answers.

For this reason also, where time and fortune allow it, young people should be led into company at proper seasons, should be carried abroad, to see the fields, the woods, the

---

From what, may we learn the evils of sin?—the patience of God?

In whom, is curiosity a hopeful sign?

Meaning of *curiosity*?

How should it be treated?

What opportunities, would Watts allow young persons for observing various objects?

First of 3 cautions relating to such observers? Their minds should not be distracted and overwhelmed, by too many objects.

Second? They should not be hurried from object to object.

Third? Their attention should be directed to the most important.

Special direction? Their minds should be improved and enriched, by various questions relating to the objects, both at the time of observing them, and afterwards.

What other means should be used for their instruction? Explanations, anecdotes and reflections.

Meaning of *anecdote*?

To what topics, should these instructions relate? To the properties, uses and history of the objects.

Why should the observer be questioned at first? To bring his attention to the subject, and to learn him to think.

Why afterward? To see, what he remembers, to fix the instructions in his mind, and to see, what farther reflections he has had.

What establishment might be exceedingly useful for such observers? A vast museum.

Meaning of *museum*?

How often should they visit it? Two or three times a week, for years, unless debarred for misconduct.

How should they be allowed to use the articles? To handle them, and examine them freely, at least, when there is no danger of injury.

What shall be done for a substitute? Collect and show them as many useful articles, as possible, and introduce them into museums, as far as it may be safe and convenient.

For what purpose, should museums be visited? Chiefly for instruction.

What seems exceedingly desirable for one, who visits a museum? A book, explaining every article.

rivers, the buildings, towns and cities, distant from their own dwelling. They should be entertained with the sight of strange birds, beasts, fishes, insects, vegetables, and productions both of nature and art of every kind, whether they are the products of their own or foreign nations. And in due time, where Providence gives opportunity, they may travel under a wise inspector or tutor, to different parts of the world, for the same end, that they may bring home treasures of useful knowledge.

III. Among all these observations, write down what is most remarkable and uncommon. Reserve these remarks in store for proper occasions, and at proper seasons, take a review of them. Such a practice will give you a habit of useful thinking. This will secure the exercises of your mind from running to waste; and by this means, even your looser moments will turn to happy account, both here and hereafter. And whatever useful observations have been made, let them be at least some part of the subject of your conversation among your friends, at the next meeting.

Let the circumstances or situations of life be what or where they will, a man should never neglect the improvement, which may be derived from observation. Let him travel into the East or West Indies, and fulfil the duties of the military or mercantile life there; let him rove through the earth or the seas, for his own humor as a traveller, or pursue his diversion in what part of the world he pleases, as a gentleman; let prosperous or adverse fortune call him to the most distant parts of the globe; still let him carry on his knowledge and the improvement of his mind by wise observations. In due time, by this means, he may render himself in some way useful to mankind.

Theobaldino, in his younger years, visited the forests of Norway, on the account of trade and timber; and besides his proper observations of the growth of trees on those northern mountains, he learnt, there was a sort of people called *Finnes* in those confines, which border upon Sweden, whose habitation was in the woods; and he lived afterwards to give a good account of them, and of some of their customs, to the Royal Society for the Improvement of Nat-

---

What observations should we write down?

What use should we make of these?

What most important habit, will such a practice conduce to form?

Meaning of *habit*? A certain state of body or mind, which enables us to do something more easily or perfectly, in consequence of having repeatedly done it before.

What do we do, from habit? Almost every thing.

ural Knowledge. Puteoli was taken captive into Turkey in his youth, and travelled with his master in their holy pilgrimage to Mecca, whereby he became more intelligent in the forms, ceremonies, and fooleries of the Mahometan worship, than perhaps ever any Briton was before; and by his manuscripts, we are more acquainted in this last century with the Turkish sacreds, than any one had ever informed us.

IV. Let us keep our minds as free as possible, from passions and prejudices; for these will give a wrong turn to our observations, both on persons and things. The eyes of a man in the jaundice make yellow observations on every thing; and the soul, tinctured with any passion or prejudice diffuses a false color over the real appearances of things, and disguises many of the common occurrences of life. It never beholds things in a true light, nor suffers them to appear, as they are. Whensoever, therefore, you would make proper observations, let self with all its influences stand aside, as far as possible; abstract your own interest and your own concern from them, and bid all friendships and enmities stand aloof, and keep out of the way, in the observations that you make relating to persons and things.

If this rule were well obeyed, we should be much better guarded against those common instances of misconduct in the observations of men, namely, the false judgments of pride and envy. How ready is envy to mingle with the notices, which we take of other persons! How often are mankind prone to put an ill sense upon the actions of their neighbors, to take a survey of them in an evil position, and in an unhappy light! And by this means, we form a worse opinion of our neighbors, than they deserve; while at the same time, pride and self-flattery tempt us to make unjust observations on ourselves, in our own favor. In all the favorable judgments we pass concerning ourselves, we should allow a little abatement on this account.

From what two evils, should we keep our minds free, in making observations?

What eyes make yellow observations upon every thing?

What often conduces to make us form a worse opinion of our neighbor, than he deserves?

Are we most likely to think too highly, or too meanly of ourselves?—Why?

Why should we make some abatement in our good opinion of ourselves?

How can we judge ourselves less excellent, than we seem to be? Just as we can judge the sun and moon, much larger, than they seem to be.

V. In making your observations on persons, take care of indulging that busy curiosity, which is ever inquiring into private and domestic affairs, with an endless desire of learning the secret history of families. It is but seldom, that such a prying curiosity attains any valuable ends. It often begets suspicions, jealousies and disturbances in households, and is a frequent temptation to persons, to defame their neighbors. Some persons cannot help telling what they know. A busy body is most liable to become a tattler upon every occasion.

VI. Let your observation even of persons and their conduct, be chiefly designed in order to lead you to a better acquaintance with things, particularly with human nature; and to inform you, what to imitate, and what to avoid, rather than to furnish out matter for the evil passions of the mind, or the impertinencies of discourse, and reproaches of the tongue.

VII. Though it may be proper sometimes to make your observations concerning persons, as well as things, the subject of your discourse in learned or useful conversation, yet what remarks you make on particular persons, especially to their disadvantage, should, for the most part, lie hid in your own breast, till some just and apparent occasions, some necessary call of providence lead you to speak them.

If the character or conduct, which you observe, be greatly culpable, it should so much the less be published. You may treasure up such remarks of the follies, indecencies or vices of your neighbors, as may be a constant guard against your practice of the same, without exposing his reputation on that account. It is a good old rule, that our conversation should rather be laid out on things, than on persons; and this rule should generally be observed, unless names be concealed, wheresoever the faults or follies of mankind are our present theme.

Our late archbishop Tillotson has written a small but excellent discourse on evil-speaking, wherein he admirably

---

Against what curiosity, should we particularly guard, in observing persons?

Meaning of *busy curiosity*?

What is a busy-body likely to become?

Meaning of *tattler*?

To what object, should our observation of persons be chiefly directed?

What is the only thing, that should ever lead us to speak unfavorably of others?

What of the maxim, that we should never speak of others, but to their advantage? It is contrary to reason and Scripture, and calculated to defeat itself.

How to defeat itself? In such a case, to say nothing of a person, who is mentioned, is often the same, as to declare, that we can say no good of him.

explains, limits and applies that general apostolic precept, "Speak evil of no man." Tit. 3: 2.

VIII. Be not too hasty to erect general theories from a few particular observations, appearances or experiments. This is what the logicians call a false induction. When general observations are drawn from so many particulars, as to become certain and indubitable, these are jewels of knowledge, comprehending great treasure in a little room; but, they are, therefore, to be made with the greater care and caution, lest errors become large and diffusive if we should mistake in these general notions.

A hasty determination of some universal principles, without a due survey of all the particular cases, which may be included in them, is the way to lay a trap for our own understandings in their pursuit of any subject; and we shall often be taken captives into mistake and falsehood. Niveo in his youth, observed that on three Christmas-days together, there fell a good quantity of snow; and now he has written it down in his almanack, as part of his wise remarks on the weather, that it will always snow at Christmas. Euron, a young lad, took notice ten times, that there was a sharp frost, when the wind was in the north-east; and therefore, in the middle of last July, he almost expected it would freeze, because the weather-cocks showed him a north-east wind; and he was still more disappointed, when he found it a very sultry season. It is the same hasty judgment, that has thrown scandal on a whole nation, for the sake of some culpable characters, belonging to several particular natives of that country; whereas all Frenchmen are not gay and airy; all the Italians are not jealous and revengeful; nor all the English over-run with the spleen.

From what, should we not hastily erect general theories?

What is this called?

What led Niveo to conclude, that it would always snow on Christmas?

On whose account, is scandal sometimes thrown upon a whole nation?

CHAPTER IV.

OF READING AND BOOKS.

I. The world is full of books; but there are multitudes, which are so ill written, that they were never worthy any man's reading; and there are thousands more, which may be good in their kind, but are worth nothing, when the month or year, or occasion is past, for which they were writtten. Others may be valuable in themselves, for some special purpose, or in some peculiar science, but are not fit to be perused by any, but those who are engaged in that particular science or business. To what use is it for a divine or physician or a tradesman, to read over the huge volumes of reports of judged cases in the law? or for a lawyer to learn Hebrew, and read the Rabbins? It is of vast advantage for improvement of knowledge and saving time, for a young man to have the most proper books for his reading recommended by a judicious friend.

II. Books of importance of any kind, and especially complete treatises on any subject, should be first read, in a more general and cursory manner, to learn a little, what the treatise promises, and what you may expect from the writer's manner and skill. And for this end, I would advise always, that the preface be read, and a survey taken of the table of contents, if there be one, before this first survey of the book. By this means, you will not only be bet-

---

What three classes of books does Watts mention, as deserving little or no attention?

How may a young person be assisted in ascertaining, what books he should read?

What qualifications should the recommender possess? Good judgment, acquaintance with the book, and circumstances of the reader.

Why should he consider the circumstances of the reader? A book may be pernicious to some, that is useful to others.

Why are recommendations of books often very injurious? By being given ignorantly, inconsiderately or wickedly.

Should we read a book, merely to gratify its recommender?—to say we have read it?—to talk about it?

Grand objects, for which we should read? Knowledge and mental improvement.

In what manner, would Watts have books first read?—Why?

What does he say of reading the preface, and table of contents?

How should the second reading be performed?

ter fitted to give the book the first reading, but you will be much assisted in your second perusal; which should be done with greater attention and deliberation; and you will learn with more ease and readiness, what the author pretends to teach. In your reading, mark what is new or unknown to you before; and review those chapters, pages or paragraphs. Unless a reader has an uncommon and most retentive memory, I may venture to affirm, that there is scarcely any book or chapter, worth reading once, that is not worthy of a second perusal. At least, take a careful review of all the lines or paragraphs, which you marked, and make a collection of the sections, which you thought truly valuable.

There is another reason also, why I would choose to take a superficial and cursory survey of a book, before I sit down to read it, and dwell upon it with studious attention; and that is, there may be several difficulties in it which we cannot easily understand and conquer at the first reading, for want of a fuller comprehension of the author's whole scheme. And therefore, in such treatises, we should not stay, till we master every difficulty at the first perusal; for perhaps, many of these will appear to be solved, when we have proceeded farther, or will vanish upon a second reading.

What we cannot reach and penetrate at first, may be noted down as matter for after consideration and inquiry, if the pages, that follow, do not happen to strike a complete light on those, which went before.

III. If three or four persons agree to read the same book, and each brings his own remarks upon it, at some set hours appointed for conversation, and they communicate mutually their sentiments on the subject, and debate about it in a friendly manner, this practice will render the reading of any author more abundantly beneficial to every one of them.

Should we stop to conquer every difficulty, at the first reading?—Why?

How shall we remember the difficulty?

To what book, does this direction more especially apply? The Bible.

What if we should never pass over a passage of scripture, without perfectly understanding it? We should probably never get through the first chapter of Genesis.

What method does he recommend for 3 or 4 persons to practise, in reading the same book?

Which of the 5 methods does this imply, as much as reading?

What objection is there, to adopting this social method in all cases? The reading must be very slow.

Chief advantage of this method? To excite greater attention to the book, fix its contents in the memory, instruct each other by remarks, produce a habit of remarking upon what is read, and improve in conversation.

IV. If several persons, engaged in the same study, take into their hands distinct treatises on one subject, and appoint a season of communication once a week, they may inform each other in a brief manner concerning the sense, sentiments and method of those several authors, and thereby promote each other's improvement, either by recommending the perusal of the same book to their companions, or perhaps by satisfying their inquiries concerning it by conversation, without every one's perusing it.

V. Remember that your business in reading or in conversation, especially on subjects of natural, moral or divine science, is not merely to know the opinion of the author or speaker; for this is but the mere knowledge of history; but your chief business is to consider, whether their opinions are right or not, and to improve your own solid knowledge of that subject, by meditation on the themes of their writing or discourse. Deal freely with every author you read and yield up your assent only to evidence, and just reasoning on the subject.

Here I would be understood to speak only of human authors, and not of the sacred and inspired writings. In these, our business indeed is only to find out the sense; and our assent then is bound to follow, when we are before satisfied,

---

Another method of reading for several, who are pursuing the same study?

Advantages? Nearly the same as of the other, with more abundant improvement.

Disadvantage of the second? Slower than the first.

What object is much more important in reading, than merely to know the opinion of the author?

With what authors, should we deal freely?

What is implied in dealing freely with an author?

To what alone, should we yield our assent, when we read human authors?

Whose reason should guide us in seeking truth?

What should be our first and grand object, in reading the scriptures?

More important object? To practise them.

Why should we yield our assent to the declarations of God? Because he certainly knows, and cannot lie.

Why cannot God lie? Because he is unchangeably good.

Why should we follow our own judgment, rather than that of others, as far as we are capable of judging?

What if we should always follow the judgment of others? Our own judgment would be in vain, and we should wickedly bury a most noble and precious talent.

When may we follow the judgment of others? When it is manifest, that they can judge for us, better than we can judge for ourselves.

What judgment, must we still exercise in such a case? We must determine, whether they can judge for us, and also, how far to follow their judgment.

On what subjects, are we more especially bound to judge for ourselves? On the most important subjects of religion and conscience.

Why? Because we must all give account for ourselves at the day of judgment.

that the writing is divine. Yet I might add also, that even this is just reasoning, and this is sufficient evidence to demand our assent.

But in the compositions of men, remember, you are a man as well as they; and it is not their reason, but your own, that is given to guide you, when you arrive at years of discretion.

Note III, by the Editor.

[*Manner of treating human Authors.*—According to the author's own direction, we should deal freely and faithfully with this treatise of his. Thus he dealt with others, however much revered and admired. Such men as Watts, would be the last to complain of such treatment. It is the very thing, they most earnestly desire. They are sensible of their imperfections. They know, that they have errors. They do not dare presume, that in this respect, their works are faultless. And they sometimes tremble, lest they should lead others into error, or confirm them in falsehood. There is no reason to think, that Watts would ever have published this or any other work, had he expected his instructions to be implicitly received. And yet we are in peculiar danger of receiving the instructions of this book, without due examination. Our love and admiration of his greatness, piety, learning, candor, caution and prayerfulness, and especially our admiration of this work, is in danger of bribing our judgment, and leading us to feel, as though such a work can contain nothing erroneous. We ought, therefore, to be continually on our guard. Nay, we should be doubly guarded; for an error imbibed from Watts, as it may have more influence, than the same error imbibed from a man less revered and loved, so it may prove more injurious. This is one reason, that I wished to publish this little appendage to a work, that I so highly estimate, and to which, I feel so much indebted. I would, if possible, lead the pupil most devoutly to inquire, whether there are not some dark spots in this sun of our literary hemisphere, though unobserved by the common eye. And yet it is possible, that

---

How should we deal with this treatise of Watts.

Why are we in peculiar danger of embracing any errors, it may contain?

What if Watts had supposed, that his instructions were likely to be received implicitly?

Why should we be doubly on our guard against embracing the errors of Watts?

Reason mentioned, for publishing the Questions and Supplement?

my queries and remarks, may induce him to doubt or discard some things, that are true, and to receive some, that are false. I must, therefore, most earnestly advise you, as a dear pupil, to deal with me, as you are here directed to deal with Watts and others. We should be cautious, however, lest excess of caution should lead us astray. We should take heed, that our jealous fearing, trembling watch for the author's errors, does not lead us to forget the danger of committing them ourselves—that our watch for enemies abroad, does not lead us to hush all suspicion of the more dangerous traitors in the camp of our own minds. Some persons, indeed, are so extremely fearful of errors from abroad, that they will scarcely give attention to what is written or spoken by others. We may expect to find the minds of such persons, an unweeded garden, overgrown with the briers and thorns, the spontaneous production of the uncultivated and noxious soil. Verily the way of truth is a strait and narrow way.]

VI. Let this, therefore, be your practice, especially after you have gone through one course of any science in your academical studies. If a writer on that subject maintains the same sentiments, as you do, yet if he does not explain his ideas, or prove his positions well, mark the faults or defects, and endeavor to do it better, either in the margin of your book, or rather in some papers of your own, or at least, let it be done in your private meditations. As for instance;

Where the author is obscure, enlighten him; where he is imperfect, supply his deficiencies; where he is too brief and concise, amplify a little, and set his notions in a fairer

---

Advice of the author of these?
Caution added?
What is then said, of the way of truth?
What if an author, would have us receive his opinions upon human authority? There is reason to suspect, that he cannot support them by argument and that most probably they are false.
What does Watts advise us to do, when we discover faults in books?
How should we mark faults, when the book is our own? With a cross in the margin.—things doubtful? With an interrogation.—things excellent? With a marginal line.—things very excellent? With two or more marginal lines.—other things, particularly noticeable? With an angle, formed by two straight lines, meeting and pointing to the important thing.
Advantages of marking, as we read? We shall be likely to read with much more attention and discrimination, can easily review the most important passages, and consult our associates concerning them.
What great and almost universal fault, will it tend to correct? Reading too rapidly.
What class of readers are more especially liable to this fault?
How much more useful, is the method of reading here recommended, than the common, careless manner?

view; where he is redundant, mark those paragraphs to be retrenched; when he trifles, and grows impertinent, abandon those passages or pages; where he argues, observe, whether his reasons be conclusive; if the conclusion be true, and yet the argument weak, endeavor to confirm it by better proofs; where he derives or infers any propositions darkly or doubtfully, make the justice of the inferences appear, and add further inferences or corollaries, if such occur to your mind; where you suppose he is in a mistake, propose your objections and correct his sentiments; what he writes so well, as to approve itself to your judgment both as just and useful, treasure it up in your memory, and count it a part of your intellectual gains.

Note, Many of the same directions, which I have now given, may be practised with regard to conversation, as well as reading, in order to render it useful in the most extensive and lasting manner.

VII. Other things also of the like nature may be usefully practised with regard to the authors, which you read. If the method of a book be irregular, reduce it into form by a little analysis of your own, or by hints in the margin; if those things are heaped together, which should be separated, you may wisely distinguish and divide them. If several things relating to the same subject, are scattered up and down separately through the treatise, you may bring them all to one view by references; or if the matter of a book be really valuable and deserving, you may throw it into a better method, reduce it to a more logical scheme, or abridge it into a lesser form. All these practices will have a tendency both to advance your skill in logic and method, to improve your judgment in general, and to give you a fuller survey of that subject in particular. When you have finished the treatise, with all your observations upon it, recollect and determine, what real improvements you have made by reading that author.

VIII. If a book has no index nor good table of contents, it is very useful to make one, as you are reading it; not with such exactness, as to include the sense of every page

---

What parts of a book should we endeavor to remember?

Meaning of *brief?—redundant?—retrench?—corollary?*

What advantages may result, from improving the method and composition of a book?

For whom, is this exercise proper? For those, who are considerably advanced in knowledge.

What if a book has no index, or good table of contents?

Use of such an exercise? To improve the mind, and to fix the most important thoughts in the memory?

and paragraph, which should be done, if you designed to print it; but it is sufficient in your index, to take notice only of those parts of the book, which are new to you, or which you think well written, and well worthy of your remembrance or review.

Shall I be so free as to assure my younger friends, from my own experience, that these methods of reading will cost some pains in the first years of your study, and especially in the first authors, which you peruse in any science, or on any particular subject; but the profit will richly compensate the pains. And in the following years of life, after you have read a few valuable books on any special subject, in this manner, it will be very easy to read others of the same kind; because you will not usually find very much new matter in them, which you have not already examined.

IX. If the writer be remarkable for any peculiar excellences or defects in his style or manner of writing, make just observations upon this also; and whatever ornaments you find there, or whatever blemishes occur in the language or manner of the writer, you may make just remarks upon them. And remember, that one book read over in this manner, with all this laborious meditation, will tend more to enrich your understanding, than skimming over the surface of twenty.

X. By perusing books in this manner, you will make all your reading subservient, not only to the enlargement of your treasures of knowledge, but also to the improvement of your reasoning powers.

There are many who read with constancy and diligence, and yet make no advances in true knowledge. They are delighted with the notions, which they read or hear, as they would be with stories that are told; but they do not weigh them in their minds, as in a just balance, in order to determine their truth or falsehood. They make no observations upon them, nor inferences from them. Perhaps their eye slides over the pages, or the words slide over their ears, and vanish, like a rhapsody of evening tales, or the shadows of a cloud, flying over a green field in a summer's day.

Or if they review them sufficiently to fix them in their remembrance, it is merely with a design to tell the tale over again, and shew, what men of learning they are. Thus they dream out their days in a course of reading, without

---

Why do many read with constancy and diligence, without advancing in knowledge?

Meaning of *rhapsody*?

What is their chief object, if they review?

real advantage. As a man may be eating all day, and for want of digestion, never be nourished; so these endless readers may cram themselves in vain with intellectual food, without real improvement, for want of digesting it by proper reflections.

XI. Be diligent, therefore, in observing these directions. Enter into the sense and argument of the authors, you read; examine all their proofs; and then judge of the truth or falsehood of their opinions; and thereby you will not only gain a rich increase of your understandings, by those truths, which the author teaches, when you see them well supported, but you will acquire also by degrees, a habit of judging justly, and of reasoning well, in imitation of the good writer, whose works you peruse.

This is laborious indeed; and the mind is backward to undergo the fatigue of weighing every argument, and tracing every thing to its original. It is much less labor to take all things upon trust. Believing is much easier, than arguing. But when Studentio had once persuaded his mind to tie itself down to this method, he sensibly gained an admirable facility to read, and judge of what he read; and the man made large advances in the pursuit of truth; while Plumbinus and Plumeo made less progress, though they had read over more folios. Plumeo skimmed over the pages, like a swallow over the flowery meads in May. Plumbinus read every line and syllable; but did not give himself the trouble of thinking and judging about them. They both could boast in company of their great reading; for they knew more titles and pages than Studentio, but were far less acquainted with science.

I confess, those whose reading is designed only to fit them for much talk, and little knowledge, may content themselves to run over their authors in such a sudden and trifling way. They may devour libraries in this manner, yet be poor reasoners at last, and have no solid wisdom nor true learning. The traveller, who walks on fair and softly, in a course that points right, and examines every turning, before he ventures upon it, will come sooner and safer to his journey's end, than he, who runs through every lane he meets, though he gallops full speed all the day.

What most important habit may we acquire, by attending closely to the sense and arguments of an author?

In what, did Studentio gain an admirable facility?—How?

Which read most, Studentio, or Plumeo and Plumbinus?

Which was the most learned?

Who may content themselves, to run over their authors in a sudden and trifling manner?

The man of much reading and a large retentive memory, but without meditation, may become, in the sense of the world, a knowing man; and if he converses much with the ancients, he may attain the fame of learning too; but he spends his days afar off from wisdom and true judgment, and possesses very little of the substantial riches of the mind.

XII. Never apply yourself to read any human author, with a determination before-hand, either for or against him, nor with a settled resolution to believe or disbelieve, to confirm or to oppose whatsoever he says; but always read with design to lay your mind open to truth, and to embrace it, as well as to reject every falsehood, though it appears under ever so fair a disguise. How unhappy are those men, who seldom take an author into their hands, but they have determined before they begin, whether they will like or dislike him! They have got some notion of his name, his character, his party or his principles, by general conversation, or perhaps by some slight view of a few pages; and having all their own opinions adjusted before hand, they read all that he writes with a prepossession either for or against him. Unhappy those, who hunt and purvey for a party, and scrape together out of every author, all those things, and those only, which favor their own tenets, while they despise and neglect all the rest!

XIII. Yet take this caution. I would not be understood here, as though I persuaded a person to live without any settled principles, by which to judge of men and books and things; or, that I would keep a man always doubting about his foundations. The chief things that I design in this advice, are these three;

1. After our most necessary and important principles of science, prudence and religion are settled upon good grounds, with regard to our present conduct and our future hopes, we should read with a just freedom of thought, all those books, which treat of such subjects, as may admit of doubt and reasonable dispute. Nor should any of our opinions be so resolved upon, especially in younger years, as never to hear or to bear an opposition to them.

To what, should we always keep our minds open, when we read?

What should we determine to reject?

With what predetermination, do many commence reading a book?

Meaning of *purvey?*—*tenet?*

What caution should we exercise, in reading authors, who defend our own sentiments?—of contrary sentiments?

2. When we peruse those authors, who defend our own settled sentiments, we should not take all their arguings for just and solid; but we should make a wise distinction between the corn and the chaff, between solid reasoning and the mere superficial colors of it. Nor should we readily swallow all the lesser opinions, because we agree with them in the greater.

3. When we read those authors, which oppose our most certain and established principles, we should be ready to receive any information from them on other points, and not abandon at once, every thing they say, though we are well fixed in opposition to their main point of arguing.

.......*Fas est, et ab hoste doceri.* VIRG.

Seize upon truth, wheré'er 'tis found,
Among your friends, among your foes,
On Christian or on Heathen ground.
The flower's divine, where'er it grows.
Neglect the prickles, and assume the rose.

XIV. What I have said hitherto on this subject, relating to books and reading, must be chiefly understood of that sort of books, and those hours of our reading and study, whereby we design to improve the intellectual powers of the mind with natural, moral or divine knowledge. As for those treatises, which are written to direct, or to enforce and persuade, our practice, there is one thing further necessary; and that is, that when our consciences are convinced, that these rules of prudence or duty belong to us, and require our conformity to them, we should then call ourselves to account, and inquire seriously, whether we have put them in practice or not, we should dwell upon the arguments, and impress the motives and methods of persuasion upon our own hearts, till we feel the force and power of them inclining us to the practice of the things, which are there recommended.

If folly or vice be represented in its open colors, or its secret disguises, let us search our hearts, and review our lives, and inquire, how far we are criminal. Nor should we

---

Meaning of *sentiment*?

Literal meaning of the Latin maxim, *Fas est ab hoste doceri*? It is lawful to be taught by an enemy.

Can you repeat the paraphrase, contained in 5 lines of poetry?

To what kind of improvement, do the preceding remarks upon reading, chiefly relate?

What inquiry should we make, when we read practical works?

Upon what, should we impress the sentiment?

What if folly and vice are discussed?

Which is most valuable, knowl-

ever think, we have done with the treatise, till we feel ourselves in sorrow for our past misconduct, and aspiring after a victory over those vices, or till we find a cure of those follies, begun to be wrought upon our souls.

In all our studies and pursuits of knowledge, let us remember, that virtue and vice, sin and holiness, and the conformation of our hearts and lives to the duties of true religion and morality, are things of far more consequence, than all the furniture of our understandings, and the richest treasures of mere speculative knowledge; and that, because they have a more immediate and effectual influence upon our eternal felicity or eternal sorrow.

XV. There is yet another sort of books, of which it is proper I should say something, while I am treating on this subject; and these are history, poesy, travels, books of diversion or amusement; among which, we may reckon also little common pamphlets, newspapers or such like. For many of these, I confess, once reading may be sufficient, where there is a tolerably good memory.

Or when several persons are in company, and one reads to the rest such writings, once hearing may be sufficient; provided, that every one be so attentive, and so free, as to make occasional remarks on such lines or sentences, such periods or paragraphs, as in his opinion, deserve it. Now all those paragraphs or sentiments deserve a remark, which are new and uncommon, are noble and excellent for the matter of them, are strong and convincing for the argument contained in them, are beautiful and elegant for the language or the manner, or in any way, worthy of a second rehearsal; and at the request of any of the company, let those paragraphs be read again.

Such parts also of these writings, as may happen to be remarkably stupid or silly, false or incorrect, should become subjects of an occasional criticism, made by some of the company; and this may give occasion to the repetition of them for confirmation of the censure, for amusement or diversion.

---

edge and mental improvement, or virtue and holiness?

What may be the effect of knowledge and mental improvement, without virtue and holiness? To sink the mind in disgrace and misery forever.—with virtue and holiness? To raise the mind in eternal honor and felicity.

Meaning of *virtue*? Practice of moral duties.—of *holiness*? Conformity of heart and life to the law of God.

Mention some kinds of books, of which once reading may in general, be thought sufficient.

Which class of these books, should be closely and abundantly studied? Those upon history, at least, such as are good.

Why is history worthy of such attention? It is full of instruction, and very improving to the mind.

What peculiar honor has God conferred upon history? More than half the Bible is history.

Why is history better than almost any other branch for children? Because it is so intelligible, interesting and instructive.

What history is most important? Sacred history.

Meaning of *sacred history*? History, contained in the Bible.

What history is next in importance to us? That of our own country, of England, and of the church generally.

What is the history of the church generally called? Ecclesiastical history.

Meaning of church, as here used? All the Christian churches, that have been known to exist.

Upon what branches of knowledge, does history throw light? Upon all.

What branches are peculiarly needful, to prepare for gaining a good acquaintance with history? Arithmetic, geography and chronology. Meaning of *chronology*?

What are called the two eyes of history? Geography and chronology.

Should these be studied before history, or in connection with it? Both; but chiefly the latter.

Meaning of *poesy*?

How has God manifested his regard for poetry? A considerable part of the Bible was originally written in poetry.

What parts? Most of Job and Isaiah, the whole of Psalms, various other songs, &c.

How has Watts manifested his regard for poetry? By writing so much.

Most useful part of Watts's works?

What two English poems, are considered more valuable than any other? Young's Night Thoughts, and Pollok's Course of Time.

What stamps superior value upon these? They are thought to contain more excellent instructions, and more lines, that are worth committing to memory, than any other poems.

Grand objections, that many have felt, to these poems? That they are too serious, dark and gloomy.

How have many others felt in relation to these objections? That these poems are on the whole, really most animating and delightful.

Whence the difference? Principally from different poetic and religious taste.

Why is it, that some serious persons do not admire the sentiments of these poems? Probably from not knowing them, or from some unhappy bias against them.

What is generally considered the greatest fault of the Night Thoughts? Its obscurity.

Meaning of *obscurity*?

Principal cause of this obscurity? Its conciseness.

Meaning of *conciseness*?

What advantage, may be derived from this obscurity? Great mental improvement, in finding out the meaning.

What other English poems, have been greatly and extensively admired? Milton's Paradise Lost, Pope's Essay on Man, Thompson's Seasons, Cowper's Task.

What striking excellence, is each of these thought to possess? Great poetic merit.

What great objection, has been made to Paradise Lost? That it is suited to bias the youthful mind in favor of Satan, and of rebellion against God; or to diminish the abhorrence, that ought to be felt in view of them.

Objection to the Essay on Man? That it is tinctured with infidelity.

Meaning of *infidelity*?

Objection to the Seasons? That it contains no gospel.

Objection to the Task? That it contains much that is trifling.

Which of these six poems, has probably been most frequently published? The Essay on Man.

Which next? Young's Night Thoughts.

What does this indicate? That the public are most fond of reading these.

What other English poems are much admired and praised? Akenside's Pleasures of Imagination,

Still, let it be remembered, that where the historical narration is of considerable moment, where the poesy, oratory, &c. shine with some degrees of perfection and glory, a single reading is neither sufficient to satisfy a mind, that has a true taste for this sort of writings; nor can we make the fullest and best improvement of them, without proper reviews, and that in our retirement, as well as in company. Who is there, that has any taste for polite writings, that would be sufficiently satisfied with hearing the beautiful pages of Steele or Addison, the admirable descriptions of Virgil or Milton, or some of the finest poems of Pope, Young or Dryden, once read, and then to lay them by forever?

XVI. Among these writings of the latter kind, we may justly reckon short miscellaneous essays on all manner of subjects; such as the Occasional Papers, the Tattlers, the Spectators, and some other books, that have been compiled out of the weekly or daily products of the press; wherein are contained a great number of bright thoughts, ingenious remarks, and admirable observations, which have had a considerable share in furnishing the present age with knowledge and politeness.

I wish every paper among these writings could be recommended, both as innocent and useful. I wish every unseemly idea and wanton expression had been banished

---

Campbell's Pleasures of Hope, and Trumbull's M'Fingal, besides a multitude of smaller poems.*

Can you name some of the poems, mentioned in the note?

Which do you like best?

Chief argument, used by many, for studying other languages? The mental improvement, derived from the effort to understand words and phrases.

By what other study, may the same advantage be gained? By studying our own poets.

Are they not too easy? They are so difficult, that probably no one ever understood perfectly all the poems, that have been just mentioned.

Why is the study of English poetry the most useful? It is vastly more instructive, and affords us much more assistance to understand English.

Poetic character of Shakspeare, Dryden and Byron? They are justly ranked among the greatest poets, that ever lived.

Grand objection to their poems? That from their immoral tendency, they are likely to do more harm than good, at least to some.

Can you mention some of Watts's remarks upon social reading?

What wish, does Watts express concerning the Spectator, &c?

---

* Among the finest of these, are Thomson's Hymn to the Seasons, Goldsmith's Traveller and Deserted Village, Porteus on Death, Byron's Dream on Darkness, and Destruction of the Assyrians, Watts's Hero's School of Morality, Pope's Messiah, Essay on Criticism and Dying Christian, Gray's Elegy in a Country Church Yard, Campbell's Battle of Hohenlinden, Tappan's Missionaries' farewell, Montgomery's Departing Christian.

from among them, and every trifling page had been excluded, when bound up in volumes. But it is not to be expected, in so imperfect a state, that every page or piece of such mixed public papers should be entirely blameless and laudable. Yet in the main, it must be confessed, there is so much virtue, prudence, ingenuity and goodness in them, especially in the eight volumes of Spectators, there is such a reverence of things sacred, so many valuable remarks for our conduct in life, that they are not improper to lie in parlors or summer-houses or places of usual residence, to entertain our thoughts in moments of leisure. There is such a discovery of the follies, iniquities and fashionable vices of mankind, contained in them, that we may learn much of the humors and madnesses of the age, and the public world, in our own solitary retirement, without the danger of frequenting vicious company, or receiving the mortal infection.

XVII. Among other books, which are proper and requisite, in order to improve our knowledge in general, or our acquaintance with any particular science, it is necessary, that we should be furnished with vocabularies and dictionaries of several sorts, namely, of common words, idioms and phrases, in order to explain their sense; of technical words, or the terms of art, to shew their use in arts and sciences; of names of men, countries, towns, rivers, &c. which are called historical and geographical dictionaries, &c. These are to be consulted, and used upon every occasion. Never let an unknown word pass in your reading, without seeking for its meaning in some of these writers.

If such books are not at hand, you must supply the want of them, as well as you can, by consulting such, as can inform you. It is useful to note down the matters of doubt and inquiry, and take the first opportunity to get them resolved, either by persons or books.

XVIII. Be not satisfied with a mere knowledge of the best authors, that treat of any subject, instead of acquainting yourselves thoroughly with the subject itself. There is many a young student, that is fond of enlarging his knowledge of books; and he contents himself with the notice he

---

What other books should be much consulted?

General rule for consulting dictionaries, in the course of reading?

Best English dictionary? (See Introduction.)

What if no such book is at hand?

What if no person near can inform you? Write down the words, and find them in a good dictionary, as soon as possible.

What direction is given respecting matters of doubt and inquiry?

has of their title-page, which is the attainment of a bookseller rather than a scholar. Such persons are under a great temptation to practise these two follies.

1. To heap up a great number of books, at greater expense than most of them can bear, and to furnish their libraries infinitely better than their understandings. And

2. When they have got such rich treasures of knowledge upon their shelves, they imagine themselves men of learning, and take a pride in talking of the names of famous authors, and the subjects of which they treat, without any real improvement of their own minds, in science or wisdom. At best, their learning reaches no farther than the indexes and tables of contents, while they know not how to judge of reason concerning the matters contained in those authors.

And indeed how many volumes of learning soever a man possesses, he is still deplorably poor in his understanding, till he has made these several parts of learning his own property, by reasoning, by judging for himself, and remembering what he has read.

NOTE IV, BY THE EDITOR.

[*Writing Questions in Connection with Reading.*—This method I have practised, more especially within a few years, and am more and more disposed to recommend it to others, at least to such, as can write with tolerable facility. It is among the best of all remedies for that evil disease—reading too fast. It is most happily fitted to promote meditation in connection with reading—most deeply to fix and invigorate attention, to ascertain in the first place, what the author means, and then, whether he is correct. It also conduces, to make us take a view of what we read in its consequences and various connection. There is perhaps no exercise, more suited to promote the flow, the delightful flow, of thought, to teach the mind to think with advantage, and to improve the performer in composition and conversation. It may promote self knowledge, as it may show in a considerable degree the state of the reader's mind. It is often, much more modest to state a remark in the form of a question, than in any other form.

Whose proper attainment is the mere knowledge of title pages? First danger of the students who are principally ambitious to know title pages?—Second? How may we make the contents of books our own? Meaning of *deplorable*?

Method. Make a book, of perhaps 3 or 4 sheets of paper, as it may contain a treasure worth preserving. Whatever important inquiry, reflection or remark occurs to you in reading, write it down in the form of a question. If one question suggests another, write that also, and so on, with a dozen questions, if they should occur, and seem sufficiently important to deserve recording. These questions will furnish excellent materials for future consideration, meditation, inquiry and conversation. If you have some learned friend, whom you may wish to consult upon certain points, mark those questions particularly, upon which you may wish for his instructions. Are you afraid you shall be mortified in looking over your questions hereafter?—that you will be tempted to say to yourself, "How could I be so foolish, as to write this question?" Is not this, the very way to trace your intellectual progress, and to lead you to perceive, and to thank God, that you grow wiser and wiser, from year to year? Experience may enable you to make important improvements in this method.]

CHAPTER V.

JUDGMENT OF BOOKS.

I. If we would form a judgment of a book, which we have not seen before, the first thing that offers, is the title-page; and we may sometimes guess a little at the import and design of a book by that; though it must be confest, that titles are often deceitful, and promise more than the book performs. The author's name, if it be known in the world, may help us to conjecture at the performance a little more, and lead us to guess, in what manner it is done. A perusal of the preface or introduction, which I before recommended, may further assist our judgment; and if there be an index of the contents, it will give us still some advancing light.

If we have not leisure or inclination to read over the book itself regularly, then by the titles of chapters, we may be

---

Give some account of the method, described in Note IV?

Mention some advantages of that method.

Subject of the fifth chapter?

Mention some of the methods of forming some general idea of a book.

In what respect, are title pages often deceitful?

directed to peruse several particular chapters or sections, and observe, whether there is any thing valuable or important in them. We shall find hereby, whether the author explains his ideas clearly, whether he reasons strongly, whether he methodizes well, whether his thoughts and sense are manly, and his manner polite; or, on the other hand, whether he is obscure, weak, trifling and confused; or, finally, whether the matter may not be solid and substantial, though the manner or style is rude and disagreeable.

II. By having run through several chapters and sections in this manner, we may generally judge, whether the treatise is worth a complete perusal or not. But if by such an occasional survey of some chapters, our expectation be utterly discouraged, we may well lay aside that book; for there is great probability, he can be but an indifferent writer on that subject, if he affords but one prize to divers blanks, and it may be, some downright blot too. The piece can hardly be valuable, if in seven or eight chapters, which we peruse, there be but little truth, evidence, force of reasoning, beauty and ingenuity of thought, &c. mingled with much error, ignorance, impertinence, dulness, mean and common thoughts, inaccuracy, sophistry, railing, &c. Life is too short, and time is too precious, to read every new book quite over, in order to find, that it is not worth reading.

III. There are some general mistakes, which persons frequently make in passing a judgment on the books, which they read. One is this. When a treatise is written but tolerably well, we are ready to pass a favorable judgment of it, and sometimes to exalt its character far beyond its merit, if it agrees with our own principles, and supports the opinions of our party. On the other hand, if the author is of different sentiments and espouses contrary principles, we can find neither wit nor reason, good sense nor good language in it. Whereas, alas, if our opinions of things were certain and infallible truth, yet a silly author may draw his pen in the defence of them, and he may attack even gross errors with feeble and ridiculous arguments. Truth in this world is not always attended and supported by the wisest

---

What if we are led to form a very low estimate of a book, by a survey of a few chapters?

Why is it not well to read a book through, in order to know, that it is not worth reading?

Meaning of *divers*?—*ingenuity*?—*sophistry*?—*railing*?

In what respect, are we likely to misjudge of a book, that favors our views or party?—a book that opposes them?

and safest methods; and error, though it can never be maintained by just reasoning, yet may be artfully covered and defended. An ingenious writer may put excellent colors upon his own mistakes. Some Socinians, who deny the atonement of Christ, have written well, and with much appearance of argument, for their own unscriptural sentiments; and some writers for the Trinity, and satisfaction of Christ, have exposed themselves and the sacred doctrine, by their feeble and foolish manner of handling it. Books are never to be judged merely by their subject, or the opinion they represent; but by the justness of their sentiments, the beauty of their manner, the force of their expression, or the strength of reason, and the weight of just and proper argument, which appears in them.

But this folly and weakness of trifling, instead of arguing, does not happen to fall to the share of Christian writers only. There are some, who have taken the pen in hand, to support the Deistical or antichristian scheme of our days, who make great pretences to reason upon all occasions, but seem to have left it quite behind them, when they are jesting with the Bible, and laughing at the books, which we call sacred. Some of these performances would scarcely have been thought tolerable, if they had not assaulted the Christian faith, though they are now grown up to a place among the admired pens. I much question whether several of the rhapsodies, called the Characteristics, would ever have survived the first edition, if they had not discovered so strong a tincture of infidelity, and now and then cast out a profane sneer at our holy religion. I have sometimes indeed been ready to wonder, how a book, in the main so loosely written, should ever obtain so many readers among men of sense. Surely they must be conscious in the perusal, that sometimes a patrician may write as idly, as a man of plebeian rank, and trifle as much, as an old school-man, though it is in another form. I am forced to say, there are few books, that ever I read, which made any pretence to a great

---

By what, can error never be maintained?

Most distinguishing characteristic of the Socinians?

Meaning of *Socinians*? Followers of Lelius and Faustus Socinus.

How were these men related? Lelius was uncle to Faustus.

Where were they born? In Italy.

When did they flourish? In the last half of the 16th century.

Where was their chief influence? In Poland.

By what characteristics shall we judge of books? By their truth, their importance, and the excellence of their style and manner.

Meaning of *characteristic*?

To what, did the Deists of the last century, make great pretensions?

Meaning of *Deist*?—of *survive*?

genius, from which I derived so little valuable knowledge, as from these treatises. There is indeed among them, a lively pertness, a parade of literature, and much of what some folks call politeness; but it is hard, that we should be bound to admire all the reveries of this author, under the penality of being unfashionable.

IV. Another mistake, which some persons fall into, is this. When they read a treatise on a subject, with which they have but little acquaintance, they find almost every thing new and strange to them; their understandings are greatly entertained and improved, by the occurrence of many thnigs, which were unknown to them before; they admire the treatise, and commend the author at once; whereas, if they had but attained a good degree of skill in that science, perhaps they would find, that the author had written very poorly, that neither his sense nor his method was just and proper, and that he had nothing but what was very common or trivial in his discourses on that subject.

Hence it comes to pass, that Cario and Faber, who were both bred up to labor, and unacquainted with the sciences, admire one of the weekly papers, or a little pamphlet, that talks pertly on some critical or learned theme, because the matter is all strange and new to them, and they join to extol the writer to the skies; and for the same reason, a young academic will dwell upon a Journal or an Observator, that treats of trade and politics in a dictatorial style, and be lavish in praise of the author. While at the same time, persons well skilled in those different subjects, hear the impertinent tattle with a just contempt; for they know, how weak and aukward many of those little diminutive discourses are; and that those very papers of science, politics or trade, which were so much admired by the ignorant, are perhaps, but very mean performances; though it must be also confessed, there are some excellent essays in those papers, and that upon science, as well as upon trade.

V. But there is a danger of mistake in our judgment of books, on the other hand also. For when we have made ourselves masters of any particular theme of knowledge, and surveyed it long on all sides, there is perhaps scarcely any writer on that subject, who much entertains and pleases us afterwards; because we find little or nothing new in him; and yet in a true judgment, perhaps his sentiments

---

How are persons likely to regard a treatise, upon a subject, of which they know very little?

How are we likely to judge of books, upon subjects, with which, we are most familiarly acquainted?

are most proper and just, his explications clear, and his reasonings strong, and all the parts of the discourse are well connected, and set in a happy light. But we knew most of those things before; and therefore, they strike us not, and we are in danger of discommending them.

Thus the learned and the unlearned have their several distinct dangers and prejudices ready to attend them in their judgment of the writings of men. These which I have mentioned are a specimen of them, and indeed but a mere specimen; for the prejudices, that wrap our judgment aside from truth, are almost infinite.

VI. Yet I cannot forbear to point out two or three more of these follies, that I may attempt something toward their correction, or at least, to guard others against them.

There are some persons of a forward and lively temper, who are fond to intermeddle with all appearances of knowledge, and will give their judgment on a book, as soon as the title of it is mentioned; for they would not willingly seem ignorant of any thing, that others know. And especially if they happen to have any superior character or passions of this world, they fancy they have a right to talk freely upon every thing that stirs or appears, though they have no other pretence to this freedom. Divito is worth forty thousand pounds; Politulus is a fine young gentleman, who sparkles in all the shining things of dress and equipage; Aulinus is a small attendant on a minister of state, and is at court almost every day. These three happened to meet on a visit, where an excellent book of warm and refined devotions lay in the window. "What dull stuff is here!" said Divito, "I never read so much nonsense in one page in my life; nor would I give a shilling for a thousand such treatises." Aulinus, though a courtier, and not used to speak roughly, yet would not allow, there was a line of good sense in the book, and pronounced him a madman, that wrote it in his secret retirement, and declared him a fool, that published it after his death. Politulus had more manners than to differ from men of such rank and character; and therefore, he sneered at the devout expressions, as he heard them read, and made the divine treatise a matter of scorn and ridicule; and yet it was well

---

What does he say of the number of the prejudices, that pervert judgment?

Why will some give their judgment of a book, as soon as the title is mentioned?

What did Divito, Politulus and Aulinus think of an excellent book of devotion?

Why did they thus misjudge?

known, that neither this fine gentleman, nor the courtier, nor the man of wealth, had a grain of devotion in them, beyond their horses, that waited at the door with their gilded chariots. But this is the way of the world. Blind men will talk of the beauty of colors, and of the harmony or disproportion of figures in painting; the deaf will prate of discords in music; and those, who have nothing to do with religion, will arraign the best treatise on divine subjects, though they do not understand the very language of the scripture, nor the common terms or phrases used in Christianity.

VII. I might here name another sort of judges, who will set themselves up to decide in favor of an author, or will pronounce him a mere blunderer, according to the company they have kept, and the judgment they have heard past upon a book by others of their own stamp or size, though they have no knowledge or taste of the subject themselves. These, with a fluent and voluble tongue, become mere echoes of the praises or censures of other men. Sonillus happened to be in the room where the three gentlemen just mentioned gave out their thoughts so freely upon an admirable book of devotion; and two days afterwards, he met with some friends of his, where this book was the subject of conversation and praise. Sonillus wondered at their dulness, and repeated the jests, which he had heard cast upon the weakness of the author. His knowledge of the book and his decision upon it were all from hearsay; for he had never seen it; and if he had read it through, he had no manner of right to judge about the things of religion, having no more knowledge, nor taste of any thing of inward piety, than a hedge-hog or a bear has of politeness.

When I had written these remarks, Probus, who knew all these four gentlemen, wished they might have opportunity to read their own character, as it is represented here. Alas! Probus, I fear, it would do them very little good, though it may guard others against their folly; for there is not one of them, would find his own name in these characters, if they read them, though all their acquaintances would acknowledge the features immediately, and see the persons almost alive in the picture.

VIII. There is yet another mischievous principle, which prevails among some persons in passing a judgment on the writings of others, and that is, when from the secret stimu-

---

What did Sonillus think of the book?—Why?

What may such judges as Sonillus be called? Echo-critics.

lation, of vanity, pride or envy, they despise a valuable book, and throw contempt upon it by wholesale; and if you ask them the reason of their severe censure, they will tell you perhaps, they have found a mistake or two in it, or there are a few sentiments or expressions, not suited to their humor. Bavius cries down an admirable treatise of philosophy, and says, there is atheism in it; because there are a few sentences, that seem to suppose brutes to be mere machines. Under the same influence, Momus will not allow Paradise Lost to be a good poem, because he had read some flat and heavy lines in it, and he thought Milton had too much honor done him. It is a paltry humor, that inclines a man to rail at any human performance, because it is not absolutely perfect.

Wise and just distinctions ought to be made, when we pass a judgment on mortal things; but envy condemns by wholesale. Envy is a cursed plant. Some fibres of it are rooted almost in every man's nature; and it works in a sly and imperceptible manner, and that even in some persons, who in the main are men of wisdom and piety. They know not, how to bear the praises, that are given to an ingenious author, especially if he be living and of their profession; and therefore they will, if possible, find some blemish in his writings, that they may nibble and bark at it. They will endeavor to diminish the honor of the best treatise, that has been written on any subject, and to render it useless, by their censures, rather than suffer their envy to lie asleep, and the little mistakes of that author to pass unexposed. Perhaps they will commend the work in general with a pretended air of candor; but pass so many sly and invidious remarks upon it afterwards, as shall effectually destroy all their cold and formal praises. I grant, when wisdom itself censures a weak and foolish performance, it will pass its severe sentence, and yet with an air of candor, if the author has any thing valuable in him; but envy will oftentimes imitate the same favorable airs, in order to make its cavils appear more just and credible, when it has a mind to snarl at some of the brightest performances of a human writer.

IX. When a person feels any thing of this invidious

Why would not Momus allow Paradise Lost to be a good poem?

From what principle, do many pour contempt upon a book, by wholesale?

In what manner, will they sometimes commend a work in general?

How will they destroy the force of their commendation?

How may a person cure such an invidious humor?

humor working in him, he may by the following considerations, attempt the correction of it. Let him think with himself, how many are the beauties of such an author whom he censures, in comparison of his blemishes, and remember, that it is a much more honorable and good natured thing to find out peculiar beauties than faults. True and undisguised candor is a much more amiable and divine talent than accusation. Let him reflect again, what an easy matter it is, to find a mistake in all human authors, who are necessarily fallible and imperfect.

I confess, where an author sets up himself to ridicule divine writers and things sacred, and yet assumes an air of sovereignty and dictatorship, to exalt and almost deify all the Pagan ancients, and cast his scorn upon all the moderns, especially if they do but savor of miracles and the gospel, it is fit the admirers of this author should know that nature and these ancients are not the same, though some writers always unite them. Reason and nature never made these ancient heathens their standard, either of art or genius, of writing or heroism. Sir Richard Steele, in his little essay called The Christian Hero, has shewn our Savior and St. Paul in a more glorious and transcendant light, than a Virgil or a Homer could do for their Achilles, Ulysses or Æneas; and I am persuaded, if Moses and David had not been inspired writers, these very men would have ranked them, at least with an Herodotus and Horace, if not given them the superior place.

But where an author has many beauties consistent with virtue, piety and truth, let not little critics exalt themselves, and shower down their ill-nature upon him, without bounds or measure; but rather stretch their own powers of soul, till they write a treatise superior to that which they condemn. This is the noblest and surest manner of suppressing what they censure.

A little wit, or a little learning, with much vanity and ill-nature, will teach a man to pour out whole pages of remark and reproach upon one real or fancied mistake of a great and good author, and this may be dressed up by the same talents, and made entertaining enough to the world, who

---

What authors, does Watts say, are not the same as nature?

How may severe critics learn to judge more favorably of the works of others?

What shall we call those who pour out the same praise or censure upon the whole of a work, that is due only to certain parts? Whole-sale critics.

Who was the most distinguished arch-bishop of Cambray? Fenelon.

Where is Cambray? In the N. E. of France.

love reproach and scandal. But if the remarker would but once make this attempt, and try to outshine the author by writing a better book on the same subject, he would soon be convinced of his own insufficiency, and perhaps might learn to judge more justly and favorably of the performance of other men. A cobler or a shoemaker may find some little fault with the latchet of a shoe, that an Apelles had painted, and perhaps with justice too, when the whole figure and portraiture is such, as none but an Apelles could paint. Every poor low genius may cavil at what the richest and the noblest has performed. But it is a sign of envy and malice, added to the littleness and poverty of genius, when such a cavil becomes a sufficient reason to pronounce at once, against a bright author, and a whole valuable treatise.

X. Another, and that a very frequent fault in passing a judgment upon books, is this, that persons spread the same praises or the same reproaches over a whole treatise, and all the chapters in it, which are due only to some of them. They judge as it were by wholesale, without making a due distinction between the several parts or sections of the performance; and this is ready to lead those, who hear them talk, into a dangerous mistake. Florus is a great and just admirer of the late arch-bishop of Cambray, and mightily commends every thing he has written, and will allow no blemish in him; whereas the writings of that excellent man are not of a piece; nor are those very books of his, which have a good number of beautiful and valuable sentiments in them, to be recommended throughout, or all at once, without distinction. There is his "Demonstration of the Existence and Attributes of God," which has justly gained a universal esteem, for bringing down some new and noble thoughts of the wisdom of the creation to the understanding of the unlearned; and they are such as well deserve the perusal of the man of science, perhaps as far as the 50th section. But there are many of the following sections which are very weakly written, and some of them built upon an enthusiastical and mistaken scheme, akin to the peculiar opinions of father Malbranche; such as Sect. 51, 53. "That we know the finite only by the ideas of the infinite." Sect. 55, 60. "That the superior reason in man, is God himself, acting in him." Sect. 61, 62. "That the idea of unity cannot be taken from creatures, but from God only;" and several of his sections, from 65, to 68, upon the

---

What kind of a writer was Fenelon?

doctrine of liberty, seem to be inconsistent. Again, toward the end of his book, he spends more time and pains, than are needful, in refuting the Epicurean fancy of atoms moving eternally through infinite changes, which might be done effectually in a much shorter and better way.

So in his Posthumous Essays and his Letters, there are many admirable thoughts in practical and experimental religion, and very beautiful and divine sentiments in devotion; but sometimes in large paragraphs, or in whole chapters together, you find him in the clouds of mystic divinity, and he never descends within the reach of common ideas or common sense.

But remember this also, that there are but few such authors, as this great man, who talks so very weakly sometimes, and yet in other places, is so much superior to the greatest part of writers.

There are other instances of this kind, where men of good sense in the main, set up for judges; but they carry too many of their passions about them, and then, like lovers, they are in rapture at the name of their fair idol. They lavish out all their incense upon that shrine, and cannot bear the thought of admitting a blemish in them.

Milton is a noble genius; and the world agrees to confess it. His Paradise Lost is a glorious performance, and rivals the most famous pieces of antiquity. But that reader must be deeply prejudiced in favor of the poet, who can imagine him equal to himself, through all that work. Neither the sublime sentiments, nor dignity of numbers, nor force or beauty of expression, are equally maintained, even in all those parts, which require grandeur or beauty, force or harmony. I cannot but consent to Mr. Dryden's opinion, though I will not use his words, that for some scores of lines together, there is a coldness and flatness, and almost a perfect absence of that spirit of poesy, which breathes and lives and flames in other pages.

XI. When you hear any person pretending to give his judgment of a book, consider with yourself, whether he be a capable judge, or whether he may not lie under some unhappy bias or prejudice, for or against it, or whether he has made a sufficient inquiry to form his justest sentiments upon it.

What does Watts say of the genius of Milton?

What does Watts say, Paradise Lost rivals?

What does he say against this poem?

When we hear a man criticising a book, what silent inquiries should we make?

Though he is a man of good sense, yet he is incapable of passing a true judgment of a particular book, if he be not well acquainted with the subject, of which it treats, and the manner in which it is written, be it verse or prose; or if he has not had opportunity or leisure to look sufficiently into the writing itself.

Again, though he is ever so capable of judging on all other accounts, by the knowledge of the subject, and of the book itself, yet you are to consider also, whether there is any thing in the author, in his manner, in his language, in his opinions, and his particular party, which may warp the sentiments of him that judges, to think well or ill of the treatise, and to pass too favourable or too severe a sentence concerning it.

If you find, that he is either an unfit judge, because of his ignorance, or because of his prejudices, his judgment of that book should go for nothing. Philographo is a good divine, a useful preacher, and an approved expositor of scripture; but he never had a taste for any of the polite learning of the age. He was fond of every thing that appeared in a devout dress; but all verse was alike to him. He told me last week, there was a very fine book of poems published on the three christian graces, Faith, Hope and Charity; and a most elegant piece of oratory on the four last things, Death, Judgment, Heaven and Hell. Do you think I shall buy either of those books merely on Philographo's recommendation?

Why would not Watts purchase a poem, on the recommendation of a certain good divine?

Miscellaneous Questions, No. 2.

Why may a book be useful to some persons, and not to others?

For what object, should children attend museums?

What is meant by dealing freely with an author?

Greatest poem of Milton?

How may we make the contents of a book our own?

What sect of professed Christians deny the atonement of Christ?

Who is most concerned to know Hebrew, a minister or a lawyer?

With what limitation, should children be allowed to handle the articles of a museum?

To what alone, should we yield our assent, when we read human authors?

Author of the Night Thoughts?

In what respect are title-pages often deceitful?

Who were Lelius and Faustus Socinus?

When should we make some abatement of our favorable opinion?

How can we be continually engaged for the improvement of our minds, and for the acquisition of knowledge?

Who is likely to become a tattler?

Why are we in peculiar danger of embracing any errors, that we may find in Watts's writings?

What fault in reading is almost universal?

Greatest poem of Young?

What does Watts say of the number of prejudices, that pervert judgment?

What should we fetch down from the clouds and from the stars?

From what two evils, should we keep ourselves free, in making observations?

What may sometimes require us to speak unfavorably of others?

To what, should we always keep our minds open, when we read?

Author of the Seasons?

How do echo-critics form their opinions of books?

Where may we see most of the works of God?

What observations are made by jaundiced eyes?

What measure with regard to evil-speaking, is calculated to defeat itself?

What if an author would have us receive his opinions on human authority?

What inquiry should we make, when we read practical works?

Greatest poem of Thomson?

What authors, does Watts say, are not the same as nature?

Where may we see most of the works of man?

Upon what, do jaundiced eyes make yellow observations?

What is false induction?

Why should we believe the declarations of God?

What is more valuable, than knowledge and mental impovement?

Author of the Essay on Man?

By what characteristics, shall we judge of books?

What are wholesale-critics?

What two branches of knowledge are most important?

Influence of envy upon our judgment of others.

How may a young person be assisted in ascertaining, what books to read?

Why cannot God lie?

What may be the effect of knowledge and mental improvement, without virtue and holiness?

Author of the Task?

Who was Fenelon?

How may we best learn the hatefulness of vice?

Of whom, are we most likely to think too favorably?

Why are recommendations of books often injurious?

What if we should always follow the judgment of others?

Effect of knowledge and mental improvement, with virtue and holiness?

Greatest poem of Cowper?

What hopeful sign should we particularly encourage in youth?

What special efforts should be made, to improve and enrich young minds, when observing new objects?

What if books are recommended ignorantly, inconsiderately or wickedly?

On what subjects, are we more especially bound to judge for ourselves?

Meaning of virtue?

Author of the Course of Time?

Against the errors of what author, should we be doubly guarded?

From what wrong motives, do persons sometimes read books?

Why should we judge for ourselves, upon the things of religion?

Meaning of *holiness*?

Author of Paradise Lost?

Greatest work of Pollok?

Grand object, for which we should read books?

What does Watts advise us to do, when we discover faults in books?

What English poems have been greatly admired?

Name, given to those, who hold to the being of God, but deny the Bible?

For whom, might museums be exceedingly useful?

With what authors, should we deal freely?

Advantages of making books, as we read?

Character of Webster's Dictionary?

From what causes or circumstances, are we in danger of judging incorrectly of books?

CHAPTER VI.

OF LIVING INSTRUCTIONS AND LECTURES—OF TEACHERS AND LEARNERS.

I. There are few persons of so penetrating a genius, and so just a judgment, as to be capable of learning the arts and sciences without the assistance of Teachers. There is scarcely any science, so safely and so speedily learned, even by the noblest genius and the best books, without a tutor. His assistance is absolutely necessary for most persons, and it is very useful for all beginners. Books are a sort of dumb teachers. They point out the way to learning; but if we labor under any doubt or mistake, they cannot answer sudden questions, or explain present doubts and difficulties. This is properly the work of a living instructor.

II. There are very few tutors, who are sufficiently furnished with such universal learning, as to sustain all the parts and provinces of instruction. The sciences are numerous, and many of them lie far wide of each other; and it is best to enjoy the instruction of two or three tutors at least, in order to run through the whole Encyclopedia or Circle of Sciences, where it may be obtained. Then we may expect, that each will teach the few parts of learning, which are committed to his care, in greater perfection. But where this advantage cannot be had with convenience, one great man must supply the place of two or three common instructors.

III. It is not sufficient that instructors be competently skilled in those sciences, which they profess and teach. They should have skill also in the art or method of teaching, and patience in the practice of it.

It is a great unhappiness indeed, when persons by a spirit of party or faction or interest or by purchase, are

---

Whose assistance do most persons need, in learning the arts and sciences?

How many teachers is it desirable to have?—Why?

Two grand qualifications, which every teacher should possess?

set up for tutors, who have neither due knowledge of science, nor skill in the way of communication. And alas, there are others, who with all their ignorance and insufficiency, have self-admiration and effrontery enough to set up themselves; and the poor pupils fare accordingly, and grow lean in their understandings.

And let it be observed also, there are some very learned men, who know much themselves, but have not the talent of communicating their own knowledge; or else they are lazy, and will take no pains. Either they have an obscure

---

Some reasons, why a learned man may be a very bad teacher?

Qualifications, desirable in a teacher? Knowledge, skill, piety, good character, zeal, affection, ingenuity, meekness, patience, authority, politeness, health.

Meaning of *ingenuity*? — of *meekness*?

Why should he be pious? He will be much more likely to use effectual means for the highest benefit of his pupils.

Why should a teacher endeavor to promote the salvation of his pupils? He has peculiar advantages for this object, and it is infinitely important.

What scripture shows it to be sinful not to improve such advantage? To him, &c. [See James 4: 17.]

Why should not a teacher be wholly employed in teaching his pupils literature, to the exclusion of religion? Religion is infinitely more important; it vastly increases the importance of the other branches, and helps the pupil's progress in them.

How does it help the pupil's progress in other branches? It conduces to render his application more constant, vigorous and persevering, and he is more likely to enjoy the special blessing of God upon his studies.

Are teachers hired to teach religion? They generally are, at least, in some degree.

How does this appear, when their employers say nothing upon the subject? It is generally understood, that teachers will give their pupils some religious instruction.

What if parents are unwilling, their children should be taught religion? Probably no one ought to take such a school.

Why should a teacher have a good moral character? That he may be respected by his pupils, and that his moral influence upon them, may be good.

Why should a teacher have zeal? He will do very little without it. The example of his zeal is also needful to awaken the genius of his pupils.

Why should a teacher be affectionate? It is a thousand times better to draw children to their studies, by the cords of love, than to drive them, by the rod of correction. It will conduce to make them love their studies, as long as they live.

Why is it desirable, that a teacher should be ingenious? To devise the best methods, and practise them in the best manner, as circumstances may vary.

Why is meekness desirable in a teacher? To fortify him against the many provocations, to which he is exposed.

Why should he be patient? He will probably find some of his pupils very ignorant, dull, stupid and slow in their progress.

What teachers are in the greatest danger of failing in regard to such scholars? Those, who are the most bright and intelligent.

Why are men of superior genius and learning very liable to fail in forming systems of education? They can hardly make due allowance for the weakness of common minds, and can hardly know the steps, by which, common minds proceed in improvement.

and perplexed way of talking; or they show their learning uselessly, and make a long periphrasis on every word of the book they explain; or they cannot condescend to young beginners; or they run presently into the elevated parts of the science, because it gives themselves greater pleasure; or they are soon angry and impatient, and cannot bear with a few impertinent questions of a young, inquisitive and

---

Why should a teacher possess authority? To render his kindness more striking and affecting, and to awe and govern those, who will not be ruled by love.

Meaning of *authority?* Dignity and energy of character.

When should a teacher's authority be directly manifested? Only when it is needful to maintain good order.

Why is politeness desirable in a teacher? To win the hearts of his pupils, and improve their manners.

What is true politeness? It is love, manifested in an easy, unaffected, graceful and winning manner.

Why is it desirable, that the pupils' manners should be improved? It may greatly conduce to their happiness and usefulness.

What passage of scripture inculcates politeness? Charity doth not behave itself unseemly.

Can we expect a teacher to possess all these qualifications? Perhaps rarely, if ever, in a high degree.

What is the daily duty of a teachas? By the most assiduous attention, watchfulness and prayer, to be as useful to his pupils, as possible.

How much time should a teacher devote to his pupils? If he is well paid for the whole of his time, justice seems to require, that the whole should be devoted; and mercy may require the same, where his compensation is little or nothing.

Why do young teachers often succeed better, than those, who have had much experience?

How shall a teacher maintain his interest in his business? By making special preparation for every recitation, and continual efforts to improve in the art of teaching.

Duties of pupils? Attendance, attention, affection, obedience, docility, respect, freedom of thought, gratitude.

Meaning of *freedom of thought?* Practice of thinking and judging for himself.

How should a teacher promote freedom of thought in his pupils? By giving the reasons of his statements, as far as possible, and also by warning them against adopting his opinions, without examination.

Why should a pupil attend school constantly? The omission of a recitation is a loss in itself, and renders the pupil less capable of understanding the next.

Tendency of several absences? To make the pupil unsteady, to destroy his relish for study, and frustrate the little efforts, that he makes.

Meaning of *frustrate?*

Why should a pupil attend punctually? Every moment's absence is a loss to himself, and his tardy coming, an interruption to others.

Meaning of *punctual?*—of *tardy?*

What important habit is punctual attendance likely to produce?

What scripture represents punctuality as a virtue? That passage in the first Psalm, which compares a godly man to a tree, that brings forth its fruit in season.

Why should a pupil love his teacher? For the sake of his own improvement.

What if the teacher is so unlovely, that the pupil cannot love him? Perhaps it may be better to be at play, than at school, at least, half of the time. It may be advisable for the pupil to quit the school, and better still for the teacher to quit.

How should a pupil honor a worthy teacher? By the best possible conduct and improvement, and by always speaking of him in a respectful and affectionate manner.

sprightly genius; or else they skim over a science in a very slight and superficial survey, and never lead their disciples into the depths of it.

IV. A good tutor has characters and qualifications, very different from all these. He is such a one, as both can and will apply himself with diligence and concern, and indefatigable patience, to effect what he undertakes; to teach his disciples, and see what they learn; to adapt his way and method, as near as may be, to the various dispositions, as well as to the capacities of those, whom he instructs, and to inquire often into their progress and improvement. And he should take particular care of his own temper and conduct, that there be nothing in him or about him which may be of ill example; nothing that may savor of a haughty temper, a mean and sordid spirit; nothing that may expose him to the aversion or to the contempt of his scholars, or create a prejudice in their minds against him and his instructions. If possible, he should have so much of a natural candor and sweetness, mixed with all the improvements of learning, as may convey knowledge into the minds of his disciples, with a sort of gentle insinuation and sovereign delight, and may draw them into the highest improvements of their reason, by a resistless and insensible force. But I shall have occasion to say more on this subject, when I come to speak more directly of the methods of the communication of knowledge

V. The learner shou.d attend with constancy and care on all the instructions of his tutor; and if he happens to be at any time unavoidably hindered, he must endeavor to retrieve the loss by double industry for time to come. He should always recollect and review his lectures, read over some other author or authors upon the same subject, confer upon it with his instructor, or with his associates, and write down the clearest result of his present thoughts, reasonings and inquiries, which he may have recourse to hereafter, either to re-examine them, and to apply them to proper use, or to improve them further to his own advantage.

VI. A student should never satisfy himself with bare attendance on the lectures of his tutor, unless he clearly takes up his sense and meaning, and understands the things, which he teaches. A young disciple should behave himself so well, as to gain the affection and the ear of his in-

---

If a pupil has difficulties, relating to his studies, how should he attempt to have them solved?

structor, that upon every occasion, he may with the utmost freedom, ask questions, and talk over his own sentiments, his doubts and difficulties with him, and in a humble and modest manner desire the solution of them.

VII. Let the learner endeavor to maintain an honorable opinion of his instructor, and heedfully listen to his instructions, as one willing to be led by a more experienced guide; and though he is not bound to fall in with every sentiment of his tutor, yet he should so far comply with him, as to resolve upon a just consideration of the matter, and try and examine it thoroughly with an honest heart, before he presumes to determine against him. And then it should be done with great modesty, with a humble jealousy of himself, and apparent unwillingness to differ from his tutor, if the force of argument and truth did not constrain him.

VIII. It is a frequent and growing folly in our age, that pert young disciples soon fancy themselves wiser, than those who teach them. At the first view, or upon a very little thought, they can discern the insignificancy, weakness and mistake of what their teacher asserts. The youth of our day, by an early petulancy and pretended liberty of thinking for themselves, dare reject at once, and that with a sort of scorn, all those sentiments and doctrines, which their teachers have determined, perhaps after long and repeated consideration, after years of mature study, careful observation, and much prudent experience.

IX. It is true, teachers and masters are not infallible, nor always in the right; and it must be acknowledged, it is a matter of some difficulty for younger minds to maintain a

---

What should a pupil do, before he decides a point against his teacher?

In what manner, should a pupil discuss a question with his teacher?

What should be the conduct of a teacher in such a case? He should encourage his pupil to ask questions, and state objections freely, and endeavor to convince and satisfy him in the most kind and affectionate manner.

What should the teacher do, if he is convinced, that his pupil is in the right? He should acknowledge his error.

Maxim relating to this subject? He that is not willing to be taught by his pupil, ought never to have a pupil.

Who should co-operate with teachers, for the improvement of their pupils? Parents, ministers, school committees and all, who can promote the object.

What does Watts mention, as a frequent and growing folly in that age?

Tendency of such a disposition? To infidelity and every evil work.

Meaning of *infidelity*?

How should a teacher check such a disposition? Chiefly by affectionate treatment and sound argument.

What qualifications should a teacher possess, in order for this? Great knowledge, and fine powers of logic.

What does Watts here mention, as a matter of difficulty for younger minds to maintain?

just and solemn veneration for the authority and advice of their parents, and the instructions of their tutors, and yet at the same time, to secure to themselves, a just freedom in their own thoughts. We are sometimes too ready to imbibe all their sentiments without examination, if we reverence and love them; or, on the other hand, if we take all freedom to contest their opinions, we are sometimes tempted to cast off that love and reverence to their persons, which God and nature dictate. Youth is ever in danger of these two extremes.

X. But I think, I may safely conclude thus; though the authority of a teacher must not absolutely determine the judgment of his pupil, yet young and inexperienced learners should pay all proper deference to the instructions of their parents and teachers, short of absolute submission to their dictates. Yet still we must maintain this, that they should never receive any opinion, whether conformable or contrary to the tutor's mind, without sufficient evidence of it, first given to their own reasoning powers.

It is thought best to omit the 7th chapter, as it would probably be useless to most learners, and of very little advantage to any.

CHAPTER VIII.

OF INQUIRING INTO THE SENSE AND MEANING OF ANY WRITER OR SPEAKER, AND ESPECIALLY THE SENSE OF THE SACRED WRITINGS.

It is a great unhappiness, that there is such an ambiguity in words and forms of speech, that the same sentence may be drawn into different significations; whereby it comes to

---

What deference should children show to parents and teachers?—Meaning of *deference*?

HERMENEUTICS.—Meaning of *hermeneutics*? The art of investigating and explaining the sense of words and phrases.

From what Greek word, is *Hermeneutics* derived? Hermeneuo.—Meaning of *hermeneuo*? To interpret.

Meaning of *phrase*? An expression, consisting of more words than one, so united as to make sense.

What is the difference between explaining a phrase, and explaining the words, of which a phrase consists? In many phrases, some of the words are used in a very peculiar sense, or have scarcely any meaning, so that the sense of the phrase cannot be gathered from

pass, that it is difficult sometimes for the reader exactly to hit upon the ideas, which the writer or speaker had in his mind. Some of the best rules to direct us in this, are such as these.

I. Be well acquainted with the tongue itself, or language, wherein the author's mind is exprest. Learn not only the true meaning of each word, but the sense, which those words obtain, when placed in such a particular situation and order. Acquaint yourself with the peculiar power and emphasis of the several modes of speech, and the various idioms of the tongue. The secondary ideas, which custom has superadded to many words, should also be known, as well as the particular and primary meaning of them, if we would understand any writer. See Logic, Part I. Chap. 4. Sec. 3.

II. Consider the signification of those words and phrases, more especially in the same nation, or near the same age, in which that writer lived, and in what sense they are used by authors of the same nation, opinion, sect, party, &c.

In this way, we may learn to interpret several phrases of the New Testament out of that version of the Hebrew Bible into Greek, which is called the Septuagint. For though that version is very imperfect and defective in many things, yet it seems to me evident, that the holy writers of the New Testament made use of that version many times in their citation of texts out of the Bible.

---

knowing the meaning of each word separately.

Can you give an example? In the phrase, *Not at all*, the word *at* is used in a peculiar sense, and the word *all*, in a sense contrary to its usual meaning.

Should we use absurd and ridiculous phrases? We should not, except such, as are so common, as to render it very difficult to drop them.

How shall we learn the meaning of phrases? As we do the meaning of words, at least, when we have dictionaries, in which phrases are explained.

What does Watts represent, as a great unhappiness, relating to language?

With what, is it very important to be well acquainted, in order to learn the sense of an author?

What language is it most important to know, in order to understand an English book, that is not a translation from another language?

In what, consists the knowledge of a language? Principally in knowing the meaning of words and phrases.

In what else, does it in some measure, consist? In knowing the relation, variation and proper collocation of words and phrases.

What branch of literature treats of these subjects? Grammar.

Meaning of *collocation*?

Three principal methods of learning the meaning of words? By observing, how they are used in conversation, how they are used in books, how they are explained in dictionaries.

What other methods are sometimes used? Showing the objects, signified by the words, making signs by motions of the hands, head, &c. and by verbal explanations.

III. Compare the words and phrases in one place of an author, with the same or kindred words and phrases, used in other places of the same author ;, which are generally called parallel places; and as one expression explains another, which is like it, so sometimes a contrary expression will explain its contrary. Remember always, that a writer best

---

What is a verbal explanation? It is telling, what a word means.

In what way, does the child begin to learn the meaning of words? By hearing them used, while he perceives the objects.

How do little children learn the meaning of words, when the objects are not perceived? By the connection, in which the words are used, and by verbal explanations.

How do children often get wrong ideas of words? By misjudging of the connection, or by guessing wrong.

When should parents and friends begin to make it a business to teach the child words? Almost as soon as he is born.

How should this be done, during his tender years? By showing him multitudes of objects, pronouncing their names, qualities, &c. and frequently asking him, "What's that? What is it good for? Where did it come from? Who made it? How do you like it?" &c.

What if the child uses a word improperly? He should be kindly corrected, and the proper word should be suggested.

Two special cautions in teaching a child words? Not attempt to teach him those, that are wholly above his comprehension, nor too many in a short time.

What should parents do, that are not qualified to teach their children, as here recommended? They must do the best in their power; and this will enable them to do better, and better continually.

Why have many parents scarcely any talent to teach their children? Because they do not improve the little talent they have.

What should parents teach children, respecting words, besides their signification? Good pronunciation, good articulation, and all the proprieties of speech.

Why will some knowledge of Latin assist us to know English? About one sixth part of our words are derived from Latin.

Can we not know the meaning of these words, without knowing their Latin origin? We can.

How does this appear? Many good English scholars know nothing of Latin; and most of our derivatives differ in signification from their foreign primitives.—Meaning of *primitive*?

What is implied in supposing that we cannot know the meaning of a word, without knowing its original in another language? That scarcely any person knows one quarter of our words, and that those which are not derived from other languages, cannot be known.

What else does it seem to imply? That in order to know a Latin or Greek word, we must know its primitive in some other language.

What injury is sometimes imparted to a person's style by his knowledge of Latin? It is sometimes rendered stately, stiff, pompous and obscure, by the copious use of high sounding words.

What compositions in English have probably been most injured by Latin? Sermons.

What part of the audience can generally understand very little of a written sermon? Probably more than half.

What then is the advantage of knowing the Latin originals? It may give us some general notion of the meaning of words, render the meaning more impressive, more permanently remembered, and more easily recalled for use.

With what should we compare an author's words and phrases, in order to understand them?

What are these generally called?

What does the author say of contraries?

Who can best interpret a writer?

interprets himself; and as we believe the Holy Spirit to be the supreme agent in the writings of the Old Testament and the New, he can best explain himself. Hence, that theological rule arises, that "Scripture is the best interpreter of scripture;" and therefore concordances, which shew its parallel places, are of excellent use for interpretation.

Note V, by the Editor.

[*Concordance.*—It is deeply to be lamented, that this admirable help for understanding and impressing Scripture, is so little used. It has been stated by some one, that "the Poor Man's Library" should always contain at least three volumes, the Bible, Psalm Book and Concordance. Surely these three ought to be the inmates of every dwelling of man. It is exceedingly useful in finding parallel passages, in fixing the scriptural meaning of words, and in finding particular passages, that we may wish to use in meditation or otherwise. The best works of this kind in our language, are unquestionably Cruden's and Butterworth's. Taylor's and Brown's are too small and imperfect, to answer the purpose in any considerable degree. Gaston's Collection of Scripture passages is a most valuable work, calculated to answer the same purpose in some respects, as a concordance. In this Collection, the Scriptures are principally inserted at large; and it is excellent indeed for those, who wish to see in a few moments, what the Scriptures say of almost any sacred subject, that may occur to mind; which, as the work has an excellent index, they can easily find. Butterworth's concordance, on account of its cheapness, will probably be preferred by most persons, to Cruden's.]

IV. Consider the subject, of which the author is treating, and by comparing other places, where he treats of the same subject, you may learn his sense in the place, which you are reading, though some of the terms, which he uses in those two places, may be very different.

And on the other hand, if the author uses the same words, where the subject of which he treats is not just the same, you cannot learn his sense by comparing those two

---

Best interpreter of scripture?
Meaning of *interpret*?
What book does he mention, as very useful in finding parallels?
What is a concordance?
Whose are the best?
Two other things, most important to be considered?

places, though the merè words may seem to agree. For some authors, when they are treating of a quite different subject, may use perhaps the same words in a very different sense, as Paul does the words faith and law and righteousness.

V. Observe the scope and design of the writer; inquire into his aim and end in that book or section or paragraph, which will help to explain particular sentences; for we suppose a wise and judicious writer directs his expressions generally toward his designed end.

VI. When an author speaks of any subject occasionally, let his sense be explained by those places, where he treats of it distinctly and professedly.—Where he treats of any subject in mystical or metaphorical terms, explain them by other places, where he treats of the same subject in terms that are plain and literal.—Where he speaks in an oratorical, affecting or persuasive way, let this be explained by other places, where he treats of the same theme in a doctrinal or instructive way.—Where the author speaks more strictly, and particularly on any theme, it will explain the more loose and general expressions.—Where he treats more largely, it will explain the shorter hints and brief intimations; and wheresover he writes more obscurely, search out some more perspicuous passages in the same writer, by which to determine the sense of that obscurer language.

VII. Consider not only the person, who is introduced speaking, but the persons, to whom the speech is directed, the circumstances of time and place, the temper and spirit of the speaker, as well as the temper and spirit of the hearers. In order to interpret scripture well, there needs a good acquaintance with the Jewish customs, some knowledge of the ancient Roman and Greek times and manners, which sometimes strike a strange and surprising light upon passages, which before were very obscure.

VIII. In particular propositions, the sense of an author may be sometimes known by the inferences, which he draws from them; and all those senses may be excluded, which will not allow of that inference.

How shall an author be explained, when he treats of a subject occasionally?—metaphorically?—very briefly?—obscurely?—Meaning of *metaphor*?—of *brief*?

In order to understand a speech, what should we particularly consider?

What customs should we know, in order to understand scripture?

How shall we gain an acquaintance with these? By studying Scripture history, Jahn's Archeology? Brown's Dictionary of the Bible, Alexander's, Malcom's, &c.

Remark upon inferences?

Note, This rule indeed is not always certain in reading and interpreting human authors; because they may mistake in drawing their inferences; but in explaining scripture, it is a sure rule; for the sacred and inspired writers always make just inferences from their own propositions. Yet even in them, we must take heed, that we do not mistake an allusion for an inference; which is many times introduced almost in the same manner.

IX. If it be a matter of controversy, the true sense of the author is sometimes known by the objections, that are brought against it. So we may be well assured, the apostle speaks against our justification in the sight of God, by our own works of holiness, in the 3d, 4th and 5th chapters of the Epistle to the Romans, because of the objection brought against him in the beginning of the 6th chapter, namely, What shall we say then? Shall we continue in sin that grace may abound? which objection could never have been raised, if he had been proving our justification by our own works of righteousness.

X. In matters of dispute, take heed of warping the sense of the writer to your own opinion, by any latent prejudices of self-love and a party spirit. It is this reigning principle of prejudices and party, that has given such a variety of senses both to the sacred writers and others, which would never have come into the mind of the reader, if he had not labored under some such prepossessions.

XI. For the same reason, take heed of the prejudices of passion, malice, envy, pride or opposition to an author, whereby you may be easily tempted to put a false and invidious sense upon his words. Lay aside therefore a carping spirit, and read even an adversary with attention and diligence, with an honest design to find out his true meaning. Do not snatch at little lapses and appearances of mistake, in opposition to his declared and avowed meaning, nor impute any sense or opinion to him, which he denies to be his opinion, unless it be proved by the most plain and express language.

Lastly, Remember that you treat every author, writer,

Why is not this a certain rule in relation to human authors?

With regard to what writings, is it a certain rule?—Why?

By what special means, may we sometimes understand controversial writings?

What special caution does he give in matters of controversy?

To what writings, does this more particularly apply?

What book has probably been more misunderstood, than any other?

With what honest design, should we read every author?

Golden rule for the treatment of authors?

or speaker, just as you yourselves would be willing to be treated by others, who are searching out the meaning of what you write or speak; and maintain upon your spirit, an awful sense of the presence of God, who is the judge of hearts, and will punish those who by a base and dishonest turn of mind wilfully pervert the meaning of the sacred writers, or even of common authors, under the influence of culpable prejudices. See more, Logic, Part I. Chap. 6. Sec. 3. Directions concerning the Definition of Names.

CHAPTER IX.

RULES OF IMPROVEMENT BY CONVERSATION.

I. If we would improve our minds by conversation, it is a great happiness to be acquainted with persons wiser than ourselves. It is a piece of useful advice, therefore, to get the favor of their conversation frequently, as far as circumstances will allow; and if they happen to be a little reserved, use all obliging methods to draw out of them, what may increase your own knowledge.

II. Whatsoever company you are in, waste not the time in trifling and impertinence. If you spend some hours among children, talk with them according to their capacity; mark the young buddings of infant reason; observe the different motions and distinct workings of the animal and the mind, as far you can discern them; take notice, by what degrees, the little creature grows up to the use of his reasoning powers, and what early prejudices beset and endanger his understanding. By this means, you will learn how to address yourself to children for their benefit, and perhaps you may derive some useful philosophemes or theorems, for your own entertainment.

III. If you happen to be in company with a merchant or a sailor, a farmer or a mechanic, a milk maid or a spinster, lead them into a discourse of the matters of their own pecu-

---

Of whose presence, should we maintain an awful sense?

With what kind of characters, is it desirable to be acquainted?

What if they are reserved?

In what situation, should we particularly guard against spending our time in trifles?

How should we talk with children?

What should we mark in them?

On what, should we converse with men of particular professions?

liar province or profession; for every one knows, or should know, his own business best. In this sense, a common mechanic is wiser than a philosopher. By this means, you may gain some improvement in knowledge from every one you meet.

IV. Confine not yourself always to one sort of company, or to persons of the same party or opinion, either in matters of learning, religion or the civil life, lest if you should happen to be nursed up or educated in early mistake, you should be confirmed and established in the same mistake, by conversing only with persons of the same sentiments. A free and general conversation with men of very various countries and of different parties, opinions and practices, so far as it may be done safely, is of excellent use to undeceive us in many wrong judgments, which we may have framed, and to lead us into juster thoughts. It is said, when the King of Siam first conversed with some European merchants, who sought the favor of trading on his coast, he enquired of them some of the common appearances of summer and winter in their country; and when they told him of water growing so hard in their rivers, that men and horses and laden-carriages passed over it, and that rain sometimes fell down as white and light as feathers, and sometimes almost as hard as stones, he would not believe a syllable they said; for ice, snow and hail, were names and things utterly unknown to him, and to his subjects in that hot climate.—He renounced all traffic with such shameful liars, and would not suffer them to trade with his people. See here the natural effects of gross ignorance.

Conversation with foreigners on various occasions, has a happy influence to enlarge our minds, and to set them free from many errors and gross prejudices, we are ready to imbibe concerning them. Domicillus has never travelled five miles from his mother's chimney; and he imagines all outlandish men are Papishes, and worship nothing but a cross. Tityrus the shepherd, was bred up all his life in the country, and never saw Rome. He fancied it to be only a huge village, and was therefore infinitely surprised to find such palaces, such streets, such glittering treasures

---

From whom, may we gain improvement?

Why should we converse with various associates? To avoid mistakes, and to gain more acquaintance with human nature.

What of the king of Siam?

From what evil, will conversation with foreigners be likely to free us?

What did Tityrus fancy Rome to be?

How was he affected, when he saw it?

and gay magnificence, as his first journey to the city shewed him, and with wonder he confesses his folly and mistake.

Conversation would have given Tityrus a better notion of Rome, though he had never happened to travel thither.

V. In mixed company among acquaintance and strangers, endeavor to learn something from all. Be swift to hear; but be cautious of your tongue, lest you betray your ignorance, and perhaps offend some of those who are present. The scripture severely censures those, who speak evil of the things they know not. Acquaint yourself, therefore, sometimes with persons and parties, which are far distant from your common life and customs. This is a way, whereby you may form a wiser opinion of men and things. Prove all things, and hold fast that which is good, is a divine rule, and it comes from the Father of light and truth. But young persons should practise it indeed with due limitation and under the eye of their elders.

VI. Be not frighted nor provoked at opinions different from your own. Some persons are so confident, they are in the right, that they will not come within the hearing of any notions but their own. They canton out to themselves, a little province in the intellectual world, where they fancy, the light shines, and all the rest is darkness. They never venture into the ocean of knowledge, nor survey the riches of other minds, which are as solid and as useful, and perhaps are finer gold, than what they ever possessed. Let not men imagine, there is no certain truth but in the sciences which they study, and among that party, in which they were born and educated.

VII. Believe, that it is possible to learn something from persons much below yourself. We are all short-sighted creatures. Our views are also narrow and limited. We often see but one side of a matter, and do not extend our sight far and wide enough, to reach every thing that has a connexion with the thing we talk of. We see but in part, and know but in part. Therefore, it is no wonder, we form not right conclusions; because we do not survey the whole of any subject or argument. Even the proudest admirer of his own parts, might find it useful to consult with others, though of inferior capacity and penetration. We have a

---

In what kind of company, should we be particularly cautious of speaking?—Why?

Of what things, should we never speak unfavorably?

To what, should we be swift when in company?—slow?

At what opinions, should we not be frightened or provoked? Meaning of *caution*?

different prospect of the same thing, if I may so speak, according to the different position of our understandings towards it. A weaker man may sometimes light on notions, which have escaped a wiser, and which the wiser man might make a happy use of, if he would condescend to take notice of them.

VIII. It is of considerable advantage, when we are pursuing any difficult point of knowledge, to have a society of ingenious correspondents at hand, to whom we may propose it; for every man has something of a different genius, and a various turn of mind, whereby the subject proposed will be shown in all its lights, represented in all its forms, and every side of it turned to view, that a juster judgment may be framed.

IX. To make conversation more valuable and useful, whether it be in a designed or accidental visit, among persons of the same or of different sexes, after the necessary salutations are finished, and the stream of common talk begins to hesitate, or runs flat and low, let some one person take a book, which may be agreeable to the whole company, and by common consent, let him read in it ten lines, or a paragraph or two, or a few pages, till some word or sentence gives an occasion for any of the company to offer a thought or two, relating to that subject. Interruption of the reader should be no blame; for conversation is the business; whether it be to confirm what the author says, or to improve it; to enlarge upon or to correct it; to object against it, or to ask any question that is a-kin to it; and let every one that pleases add his opinion, and promote the conversation. When the discourse sinks again, or diverts to trifles, let him that reads pursue the page, and read on further paragraphs or pages, till some occasion is given by a word or sentence, for a new discourse to be started, and that with the utmost ease and freedom. Such a method as this would prevent the hours of a visit from running all to waste; and by this means, even among scholars, they will seldom find occasion for that too just and bitter reflection, "I have lost my time in the company of the learned."

Why may we learn something from inferiors?

Why is it desirable to converse with others upon difficult points?

How may time be profitably spent, when conversation declines?

When may any one interrupt the reader?

Why is not this uncivil?

When should the reading recommence?

What evil may this method prevent?

What bitter reflection might it prevent among scholars?

By such practice as this, young ladies may very honorably and agreeably improve their hours. While one applies herself to reading, the others may employ their attention, among the various artifices of the needle. But let all of them make their occasional remarks or inquiries. This will guard a great deal of that precious time from modish trifling impertinence or scandal, which might otherwise afford matter for painful repentance.

Observe this rule in general; whensoever it lies in your power to lead the conversation, let it be directed to some profitable point of knowledge or practice, so far, as may be done with decency; and let not the discourse and the hours be suffered to run loose without aim or design; and when a subject is started, pass not hastily to another, before you have brought the present theme or discourse to some tolerable issue; or there be a joint consent to drop it.

X. Attend with sincere diligence, while any one of the company is declaring his sense of the question proposed. Hear the argument with patience, though it differ ever so much from your sentiments; for you yourself are very desirous to be heard with patience by others who differ from you. Let not your thoughts be active and busy all the while, to find out something to contradict, and by what means to oppose the speaker, especially in matters which are not brought to an issue. This is a frequent and unhappy temper and practice. You should rather be intent and solicitous to take up the mind and meaning of the speaker, zealous to seize and approve all that is true in his discourse; nor yet should you want courage to oppose where it is necessary; but let your modesty and patience, and a friendly temper, be as conspicuous as your zeal.

XI. When a man speaks with much freedom and ease, and gives his opinion in the plainest language of common sense, do not presently imagine you shall gain nothing by his company. Sometimes you will find a person, who in

---

How may this method be improved by a circle of ladies?

To what, should we direct the conversation, when we can take the lead?

How shall we decide, whether we ought to take the lead in conversation? By considering our age, qualifications and circumstances.

First of 3 great rules for those, who are qualified to lead in conversation? Be willing to take the lead, when duty requires.

Second? Never engross conversation, when others should speak.

Third? Always keep the conversation upon some profitable subject.

What does Watts say with regard to changing subjects?

In what manner, should we hear the remarks of others?

What should we do, rather than find out something to contradict?

his conversation or his writings, delivers his thoughts in so plain, so easy, so familiar and perspicuous a manner, that you both understand and assent to every thing he says, as fast as you read or hear it. Hercupon some hearers have been ready to conclude in haste, "Surely this man says none but common things. I knew as much before, or I could have said all this myself." This is a frequent mistake. Pellucido was a very great genius. When he spoke in the senate, he was wont to convey his ideas in so simple and happy a manner, as to instruct and convince every hearer, and to inforce the conviction through the whole illustrious assembly; and that, with so much evidence, that you would have been ready to wonder, that every one who spoke had not said the same things. But Pellucido was the only man that could do it, the only speaker who had attained this art and honor.

XII. If any thing seems dark in the discourse of your companion, so that you have not a clear idea of what is spoken, endeavor to obtain a clearer conception of it by a decent manner of inquiry. Do not charge the speaker with obscurity, either in his sense or his words; but intreat his favor to relieve your own want of penetration, or to add an enlightening word or two, that you may take up his whole meaning.

If difficulties arise in your mind, and constrain your dissent to the things spoken, represent what objections some persons would be ready to make against the sentiments of the speaker, without telling him, you oppose. This manner of address carries something more modest and obliging in it, than to appear to raise objections of your own, by way of contradiction to him that spoke.

XIII. When you are forced to differ from him, who delivers his sense on any point, yet agree as far as you can, and represent how far you agree; and if there be any room for it, explain the words of the speaker in a sense, to which you can in general assent, and so agree with him; or at least, by a small addition or alteration of his sentiments, shew your own sense of things. It is the practice and de-

---

In what manner, did Pellucido speak in the senate?
With what effect?
At what, would the hearers be ready to wonder?
Who else could speak like Pellucido?
What if the speaker's remarks are obscure?
With what, should we not charge an obscure speaker?
What if you dissent from him?
Benefit of this manner of address?
When you are forced to differ from the speaker, in what manner, should you express the difference?

light of a candid hearer, to make it appear, how unwilling he is to differ from him that speaks. Let the speaker know, that it is nothing but truth constrains you to oppose him; and let the difference be always exprest in few and civil and chosen words, such as give the least offence. And be careful always to take Solomon's rule with you, and let your correspondent fairly finish his speech before you reply: for he that answereth a matter, before he heareth it, it is folly and shame unto him. Prov. 18:13.

A little watchfulness, care and practice in younger life, will render all these things more easy, familiar, and natural to you, and will grow into habit.

XIV. As you should carry about with you a constant and sincere sense of your own ignorance, so you should not be afraid nor ashamed to confess this ignorance, by taking all proper opportunities to inquire for farther information; whether it be the meaning of a word, the nature of a thing, the reason of a proposition, the custom of a nation, &c. Never remain in ignorance for want of asking.

Many a person had arrived at some considerable degree of knowledge, if he had not been full of self-conceit, and imagined, that he had known enough already, or else was ashamed to let others know, that he was unacquainted with it. God and man are ready to teach the meek, the humble and the ignorant; but he that fancies himself to know any particular subject well, or that will not venture to ask a question about it, such a one will not put himself into the way of improvement, by inquiry and diligence. A fool may be wiser in his own conceit, than seven men who can render a reason; and such a one is very likely to be an everlasting fool; and perhaps also it is a silly shame, which renders his folly incurable.

XV. Be not too forward, especially in the younger part of life, to determine any question in company, with an infallible and peremptory sentence, nor speak with assuming airs, and a decisive tone of voice. A young man in the presence of his elders, should rather hear and attend, and

---

Why should we wait, till the speaker has finished his remark, before we reply to it?

For want of what, should we never remain in ignorance?

Why are some ashamed to ask questions?

Effect of self-conceit upon improvement in knowledge?

Whom are God and man willing to instruct?

Who is wiser in his own conceit, than 7 men, that can render a reason?

Who should especially guard against forwardness in deciding a question?

How should a young man generally conduct in the presence of his elders?

weigh the arguments, which are brought for the proof or refutation of any doubtful proposition. When it is your turn to speak, propose your thoughts rather in way of inquiry. By this means your mind will be kept in a fitter temper to receive truth, and you will be more ready to correct and improve your own sentiments, where you have not been too positive in affirming them. But if you have magisterially decided the point, you will find a secret unwillingness to retract, though you should feel an inward conviction, that you were in the wrong.

XVI. It is granted, indeed, that a season may happen, when some bold pretender to science may assume haughty and positive airs to assert and vindicate a gross and dangerous error, or to denounce and vilify some very important truth; and if he has a popular talent of talking, and there be no remonstrance made against him, the company may be tempted too easily to give their assent to the impudence and infallibility of the presumer. They may imagine, a proposition so much vilified can never be true, and that a doctrine, which is so boldly censured and denounced, can never be defended. Weak minds are too ready to persuade themselves, that a man would never talk with so much assurance, unless he were certainly in the right, and could well maintain and prove what he said. By this means, truth itself is in danger of being betrayed or lost, if there be no opposition made to such a pretending talker.

Now in such a case, even a wise and a modest man may assume airs too, and repel insolence with its own weapons. There is a time, as Solomon the wisest of men teaches us, when a fool should be answered according to his folly, lest he be wise in his own conceit, and lest others too easily yield up their faith and reason to his imperious dictates. Courage and positiveness are never more necessary than on such an occasion. But it is good to join some argument with them, of real and convincing force; and let it be strongly pronounced too.

When such a resistance is made, you will find some of

In what manner, should he propose his thoughts?—Why?

What if he decides a point with great confidence, and is afterwards convinced of his error?

What are weak minds ready to conclude concerning a man who talks with great assurance?

With what, may we sometimes repel the insolence of such a man?

What caution should we use in such a case? Not thus to oppose, unless we are very sure to conquer.

Of what, is there danger in such a case? Furious debate.

these bold talkers will draw in their horns, when their fierce and feeble pushes against truth and reason are repelled with pushing and confidence. It is a pity indeed, that truth should ever need such sort of defences. But we know, that a triumphant assurance has sometimes supported gross falsehoods, and a whole company have been captivated to error by this means, till some man with equal assurance has rescued them. It is a pity that any momentous point of doctrine should happen to fall under such reproaches, and require such a mode of vindication; though if I happen to hear it, I ought not to turn my back and sneak off in silence, and leave the truth to lie baffled, bleeding and slain. Yet I must confess, I should be glad to have no occasion ever to fight with any man of this sort of weapons, even though I should be so happy as to silence his insolence, and obtain an evident victory.

XVII. Be not fond of disputing every thing *Pro* and *Con*, nor indulge yourself, to shew your talent of attacking and defending. A logic, which teaches nothing else, is little worth. This temper and practice will lead you just so far out of the way of knowledge, and divert your honest inquiry after the truth, which is debated or sought. In set disputes, every little straw is often seized, to support our own cause; every thing, that can be drawn in any way, to give color to our argument, is advanced, and that perhaps with vanity and ostentation. This puts the mind out of a proper posture to seek and receive the truth.

XVIII. Do not bring a warm party-spirit into free conversation, which is designed for mutual improvement in the search of truth. Take heed of allowing yourself in those self-satisfied assurances, which keep the doors of the understanding barred fast against the admission of any new sentiments. Let your soul be ever ready to hearken to further discoveries, from a constant and ruling consciousness of our present fallible and imperfect state; and make it appear to your friends, that it is no hard task for you to learn and pronounce those little words, *I was mistaken,* how hard soever it is for the bulk of mankind to pronounce them.

XIX. As you may sometimes raise inquiries for your own instruction and improvement, and draw out the learn-

---

Influence of a disputatious spirit upon the acquisition of truth?

What is said of a logic, that teaches nothing else?

What little humiliating words should we be willing to pronounce, when convinced of error?

ing, wisdom and fine sentiments of your friends, who perhaps may be too reserved or modest; so at other times, if you perceive a person unskilful in the matter of debate, you may by questions aptly proposed in the Socratic method, lead him into a clearer knowledge of the subject. Then you become his instructor, in such a manner, as may not appear to make yourself his superior.

XX. Take heed of affecting always to shine in company, above the rest, and to display the riches of your own understanding or your oratory, as though you would render yourself admirable to all that are present. This is seldom well taken in polite company. Much less should you use such forms of speech, as would insinuate the ignorance or dulness of those, with whom you converse.

XXI. Though you should not affect to flourish in a copious harangue and diffusive style in company, yet neither should you rudely interrupt and reproach him that happens to use it; but when he has done speaking, reduce his sentiments into a more contracted form; not with a show of correcting, but as one who is doubtful whether you hit upon his true sense or not. Thus matters may be brought more easily from a wild confusion, into a single point, questions may be sooner determined, and difficulties more easily removed.

XXII. Be not so ready to charge ignorance, prejudice and mistake upon others, as you are to suspect yourself of them; and in order to show, how free you are from prejudices, learn to bear contradiction with patience. Let it be easy to you to hear your own opinion strongly opposed, especially in matters, which are doubtful and disputable among men of sobriety and virtue. Give a patient hearing

---

What if you see a person unskilful in debate?

What is said of attempting to gain admiration in company? We should never attempt it.

What should we be more ready to suspect in ourselves, than to charge upon others?

When charged with these, what reply may we sometimes make? This remark of Watts.

With what feelings, should we learn to bear contradiction?

What advantage will this give us? We shall be much better able to perceive and defend the truth.

Why should we be willing to listen patiently to arguments on all sides? For the sake of gaining and supporting truth, and maintaining a character for candor.

Why should we be willing sometimes, to listen to remarks, that appear frivolous? The remarks may really be much better, than they seem; and our remarks may sometimes appear equally frivolous to others.

Meaning of *frivolous*?

What if we certainly know, that another's remarks are frivolous? We may perhaps do him much good by kindly showing him, that they are so

to arguments on all sides. Otherwise you give the company occasion to suspect, that it is not the evidence of truth, which has led you into this opinion, but some lazy anticipation of judgment, some beloved presumption, some long and rash possession of a party scheme, in which you desire to rest undisturbed. If your assent has been established upon just and sufficient grounds, why should you be afraid to let the truth be put to the trial of argument?

XXIII. Banish utterly out of all conversation, and especially out of all learned and intellectual conference, every thing, that tends to provoke passion, or raise a fire in the blood. Let no sharp language, nor noisy exclamation, no sarcasms or biting jests be heard among you; no perverse or invidious consequences be drawn from each other's opinions, and imputed to the person. Let there be no wilful perversion of another's meaning; no sudden seizure of a lapsed syllable to play upon it, nor any abused construction of an innocent mistake. Suffer not your tongue to insult a modest opponent, that begins to yield. Let there be no crowing and triumph, even where there is evident victory on your side. All these things are enemies to friendship, and the ruin of free conversation. The impartial search of truth requires all calmness and serenity, all good temper and candor. Mutual instruction can never be attained in the midst of passion, pride and clamor, unless we suppose, in the midst of such a scene, there is a loud and penetrating lecture read by both sides on the folly and shameful infirmities of human nature.

XXIV. Whensoever, therefore, any unhappy word shall arise in company, that might give you a reasonable disgust, suppress the rising resentment, be it ever so just, and command your soul and your tongue into silence, lest you cancel the hopes of all improvement for that hour, and transform the learned conversation into the mean and vulgar form of reproaches and railing. The man, who begun to break the peace in such a society, will fall under the shame and conviction of such a silent reproof, if he has any thing

---

What should we banish from conversation, in order to preserve peace?

What caution should we exercise, when our opponent begins to yield?

What is the only instruction, we can gain from passion, pride and clamor?

Should we sin, and play the fool, for the sake of learning the evils of sin and folly?

What does the Scripture say of the damnation of those, who do evil, that good may come? Rom. 3: 8.

What if something occurs, that is very irritating?

Who will be likely to feel such a silent reproof?—Meaning of *irritate*?

ingenuous about him. If this should not be sufficient, let a grave admonition, or a soft and gentle turn of wit, with an air of pleasantry, give the warm disputer an occasion to stop the progress of his indecent fire, if not to retract the indecency, and quench the flame.

XXV. Inure yourself to a candid and obliging manner in all your conversation, and acquire the art of pleasing address, even when you teach, as well as when you learn, and when you oppose, as well as when you assert or prove. This degree of politeness is not to be attained, without a diligent attention to such directions, as are here laid down, and a frequent exercise and practice of them.

XXVI. If you would know what sort of companions you should select for the cultivation and advantage of the mind, the general rule is, choose such as by their brightness of parts and their diligence in study, or by their superior advancement in learning, or peculiar excellency in any art, science or accomplishment, divine or human, may be capable of administering to your improvement; and be sure to maintain and keep some due regard to their moral character always, lest while you wander in quest of intellectual gain, you fall into the contagion of irreligion and vice. No wise man would venture into a house infected with the plague, in order to see the finest collections of any virtuoso in Europe.

XXVII. Nor is it every sober person of your acquaintance, no, nor every man of bright parts, or rich in learning, that is fit to engage in free conversation for the inquiry after truth. Let a person have ever so illustrious talents, yet he is not a proper associate for such a purpose, if he lie under any of the following infirmities;

To what manner of conversation, should we inure ourselves?—Meaning of *inure*?

What will afford the best opportunity to cultivate such a manner? Good company.

Where is it most desirable, that every person should find such company? At home.

How might the members of most families greatly improve their manners? By treating each other much more kindly and politely, and by special efforts to cultivate propriety of speech and behavior.

Against what, should such reformers particularly guard? Affectation.

What if any one should exchange awkwardness and rusticity for affectation? He would make a bad bargain.

What shall we think of those, who consider it of very little importance, how they regulate their manners in the family circle? They do exceedingly err.

Qualities, desirable in a companion?

Qualities, undesirable in a companion? Reserve, pride, dogmatism, assuming forwardness, impertinent loquacity, fretfulness, affectation of wit, jealousy, &c.

1. If he be exceedingly reserved, and has either no inclination to discourse, or no tolerable capacity of speech and language for the communication of his sentiments;

2. If he be haughty and proud of his knowledge, imperious in his airs, and always fond of imposing his sentiments on all the company;

3. If he be positive and dogmatical in his own opinions, and will dispute to the end; if he will resist the brightest evidence of truth, rather than suffer himself to be overcome, or yield to the plainest and strongest reasonings;

4. If he be one, who always affects to outshine all the company, and delight to hear himself talk and flourish upon a subject, and make long harangues, while the rest must be all silent and attentive;

5. If he be a person of a whiffling and unsteady turn of mind, who cannot keep to a point of controversy; but wanders from it perpetually, and is always solicitous to say something, whether it be pertinent to the question or not;

6. If he be fretful and peevish, and given to resentment upon all occasions; if he know not how to bear contradiction, or be ready to take things in a wrong sense; and if he be swift to feel a supposed offence, or to imagine himself affronted, and then break out into a sudden passion, or retain silent and sullen wrath;

7. If he affect wit on all occasions, and be full of his conceits and puns, quirks or quibbles, jests and repartees; these may agreeably entertain and animate an hour of mirth; but they have no place in the search after truth;

8. If he carry always about him, a sort of craft and cunning and disguise, and act rather like a spy, than a friend. Have a care of such a one, as will make an ill use of freedom in conversation, and immediately charge heresy upon you, when you happen to differ from those sentiments, which authority or custom has established.

In short, you should avoid the man in such select conversation, who practises any thing, that is unbecoming the character of a sincere, free and open searcher after truth.

Now though you may pay all the relative duties of life to persons of these unhappy qualifications, and treat them with decency and love, so far as religion and humanity oblige you, yet take care of entering into a free debate of matters of truth or falsehood in their company, and especially about the principles of religion. I confess, if a person of such a

---

Can you think of any others, not here mentioned?

Where should we especially watch against these evils?

temper happens to judge and talk well on such a subject, you may hear him with attention, and derive what profit you can from his discourse; but he is by no means to be chosen for a free conference in matters of inquiry and knowledge.

XXVIII. While I would persuade you to beware of such persons, and abstain from too much freedom of discourse among them, it is very natural to infer, that you should watch against the working of these evil qualities in your own breast, if you happen to be tainted with any of them yourself. Men of learning and ingenuity will justly avoid your acquaintance, when they find such an unhappy and unsociable temper prevailing in you.

XXIX. To conclude; when you retire from company, then converse with yourself in solitude, and inquire, what you have learnt for the improvement of your understanding, or for the rectifying your inclinations; for the increase of your virtues, or the meliorating of your conduct and behavior in any future parts of life. If you have seen some of your company candid, modest, humble in their manner, wise and sagacious, just and pious in their sentiments, polite and graceful, as well as clear and strong in their expression, and universally acceptable and lovely in their behavior, endeavor to impress the idea of all these upon your memory, and treasure them up for your imitation.

XXX. If the laws of reason, decency and civility have not been well observed among your associates, take notice of those defects, for your own improvement; and from every occurrence of this kind, remark something to imitate or to avoid, in elegant, polite and useful conversation. Perhaps you will find, that some persons present have really displeased the company, by an excessive and too visible affectation to please; that is, by giving loose to servile flattery, or promiscuous praise; while others were as ready to oppose and contradict every thing said. Some have deserved just censure for a morose and affected taciturnity. Others have been anxious and careful, lest their silence should be interpreted a want of sense; and therefore, they

---

What inquiry should we make of ourselves, when we retire from company?—Meaning of *meliorate*?

What improvement should we make of the example of those, who have shone in company with superior lustre and loveliness?—of bad examples?

What may sometimes be an unhappy effect of too great a desire to please?

Whom should we strive to please, more than men?

For what object may we please men? Rom. 15: 2.

What class of men, is it most desirable to please? The wise and good.

Best way to please the wise and good? To please God.

have ventured to make speeches, though they had nothing to say, which was worth hearing. Perhaps you will observe, that one was ingenious in his thoughts, and bright in his language; but he was so full of himself, that he let it fall on all the company; that he spoke well indeed, but that he spoke too long, and did not allow equal liberty or time to his associates. You will remark, that another was full charged, or let out his words, before his friend had done speaking, or impatient of the least opposition to any thing he said. You will remember, that some persons have talked at large, and with great confidence, of things, which they understood not, and others counted every thing tedious and intolerable, that was spoken upon subjects out of their own sphere, and they would fain confine the conference entirely within the limits of their own narrow knowledge and study. The errors of conversation are almost infinite.

XXXI. By a review of such irregularities as these, you may learn to avoid those follies and instances of ill conduct, which spoil good conversation, or make it less agreeable and less useful; and by degrees you will acquire that delightful and easy manner of address and behavior in all useful correspondences, which may render your company every where desired and beloved; and at the same time, among the best of your companions, you may make the highest improvement in your own intellectual acquisitions, that the discourse of mortal creatures will allow, under all our disadvantages in this sorry state of mortality. But there is a day coming, when we shall be seized away from this lower class in the school of knowledge, where we labor under the many dangers and darknesses, the errors and the incumbrances of flesh and blood, and our conversation will be with angels, and more illuminated spirits in the upper regions of the universe.

Why do many make speeches, when they have nothing to say worth hearing?

By imitating the excellences and avoiding the faults, that we witness in company, what manner of address may we gradually acquire?

What more solid acquisitions may we gain?

With whom, will good men converse hereafter?

Five qualifications most desirable for conversation? Piety, knowledge, mental improvement, eloquence and good manners.

If a person can converse properly, fluently, pleasingly and forcibly, is it needful, that he should be eloquent? Speaking thus is eloquence

Miscellaneous Questions, No. 3.

What branch of knowledge most helps all others?

What important instructions may we receive from that scripture, which represents the good man as bringing forth his fruit in his season?

In what manner, should a pupil discuss a point with his teacher?

How may time be profitably spent, when conversation declines?

How should a young man generally conduct in presence of his elders?

What are some reasons, why a learned man may be a very bad teacher?

Why should a teacher have a good moral character?

How should a pupil honor his teacher?

What science investigates and explains the sense of words and phrases?

To what, should we direct the conversation, when we take the lead?

With what feelings, should we learn to bear contradiction?

Qualifications desirable in a teacher?

Why should a teacher have zeal?

Why should a pupil attend school punctually?

What should a pupil do before he decides a point against his teacher?

Three principal methods of learning the meaning of words?

How shall we decide, whether we ought to take the lead in conversation?

Why should we listen patiently to arguments on all sides?

Why should a teacher be pious?

Why should a teacher be affectionate?

What should we think of a teacher, who is unwilling to be taught by his pupil?

How does a child begin to learn the meaning of words?

In order to understand a speech, what should we particularly consider?

In what manner, did Pellucido speak in the senate?

Why should we be willing sometimes to listen to remarks that appear frivolous?

Whose salvation should a teacher make special efforts to promote?

What should a pupil do, before he decides a point against his teacher?

Why is meekness desirable in a teacher?

How should we talk with children?

In what kind of company, should we be particularly cautious of speaking?

When we differ from a speaker, in what manner, should we express the difference?

Why should we banish from conversation, all provocatives to passions?

What if we know to do good, and do it not?

What is true politeness?

Why should a pupil attend school constantly?

Who should co-operate with teachers for the improvement of their pupils?

With what honest design, should we read every author?

Why are some ashamed to ask questions?

Five qualifications most desirable in a companion?

What branch of instruction is it most important for a teacher to inculcate?

What is inculcated by that scripture, which says, Charity doth not behave itself unseemly?

For what purpose, should parents, teachers, ministers, school committees, &c. co-operate?

Golden rule for the treatment of authors?

To what king, did some European merchants give some account of the effects of cold?

Mention some qualities, that appear undesirable in a companion?

How does religion help a pupil's progress in all other branches?

How should a teacher promote freedom of thought in his pupils?

How do children often get wrong ideas of words?

With what, should we compare an author's words and phrases, in order to understand them?

Why should we converse with various associates?

CHAPTER X.

OF DISPUTES.

I. UNDER the general head of Conversation for the Improvement of the Mind, we may rank the practice of disputing; that is, when two or more persons appear to maintain different sentiments, and defend their own, or oppose the other's opinion, in alternate discourse, by some methods of argument.

II. As these disputes often arise in good earnest, where the two contenders do really believe the different propositions, which they support; so sometimes they are appointed, as mere trials of the students' skill in academies, or schools. Sometimes they are practised, and that with apparent fervor in courts of judicature, by lawyers, in order to gain the fees of their clients, while both sides perhaps are really of the same sentiment, with regard to the cause which is tried.

III. In common conversation, disputes are often managed without any forms of regularity or order; and they turn to good or evil purposes, chiefly according to the temper of the disputants. They may sometimes be successful to search out truth, sometimes effectual to maintain truth, and convince the mistaken; but at other times, a dispute is a mere scene of battle, in order to victory and vain triumph.

DISPUTES.—Meaning of *dispute*?

How are disputes generally managed in conversation?

According to what, do disputes generally produce good or evil?

What may disputes sometimes enable us to search out and maintain?

What Scripture authority have we to show, that disputing may be right? Paul disputed daily in the school of Tyrannus; and we are exhorted to contend earnestly for the faith, once delivered to the saints. Acts 19: 9. Jude: 3.

How does the latter text show, that we should sometimes dispute? We must doubtless contend for the faith by argument; and this is disputing.

What shall we think of the maxim, adopted by some, "Never dispute about religion?" It seems to be as unscriptural, as it is unreasonable.

Has not disputing done more harm than good? Probably not.

What good has ever been done by disputing? Most important truths have been maintained, and spread far and wide.

How do missionaries propagate the gospel? In a great measure, by disputing.

Would it not be better to propagate the gospel by preaching? The missionaries do preach; but, their doctrine being disputed, they must, like Paul, defend it by disputation.

IV. There are some few general rules, which should be observed in all debates whatever, if we would find out truth by them, or convince a friend of his error, even though they be not managed according to any settled forms of disputation. As there are almost as many opinions and judgments of things, as there are persons, so when several persons happen to meet, and confer together upon any subject, they are ready to declare their different sentiments, and support them by such reasonings, as they are capable of. This is called debating, or disputing, as is above described.

V. When persons begin a debate, they should always take care, that they are agreed in some general principles or propositions, which either more nearly or remotely affect the question in hand; for otherwise, they have no foundation or hope of convincing each other. They must have some common ground to stand upon, while they maintain the contest.

When they find that they agree in some remote propositions, then let them search farther, and inquire, how near they approach to each other's sentiments; and whatsoever propositions they agree in, let these lay a foundation for the mutual hope of conviction. Hereby you will be prevented from running, at every turn, to some original and remote propositions and axioms, which practice both entangles and prolongs a dispute. As for instance, if there was a debate proposed between a Protestant and a Papist, whether there be such a place as purgatory; let them remember, that they both agree in this point, that Christ has made satisfaction or atonement for sin, and upon this ground, let them both stand, while they search out the controverted doctrine of purgatory, by way of conference or debate.

VI. The question should be cleared from all doubtful terms and needless additions; and all things, that belong to the question, should be expressed in plain and intelligible language. This is so necessary a thing, that without it, men will be exposed to such sort of ridiculous contests as was found one day between the two unlearned combatants Sartor and Sutor, who assaulted and defended the

---

In what, does it seem needful, that disputants should be agreed?

Why? Unless they are agreed in some points, there seems to be no foundation, upon which, to rest an argument.

What inquiry should disputants make, when they find, they are agreed in some points?

From what, should the question be cleared?

In what kind of language, should the question be stated?

Upon what doctrine, did Sartor

doctrine of transubstantiation with much zeal and violence. But Latino happening to come into their company, and inquiring the subject of their dispute, asked each of them, what he meant by that long hard word *transubstantiation.* Sutor readily informed him, that he understood bowing at the name of Jesus. But Sartor assured him, that he meant nothing but bowing at the high altar. "No wonder then," said Latino, "that you cannot agree, when you neither understand one another, nor the word, about which you contend." I think the whole family of the Sartors and Sutors would be wiser, if they avoided such kind of debates, till they understood the terms better. But alas! even their wives carry on such conferences. The other day, one was heard in the street, explaining to her less learned neighbor, the meaning of metaphysical science; and she assured her, that as physics were medicines for the body, so metaphysics was physic for the soul. Upon this, they went on to dispute the point, how far the divine excelled the doctor.

VII. And not only the sense and meaning of the words used in the question, should be settled and adjusted between the disputants, but the precise point of inquiry should be distinctly fixed; the question in debate should be limited precisely to its special extent, or declared to be taken in its more general sense. As for instance, If two men are contending whether civil government be of divine right or not; here it must be observed, the question is not whether monarchy in one man, or a republic in multitudes of the people, or an aristocracy in a few of the chief, is appointed of God as necessary; but whether civil government in its most general sense, or in any form whatsoever, is derived from the will and appointment of God? Again, The point of inquiry should be limited further. Thus, the question is not whether government comes from the will of God, by the light of revelation; for that is granted; but whether it is derived from the will of God, by the light of reason too. This sort of specification or limitation of the question prevents the disputants from wandering away from the precise point of inquiry.

---

and Sutor dispute?

Meaning of *transubstantiation*?

What did Sutor suppose, it meant?

What did Sartor?

What did Latino say to them?

How long should the whole family of Sartors and Sutors avoid debate?

What precise point should be clearly settled in every dispute?

What evil does this specification tend to prevent?

What if the terms could be clearly defined, and the precise point of inquiry settled, in relation to every

It is this trifling humor or dishonest artifice of changing the question, and wandering away from the first point of debate, which gives endless length to disputes, and causes both the disputants to part without any satisfaction. And one chief occasion of it is this. When one of the combatants feels his cause run low and fail, and is just ready to be confuted and demolished, he is tempted to step aside, to avoid the blow, and betakes himself to a different question. Thus, if his adversary be not well aware of him, he begins to entrench himself in a new fastness, and holds out the siege with a new artillery of thoughts and words. It is the pride of man, which is the spring of this evil, and an unwillingness to yield up their own opinions, even to be overcome by truth itself.

VIII. Keep this always, therefore, upon your mind, as an everlasting rule of conduct in your debates, to find out truth, that a resolute design, or even a warm affectation of victory, is the bane of all real improvement, and an effectual bar against the admission of the truth, which you profess to seek. This works with a secret but powerful and mischievous influence in every dispute, unless we are much upon our guard. It appears in frequent conversation; every age, each sex, and each party of mankind are so fond of being thought in the right, that they know not how to renounce this unhappy prejudice, this vain love of victory.

When truth with bright evidence, is ready to break in upon a disputant, and to overcome his objections and mistakes, how swift and ready is the mind to engage wit and fancy, craft and subtilty, to cloud and perplex and puzzle the truth, if possible? How eager is he to throw in some impertinent question to divert attention from the main subject? How swift to take hold of some occasional word, thereby to lead the discourse off from the point in hand? So much afraid is human nature of parting with its errors, and being overcome by truth. Just thus a hunted hare calls

---

disputed question? Perhaps three quarters of the disputes would be prevented.

Effect of changing the question, and wandering away from the first point of dispute?

What is generally the occasion of changing the question?

Does he intend evasion? Probably not always, and perhaps, not generally.

What can cause him to commit such a fault, without knowing it? Self love, want of discernment or both.

What should be the grand object of disputation?

What does the author say of the love of victory?

Why are most persons so very fond of victory?

To what, does he compare attempts to evade the truth?

up all the shifts that nature has taught her. She treads back her mazes, crosses and confounds her former track, and uses all possible methods, to divert the scent, when she is in danger of being seized and taken. Let puss practise what nature teaches; but would one imagine, that any rational being should take such pains to avoid truth, and to escape the improvement of his understanding?

IX. When you come to a dispute, in order to find out truth, do not presume that you are certainly possessed of it beforehand. Enter the debate with a sincere design of yielding to reason, on which side soever it appears. Use no subtle arts to cloud and entangle the question; hide not yourself in doubtful words and phrases; do not affect little shifts and subterfuges to avoid the force of an argument; take a generous pleasure to espy the first rising beams of truth, though it be on the side of your opponent; endeavor to remove the little obscurities that hang about it, and suffer and encourage it to break out into open and convincing light; that while your opponent, perhaps, may gain the better of your reasonings, yet you yourself may triumph over error; and I am sure, that is a much more valuable acquisition and victory.

X. Watch narrowly in every dispute, that your opponent does not lead you unwarily to grant some principle or proposition, which will bring with it a fatal consequence, and lead you insensibly into his sentiment, though it be far astray from the truth. By this wrong step, you may be plunged into dangerous errors, before you are aware.

What does he mention, that we should not presume, when we are disputing, to find out truth?

Over what, may we sometimes gain a victory, when our opponent gains a victory over us?

Why should we dispute only for truth? If we dispute for any thing else, we shall be in danger of promoting error, and diminishing our love and thirst for truth.

Is it right to dispute in favor of an opinion, that we do not believe? Probably not.

Why? We can hardly expect to promote truth by advocating error. —Meaning of *advocate*?

By what arguments, should we defend truth? Only such, as we consider sound.

Why not by others? It is an attempt to convince others by arguments, that do not convince ourselves.

To what wicked traffic, may it be compared? Passing counterfeit money, to promote a good object.

What caution does Watts give, with regard to concession in disputes?

When is this caution scarcely needful? When our opponent allows us to retract any concession we have made.

Why should this privilege be allowed on both sides? All are liable to make false concessions.

Who seem the most liable to make false concessions? Those who are most candid.

What are we bound to do, when we retract a concession? To answer the arguments, that led us to make it.

Polonides in free conversation, led Incauto to agree with him in this proposition, that the blessed God has too much justice, in any case to punish any being, who is in itself innocent, till he not only allowed it with an unthinking alacrity, but asserted it in most universal and unguarded terms. A little after Polonides came in discourse, to commend the virtues, the innocence and the piety of our blessed Savior; and thence inferred, it was impossible that God should ever punish so holy a person, who was never guilty of any crime. Then Incauto espied the snare, and found himself robbed and defrauded of the great doctrine of the atonement by the death of Christ; upon which he had placed his immortal hopes according to the gospel. This taught him to bethink himself, what a dangerous concession he had made in so universal a manner, that God would never punish any being who was innocent, and he saw it needful to recal his words, or to explain them better, by adding this reflection or limitation, namely, Unless this innocent being were some way involved in another's sin, or stood as a voluntary surety for the guilty. By this limitation, he secured the great and blessed doctrine of the sacrifice of Christ for the sins of men, and learnt to be more cautious in his concessions for time to come.

Two months ago Fatalio had almost tempted his friend Fidens to leave off prayer, and to abandon his dependence on the providence of God in the common affairs of life, by obtaining of him a concession of the like kind. "Is it not evident to reason," says Fatalio, "that God's immense scheme of transactions in the universe, was contrived and determined long before you and I were born? Can you imagine, my dear Fidens, that the blessed God changes his original contrivances, and makes new interruptions in the course of them so often, as you and I want his aid, to prevent the little accidents of life, or to guard us from them? Can you suffer yourself to be persuaded, that the great Creator of this world takes care to support a bridge, which was quite rotten, and to make it stand firm a few minutes longer, till you had rode over it? Or will he uphold a falling tower, while we two are passing by it, that such worms as you and I, may escape the ruin?

What doctrine did Polonides almost lead Incauto to renounce?—How?—Meaning of *atonement*?

How did Incauto secure the doctrine?

What duty did Fatalio almost persuade Fidens to omit?

How may the propriety of prayer be vindicated against the objection of Fatalio? By supposing, that God had respect to the prayer, in his eternal arrangements.

But you say, you prayed for his protection in the morning; and he certainly hears prayer. I grant, he knows it. But are you so fond and weak, as to suppose, that the universal Lord of all had such a regard to a word or two of your breath, as to make alterations in his own eternal scheme upon that account? Nor is there any other way, whereby his providence can preserve you in answer to prayer, but by creating such perpetual interruptions and changes in his own conduct according to your daily behavior."

"I acknowledge," says Fidens, "there is no other way to secure the doctrine of divine providence in all these common affairs; and therefore, I begin to doubt, whether God does or ever will exert himself so particularly in our little concerns."

Have a care, good Fidens, that you yield not too far. Take heed, lest you have granted too much to Fatalio. Pray let me ask of you, Could not the great God, who grasps and surveys all future and distant things in one single view, could not he from the beginning, foresee your morning prayer, for his protection, and appoint all second causes to concur for the support of that crazy bridge, or to make that old tower stand firm, till you had escaped the danger? Or could not he cause all the mediums to work, so as to make it fall before you come near it? Can he not appoint all his own transactions in the universe, and every event in the natural world, in a way of perfect correspondence, with his own fore-knowledge of all the events, actions and appearances of the moral world in every part of it? Can he not direct every thing in nature, which is but his servant, to act in perfect agreement with his eternal prescience of our sins, or of our piety? And hereby all the glory of providence, and our necessary dependence upon it by faith and prayer, are as well secured, as if he interposed to alter his own scheme every moment.

Let me ask again, Did not he in his own counsels or decrees appoint thunders and lightnings and earthquakes, to burn up and destroy Sodom and Gomorrah, and turn them into a dead sea, just at the time, when the iniquities of those cities were raised to their supreme height? Did he not ordain the fountains of the deep to be broken up, and overwhelming rains to fall from heaven, just when a guilty world deserved to be drowned; while he took care of the security of righteous Noah, by an ark, which should float upon that very deluge of waters? Thus, he can punish the criminal, when he pleases, and reward the devout worshipper in the proper season, by his original and eternal schemes of appointment, as well as if he interposed every moment anew. Take heed, Fidens, that you be not tempted away by such sophisms of Fatalio, to withhold prayer from God, and to renounce your faith in his providence.

Remember this short and plain caution of the subtle errors of men. Let a snake but once thrust in his head at some small unguarded fold of your garment; and he will insensibly and unavoidably wind his whole body into your bosom, and give you a pernicious wound.

XI. On the other hand, when you have found your opponent make any such concession as may turn to your real advantage in maintaining the truth, be wise and watchful to observe it, and make a happy improvement of it. Rhapsodus has taken a great deal of pains to detract from the honor of Christianity, by sly insinuations, that the sacred writers are perpetually promoting virtue and piety by promises and threatenings; whereas, neither the fear of future punishment, nor the hope of future reward can possibly be called good affections, or such as are the acknowledged springs and sources of all actions truly good. He adds further, that this fear or this hope cannot consist in reality with virtue or goodness, if it either stands as essential to any moral performance, or as a considerable motive to any good action. Thus he would fain lead Christians to be ashamed of the gospel of Christ, because of its future and eternal promises and threatenings, as being inconsistent with his notion of virtue; for he supposes, virtue should be so beloved and practised for the sake of its own beauty and loveliness, that all other motives arising from rewards or punishments, fear or hope, do really take away just so much from the very nature of virtue, as their influence reaches to; and that no part of those good practices are really valuable, but what arises from the mere love of virtue itself, without any regard to punishment or reward.

But observe in two pages afterwards he grants, that this principle of fear of future punishment, and hope of future

---

What if your opponent makes some important concession?

What objection did Rhapsodus make to the Bible?

Why would Rhapsodus have virtue practised?

What concession does Rhapsodus afterwards make?

How may fears and hopes be a great security to virtue? They may prevent its being swept away by some violent temptation.

What seems to be a complete answer to Rhapsodus? That virtue is just as mercenary, when practised for present satisfaction, as for future.

reward, how mercenary and servile soever it may be accounted, is yet in many circumstances, a great advantage, security and support to virtue; especially where there is danger of the violence of rage or lust, or any counterworking passion to control and overcome the good affections of the mind.

Now the rule and the practice of Christianity, or the gospel, as it is closely connected with future rewards and punishments, may be well supported by this concession. Pray, Rhapsodus, tell me, if every man in this present life, by the violence of some counter-working passion, may not have his good affections to virtue controlled or overcome? May not therefore his eternal fears and hopes be a great advantage, security, and support to virtue in so dangerous a state and situation, as our journey through this world towards a better? And this is all, that the defence of Christianity necessarily requires.

And yet further, let me ask our Rhapsodist, If you have nothing else, Sir, but the beauty and excellency, and loveliness of virtue to preach and flourish upon before such sorry and degenerate creatures, as the bulk of mankind are, and you have no future rewards or punishments, with which to address their hopes and fears, how many of these vicious wretches will you ever reclaim from all their varieties of profaneness, intemperance and madness? How many have you ever actually reclaimed by this smooth, soft method, and these fine words? What has all that reasoning and rhetoric done, which have been displayed by your predecessors the Heathen moralists, upon this excellency and beauty of virtue? What has it been able to do towards the reforming of a sinful world? Perhaps now and then a man of better natural mould has been a little refined, and perhaps also there may have been here and there a man restrained or recovered from injustice and knavery, from drunkenness and lewdness, and vile debaucheries, by this fair reasoning and philosophy. But have the passions of revenge and envy, of ambition and pride, and the inward secret vices of the mind been mortified merely by this philosophical language? Have any of these men been made new creatures, men of real piety and love to God?

Go, dress up all the virtues of human nature in all the beauties of your oratory, and declaim aloud among the looser herds of mankind, on the praise of social virtue, and

---

What success have philosophers had, in preaching the beauty of virtue?

the amiable qualities of goodness, till your heart or your lungs ache, and you will ever find, as your Heathen fathers have done before, that the wild passions and appetites of men are too violent to be restrained by such mild and silken language. You may as well build up a fence of straw and feathers, to resist a cannon-ball, or try to quench a flaming grenado with a shell of fair water, as hope to succeed in these attempts. But an eternal heaven and an eternal hell carry divine force and power with them. This doctrine from the mouth of Christian preachers has begun the reformation of multitudes. This gospel has recovered thousands among the nations from iniquity and death. They have been awakened by these awful scenes to begin religion; and afterwards their virtue has improved into superior and more refined principles and habits by divine grace, and risen to high and eminent degrees, though not to a consummate state. The blessed God knows human nature much better than Rhapsodus, and has throughout his word appointed a more proper and more effectual method of address to it, by the passions of hope and fear, by punishments and rewards.

If you read on four pages further in these writings, you will find, the author makes another concession. He allows, that the master of a family, using proper rewards, and gentle punishments toward his children, teaches them goodness, and by this help, instructs them in a virtue, which afterwards they practise upon other grounds, and without thinking of a penalty or a bribe; and this, says he, is what we call a liberal education and a liberal service.

This new concession of that author may also be very happily improved in favor of Christianity. What are the best of men in this life? They are by no means perfect in virtue. We are all but children here under the great Master of the family; and he is pleased by hopes and fears, by mercies and corrections, to instruct us in virtue, and to conduct us onward towards the sublimer and more perfect practice of it in the future world, where it will be performed, as in his own language, perhaps without thinking of penalties and bribes. And since he has allowed, that this conduct may be called "a liberal education, and a liberal service," let Christianity, then, be indulged the title of a "liberal

---

Effect of preaching eternal rewards and punishments?

What is a personal argument? One, that is addressed to a person, upon his own principle, and may not apply to a person of different principles.

education" also; and it is admirably fitted for such frail and sinful creatures, while they are training up toward the sublimer virtues of the heavenly state.

XII. When you are engaged in a dispute with a person of very different principles from yourself, and you can find any ready way to prevail with him to embrace the truth by principles, which you both freely acknowledge, you may fairly make use of his own principles to shew him his mistake, and thus convince or silence him, from his own concessions.

If your opponent should be a Stoic philosopher, or a Jew, you may pursue your argument in defence of some Christian doctrine or duty against such a disputant, by axioms or laws, borrowed either from Zeno or Moses. And though you do not enter into the inquiry, how many of the laws of Moses are abrogated, or whether Zeno was right or wrong in his philosophy; yet if from the principles and concession of your opponent, you can support your argument for the gospel of Christ, this has been always counted a fair treatment of an adversary, and it is called *Argumentum ad hominem*, or *Ratio ex concessis*. Paul sometimes makes use of this sort of disputation, when he talks with Jews or Heathen philosophers; and at least, he silences if not convinces them; which is sometimes necessary to be done against an obstinate and clamorous adversary, that just honor may be paid to truths, which he knew were divine, and that the only true doctrine of salvation might be confirmed and propagated among sinful and dying men.

XIII. Yet great care must be taken, lest your debates break in upon your passions, and awaken them to take part in the controversy. When the opponent pushes hard, and gives just and mortal wounds to our own opinion, our passions are very apt to feel the strokes, and to rise in resentment and defence. Self is so mingled with the sentiments, which we have chosen, and has such a tender feeling of all the opposition, which is made to them, that personal brawls are very ready to come in as seconds, to succeed and finish

---

Latin name?

Literal meaning of *argumentum ad hominem*? An argument to a man.

Meaning of *ratio ex concessis*? A reason from what is conceded.

When may we use personal arguments? Whenever there is opportunity, especially when our opponent appears inconsistent with himself.

Excellence of personal argument? It is perhaps the best weapon, that logic can furnish, for the destruction of error.

If our opponent presses us very hard with argument, what is likely to be the effect, upon our passions?

What will be likely to be the effect, if our bad passions are engaged?

the dispute of opinions. Then noise and clamor and folly appear in all their shapes, and chase reason and truth out of sight.

How unhappy is the case of frail and wretched mankind, in this dark or dusky state of strong passion and glimmering reason? How ready are we, when our passions are engaged in the dispute, to consider more, what loads of nonsense and reproach we can lay upon our opponent, than what reason and truth require in the controversy itself. Dismal are the consequences mankind are too often involved in by this evil principle. It is this common and dangerous practice, that carries the heart aside from all that is fair and honest in our search after truth, or the propagation of it in the world. One would wish, that none of the Christian fathers had been guilty of such follies as these. But Jerome fairly confesses this evil principle in his apology for himself to Pammachius, "that he had not so much regarded what was exactly to be spoken in the controversy he had in his hand, as what was fit to lay a load on Jovinian." And indeed, I fear this was the vile custom of many writers even in the church-affairs of those times. But it will be a double scandal upon us in our more enlighted age, if we allow ourselves in a conduct so criminal and dishonest. Happy souls, who keep such a sacred dominion over their inferior and animal powers, and all the influences of pride, and secular interest, that the sensitive tumults, or these vicious influences, never rise to disturb the superior and better operations of the reasoning mind!

XIV. These general directions are necessary, or at least useful, in all debates whatsoever, whether they arise in occasional conversation, or are appointed at any certain time or place; whether they are managed with or without any formal rules to govern them. But there are three sorts of disputation, in which there are some forms and orders observed, and which are distinguished by these three names, namely, Socratic, Forensic, and Academic, that is, the disputes of the schools.

Concerning each of these it may not be improper to discourse a little, and give a few particular directions or remarks about them.

Confession of St. Jerome upon this point?

Who was St. Jerome? The most learned of the Latin fathers.

Who were the Latin fathers? Those Christian fathers, who wrote in Latin.

What were those called, who wrote in Greek? Greek fathers.

Meaning of *Christian fathers*? Distinguished early writers, who were professed Christians.

When did Jerome live? In the 4th and 5th centuries.

CHAPTER XI.

THE SOCRATIC WAY OF DISPUTATION.

I. This method of dispute derives its name from Socrates, by whom it was practised, and by other philosophers in his age, long before Aristotle invented the particular forms of syllogism in mood and figure, which are now used in scholastic disputations.

II. The Socratic way is managed by questions and answers in such a manner as this, namely, If I would lead a person into the belief of a heaven or hell, or a future state of rewards and punishments, I might begin in some such manner of inquiry, as the following, and suppose the most obvious and easy answers.

Q. Does not God govern the world? *A.* Surely, he that made it governs it.

Q. Is not God both a good and a righteous governor? *A.* Both these characters doubtless belong to him.

Q. What is the true notion of a good and righteous governor? *A.* That he punishes the wicked, and rewards the good.

Q. Are the good always rewarded in this life? *A.* No, surely; for many virtuous men are miserable here, and greatly afflicted.

Q. Are the wicked always punished in this life? *A.* No, certainly; for many of them live without sorrow, and some of the vilest of men are often raised to great riches and honor. *Q.* Wherein then does God make it appear, that he is good and righteous? *A.* I own, there is but little appearance of it on earth.

Q. Will there be not a time, then, when the tables will be turned, and the scene of things changed, since God governs mankind righteously? *A.* Doubtless there must

Socratic Disputation. — From whom, does this method derive its name?

Who was Socrates? The most distinguished Grecian philosopher.

Of what city? Athens.

When did he die? B. C. 400.

At what age? 70—How long ago?

When was he born?

What more do you know about Socrates?

In what manner, is the Socratic method managed?

be a proper time, wherein God will make that goodness and that righteousness to appear.

Q. If this be not before their death, how can it be done? *A.* I can think of no other way, but by supposing man to have some existence after this life.

Q. Are you not convinced, then, that there must be a state of reward and punishment after death? *A.* Yes, surely, I now see plainly, that the goodness and righteousness of God, as governor of the world, necessarily require it.

III. Now the advantages of this method are very considerable.

1. It represents the form of a dialogue or common conversation, which is a much more easy, more pleasant and a more sprightly way of instruction, and more fit to excite the attention and sharpen the penetration of the learner, than solitary reading, or silent attention to a lecture. Man being a sociable creature, delights more in conversation, and learns better this way, if it could always be wisely and happily practised.

2. This method has something very obliging in it, and carries a very humble and condescending air, when he that instructs seems to be the inquirer, and seeks information from him who learns.

3. It leads the learner into the knowledge of truth, as it were by his own invention; which is a very pleasing thing to human nature; and by questions pertinently and artificially proposed, it does as effectually draw him on to discover his own mistakes, which he is much more easily persuaded to relinquish, when he seems to have discovered them himself.

4. It is managed in a great measure in the form of the most easy reasoning, always arising from something asserted or known in the foregoing answer, and so proceed-

---

First class of advantages, mentioned by Watts?

Second class?

How does it lead the learner, into the knowledge of truth?

For, what, does the Socratic method give a teacher, peculiar advantages? To adapt his ideas and words to the capacities of his pupils.

When may this method, become very unreasonable and oppressive? When one party insists upon asking all the questions, and answering none.

Grand rule upon this method? That each party, should he allowed to ask as many questions as, the other.

When one answers the questions of his opponent, what is the exercise often called? Using the laboring oar.

How much ought each to be willing to use the laboring oar?

Why is it so called? Because it is generally much easier to ask questions, than to answer them.

Who can ask questions, that no philosopher can answer? A little child

ing to inquire something unknown in the following question, which again makes way for the next answer. Now such an exercise is very alluring and entertaining to the learner, while his own reasoning powers are all along employed, and that without labor or difficulty; because the querist finds out and proposes all the intermediate ideas or middle terms.

IV. There is a method very near akin to this, which has much obtained of late, namely, writing controversies by questions only, or confirming or refuting any position, or persuading to, or dehorting from, any practice, by the mere proposal of queries. The answer to each question is supposed to be so plain and so necessary, that it is not expressed; because the query itself carries a convincing argument in it, and seems to determine, what the answer must be.

V. If Christian catechisms could be framed in the manner of a Socratic dispute, by question and answer, it would wonderfully enlighten the minds of children, and it would improve their intellectual and reasoning powers, at the same time, that it would lead them into the knowledge of religion. It is upon one account, well suited to the capacity of children; for the questions may be pretty numerous, and the querest must not proceed too swiftly toward the determination of his point proposed, that he may with more ease, with brighter evidence, and with surer success, draw the learner on to assent to those principles step by step, from whence the final conclusion will naturally arise. The only inconvenience would be this, that if children were to reason out all their way entirely into the knowledge of every part of their religion, it would draw common catechisms into too large a volume for their leisure, attention or memory.

Yet those who explain their catechisms to them may, by due application and forethought, instruct them in this manner.

Method of instruction, nearly allied to the Socratic?

Why are not the answers given?

What effect does Watts think a catechism upon the Socratic method might have upon children?

Why should the querist be cautious not to proceed too rapidly?

What would be the inconvenience of a catechism, consisting of a vast number of questions and answers?

Miscellaneous Questions, No. 4.

In what language, should disputants state the question of debate?
According to what, do disputes generally produce good or evil?
Whom does Watts represent as disputing upon transubtantiation?
Of what, shall we be in danger, if we dispute for any think but truth?
Who was the most distinguished Grecian philosopher?
What method of disputation seems the most kind and conciliating?
What good has ever been done by disputing?
Where did Paul dispute daily?
How long should Sartors and Sutors avoid debate?
Why should we not attempt to defend truth by unsound arguments?
What is the Socratic method of disputation?
What class of ministers propagate the gospel in a great measure by disputation?
Upon what, did Sartor and Sutor dispute?
How often did Paul dispute in the school of Tyrannus?
What word signifies the supposed change of bread and wine into the body and blood of Christ?
What method of disputation is conducted principally by questions?
Why is it needful for missionaries to dispute upon religion?
What precise point should be clearly settled in every dispute?
For what faith, should Christians earnestly contend?
What precise point should be clearly settled in every dispute?
What name is given to an argument, that is addressed to a person on his own principles?
When may the Socratic method become oppressive?
Over what may we sometimes gain a victory, when our opponent gains a victory over us?
When the doctrines of a missionary are denied, how should he generally defend them?
What should be the grand object of disputation?
Who were the Latin fathers?
Grand rule to be used in the Socratic method of reasoning?
What may disputes sometimes enable us to search out and maintain?
What if our opponent makes some important concession?
What maxim relating to religion seems to be as unscriptural, as it is unreasonable?
What does Watts compare to the flight of a hunted hare?
Who were the Greek fathers?
In what school, did Paul dispute daily?
What scripture authority have we for disputing?
Why should we dispute only for truth?
What good has ever been done by disputing?
Most learned of the Latin fathers?
What shall we think of the maxim *never to dispute about religion*?
What effect have philosophers had in preaching the beauty of virtue?
Why is it needful, that disputants should be agreed in some points?
Effect of changing the question in a dispute?

It is thought best to omit the two next chapters, as Forensic and Scholastic disputations are now perhaps, on the whole of no use, and would probably never be practised by one of a hundred, who may study this book. Though some of the instructions of these chapters are in themselves valuable, in relation to other disputes, perhaps most of them have been superseded.

CHAPTER XIV.

OF STUDY, OR MEDITATION.

I. It has been proved and established in some of the foregoing chapters, that neither our own observations, nor our reading the labors of the learned, nor the attendance on the best lectures of instruction, nor enjoying the brightest conversation, can ever make us truly knowing and wise, without the labors of our reason in surveying, examining and judging concerning all subjects, upon the best evidence we can acquire. A good genius, or sagacity of thought, a happy judgment, a capacious memory, and large opportunities of observation and converse, will do much of themselves toward the cultivation of the mind, where they are well improved. But where to the advantage of learned lectures, living instructions and well chosen books, diligence and study are superadded, this man has all human aids concurring, to raise him to a superior degree of wisdom and knowledge.

Under the preceding heads of discourse, it has been already declared, how our own meditation and reflection should examine, cultivate and improve all other methods and advantages of enriching the understanding. What remains in this chapter, is to give some further occasional hints, how to employ our own thoughts, what sort of subjects we should meditate on, and in what manner, we should regulate our studies, and how we may improve our judgment, so as in the most effectual and compendious way, to attain such knowledge, as may be most useful for every man in his circumstances of life, and particularly for those of the learned professions.

II. The first direction for youth is this, Learn betimes to distinguish between words and things. Get clear and plain ideas of the things you are set to study. Do not con-

---

What is the grand, and crowning method of gaining knowledge and mental improvement?

Between what objects, should we learn betimes to distinguish?—Meaning of *betimes*?

Why should we not content ourselves with mere words?

What gives words, their whole value? Their representing other objects.

What, if we do not know, what objects, certain words represent? Those words are useless to us.

What is implied in knowing, what objects, words represent? It is the

tent yourselves with mere words and names, lest your labored improvements only amass a heap of unintelligible phrases, and you feed upon husks instead of kernels. This rule is of unknown use in every science.

But the greatest and most common danger is in the sacred science of theology, where settled terms and phrases have been pronounced divine and orthodox, which yet have had no meaning. The scholastic divinity would furnish us with numerous instances of this folly; and yet for many ages, all truth and all heresy were determined by such senseless tests, and by words without ideas. Such Shibboleths as these, have decided the secular fates of men; and bishopricks or burning, mitres or faggots, have been the rewards of different persons, according as they pronounced these consecrated syllables, or not pronounced them. To defend them was all piety and pomp and triumph; to despise them, or to doubt or deny them, was torture and death. A thousand thank-offerings are due to that Providence, which has delivered our age and our nation from these absurd iniquities! O that every specimen and shadow of this madness, in every shape, were banished from our schools and churches.

III. Let not young students apply themselves to search out deep, dark and abstruse matters, far above their reach,

---

same as knowing the meaning of the words.

What are the two grand divisions of words? Spoken and written.

By which of the 5 senses, are spoken words perceived?—written?

What four things, most intimately connected together, and connected with study, should be carefully distinguished? Things, ideas, spoken words, and written words.

What do written words immediately represent? In general, they immediately represent spoken words.

What do spoken words, immediately represent? Generally ideas; sometimes, things directly, without representing ideas.

When we study words, of what, should we endeavor to gain clear conceptions?

Why is it necessary, to pay very particular attention to words, in pursuing our studies? We can scarcely study without them.

In what science, is the greatest and most common danger of not having clear ideas annexed to words.

Meaning of *annex*?

Why is it peculiarly desirable, to have clear ideas upon this subject? Because these ideas relate more immediately to our eternal welfare.

By what tests, were all truth and heresy determined, for ages?

What are due to Providence, for delivering us from such absurd iniquities?

What branch of literature, has been highly conducive to such deliverance? Hermeneutics.

Who have been the greatest instruments in effecting this deliverance? Luther and his coadjutors in the Reformation.

Meaning of *coadjutor*?

Who, since their day, has done the most, to promote this cause of truth, candor and holiness? Probably Watts.

Who should be especially cautious, not to search for things above their reach?

or spend their labor in any subjects, for which they have not the advantages of necessary antecedent learning or books or observations. Let them not be too hasty to know things above their present powers, nor plunge their inquiries at once into the depths of knowledge, nor begin to study any science in the middle. This will confound, rather than enlighten, the understanding. Such practices may happen to discourage and harass the mind by an attempt above its power; it may balk the understanding, and create an aversion to future diligence, and perhaps by despair, may forbid the pursuit of that subject for ever afterwards; as a limb overstrained by lifting a weight above its power, may never recover its former agility and and vigor; or if it does, the man may be frighted from ever exerting his strength again.

IV. Nor yet let any student on the other hand frighten himself at every turn, with insurmountable difficulties; nor imagine, that the truth is wrapt up in impenetrable darkness. These are formidable spectres, which the understanding raises sometimes, to flatter its own laziness. Those things, which in a remote and confused view, seem very obscure and perplexed, may be approached by gentle and regular steps, and may then unfold and explain themselves at large to the eye. The hardest problems in geometry, and the most intricate schemes or diagrams may be explicated and understood step by step. Every great mathematician bears a constant witness to this observation.

V. In learning any new thing, there should be as little as possible first proposed to the mind at once. That being understood, and fully mastered, proceed to the next adjoining part yet unknown. This is a slow, but safe and sure way to arrive at knowledge. If the mind apply itself at first to easier subjects, and things near akin to what is already known, and then advance to the more remote and knotty parts of knowledge, by slow degrees, it will be able in this manner, to cope with great difficulties, and prevail over them, with amazing and happy success.

Mathon happened to dip into the two last chapters of a

Where should we not begin to study any science?—Why?

Why does the understanding sometimes raise formidable spectres, in the course of study?

How may we learn very difficult truths? By proceeding systematically, gradually, vigorously patiently and perseveringly

Effect of such proceeding upon the faculties of the mind? Great improvement.

In learning any new thing, how much should be proposed at once?

How was Mathon affected, when he first attended to the latter part of a work on Geometry?

new book of geometry and mensuration. As soon as he saw it, and was frighted with the complicated diagrams, which he found there, about the frustums of cones and pyramids, &c. and some deep demonstrations among conic sections, he shut the book in despair; and imagined none but a Sir Isaac Newton was ever fit to read it. But his tutor happily persuaded him to begin the first pages about lines and angles. And he found such surprising pleasure in three weeks time in the victories he daily obtained, that at last, he became one of the chief geometers of his age.

VI. Engage not the mind in the intense pursuit of too many things at once; especially such, as have no relation to one another. This will be ready to distract the understanding, and hinder it from attaining perfection in any one subject of study. Such a practice gives a slight smattering of several sciences, without any solid and substantial knowledge of them, and without any real and valuable improvement. Though two or three sorts of study may be usefully carried on at once, to entertain the mind with variety, that it may not be over-tired with one sort of thoughts, yet a multitude of subjects will too much distract the attention, and weaken the application of the mind to any one of them.

Where two or three sciences are pursued at the same time, if one of them be dry, abstracted and unpleasant, as logic, metaphysics, law, languages, let another be more entertaining and agreeable, to secure the mind from weariness. Delight should be intermingled with labor, as far as possible, to allure us to bear the fatigue of dry studies the

---

What did Mathon finally become? How?

Effect of pursuing too many studies at once?

How many principal studies, may usually be pursued collaterally?—Meaning of *collaterally*?

What else may be attended to, at the same time? Reading, writing, spelling and perhaps, one or two subordinate branches, that require but little attention.

Why should more than one sort of study be carried on at once?

Why should they not be very numerous?

What studies should be pursued in connection with such, as are more dry and uninteresting?

Can you mention some of these dry studies?

How can the driest studies be rendered agreeable? By excellent teaching, and excellent learning.

How far, should delight be mingled with study?—Why?

What advantage may it afford, besides this allurement? It may improve bodily health, and intellectual vigor.

How far should our studies be made amusements? If possible, every study should be made an amusement, in relation to others, pursued at the same time.—Meaning of *amusement*, as here used? That which refreshes the mind, and prepares it, to attend with more vigor, to something else.

What effect upon many wandering geniuses, has the pursuit of incidental themes?

Meaning of *theme*?

better. Poetry, practical mathematics, history, &c. are generally esteemed entertaining studies, and may be happily used for this purpose. Thus, while we relieve a dull and heavy hour, by some alluring employments of the mind, our very diversions enrich our understandings; and our pleasure is turned into profit.

VII. In the pursuit of every valuable subject of knowledge, keep the end always in your eye, and be not diverted from it by every petty trifle you meet with in the way. Some persons have such a wandering genius, that they are ready to pursue every incidental theme or occasional idea, till they have lost sight of their original subject. These are the men, who, when they are engaged in conversation, prolong their story by dwelling on every incident, and swell their narrative with long parentheses, till they have lost their first design; like a man, who is sent in quest of some great treasure; but steps aside to gather every flower he finds, or stands still to dig up every shining pebble he meets with, till the treasure is forgotten, and never found.

VIII. Exert your care, skill and diligence about every subject and every question, in a just proportion to the importance of it, together with the danger and bad consequences of ignorance or error therein. Many excellent advantages flow from this one direction.

1. This rule will teach you to be very careful in gaining some general and fundamental truths both in philosophy, in religion and in human life; because they are of the highest moment, and conduct our thoughts with ease, into a thousand inferior and particular propositions. Such is that great principle in natural philosophy, the doctrine of gravitation, or mutual tendency of all bodies toward each other, which Sir Isaac Newton has so well established, and from which he has drawn the solution of a multitude of appearances in the heavenly bodies, as well as on earth.

Such is that golden principle of morality, which our

How do some men most painfully prolong their stories, in conversation?—Meaning of *guest*?—of *pebble*?—of *parenthesis*?

In proportion to what, should we pursue every study?

By whom, is this rule violated? Probably by most persons, who direct, what studies shall be pursued.

What mistakes are often made, by disregarding this rule? Persons often content themselves with the consideration, that a study is really useful, without inquiring, whether it is useful, in proportion to the attention paid to it; or whether it is more useful, than some other study, less attended to, or wholly neglected.

In what, will this rule teach us, to be very cautious, in gaining some fundamental truths?

Meaning of *fundamental*?—of *gravitation*?

blessed Lord has given us, Do that to others, which you think just and reasonable, that others should do to you; which is almost sufficient in itself to solve all cases of conscience, which relate to our neighbor.

Such are those principles in religion, that a rational creature is accountable to his Maker for all his actions; that the soul of man is immortal; that there is a future state of happiness and of misery, depending on our behavior in the present life, on which all our religious practices are built or supported.

We should be very critical in examining all propositions, that pretend to this honor of being general principles. We should not, without just evidence, admit into this rank mere matters of common fame, or commonly received opinions; no, nor the general determinations of the learned, nor the established articles of any church or nation, &c. for there are many learned presumptions, many synodical and national mistakes, many established falsehoods, as well as many vulgar errors, wherein multitudes of men have followed one another for whole ages almost blindfold. It is of great importance for every man to be careful, that these general principles are just and true. For one error may lead us into thousands, which will naturally follow, if once a leading fasehood be admitted.

2. This rule will direct us to be more careful about practical points, than mere speculations; since they are commonly of much greater use and consequence. Therefore, the speculations of algebra, the doctrine of infinites, and the quadrature of curves in mathematical learning, together with all the train of theorems in natural philosophy, should by no means intrench upon our studies of morality and virtue. Even in the science of divinity itself, the sublimest speculations of it are not of that worth and value, as the rules of duty toward God and toward man.

3. In matters of practice, we should be most careful to fix our end right, and wisely determine the scope, at which

---

What are some of the fundamental principles in religion?

What propositions should we be very critical in examining?

Into how many smaller errors, may one great error lead us?

What points are more important, than mere speculations?

Meaning of *speculation*?

Why are speculations useful? Principally on account of their connection with practice.

What speculations are most important? Those, which are most intimately connected with the most important practice.

Grand negative maxim for regulating our studies? Never neglect a more important, for the sake of pursuing a less important.

What should we be most careful to fix right, in matters of practice?

we aim; because that is to direct us in the choice and use of all the means to attain it. If our end be wrong, all our labor in the means will be vain, or perhaps so much the more pernicious, as they are better suited to attain that mistaken end. If mere sensible pleasure or human grandeur or wealth be our chief end, we shall choose means contrary to piety and virtue, and proceed apace toward real misery.

4. This rule will engage our best powers and deepest attention in the affairs of religion, and things that relate to a future world. For those propositions, which extend only to the interest of the present life, are but of small importance, when compared with those, that have influence upon our everlasting concernments.

5. And even in the affairs of religion, if we walk by the conduct of this rule, we shall be much more laborious in our inquiries into the necessary and fundamental articles of faith and practice, than the lesser appendices of Christianity. The great doctrines of repentance toward God, faith in our Lord Jesus Christ, with love to men, and universal holiness, will employ our best and brightest hours and meditations; while the mint, anise and cummin, the gestures and vestures and fringes of religion, will be regarded no further, than they have a plain and evident connection with faith and love, with holiness and peace.

6. This rule will make us solicitous not only to avoid such errors, whose influence will spread wide into the whole scheme of our own knowledge and practice, but such mistakes also, whose influence would be yet more extensive and injurious to others, as well as to ourselves; perhaps to many persons or many families, to a whole church, a town, a country or a kingdom. Upon this account, persons, who are called to instruct others, who are raised to any eminence either in church or state, ought to be careful in settling their principles in matters relating to the civil, the moral or the religious life, lest a mistake of theirs should

---

What if our end be wrong?

What if our end be mere sensual enjoyment?

In what affairs, should our best powers and deepest attention be engaged?

To what doctrines of religion, should we pay most attention?

How far should the circumstantials of religion be regarded?

Who should pray kneeling? Those who find that posture most conducive to devotion, and especially those, who think it most agreeable to scripture.

Against what mistakes, should we most earnestly guard?

Why should we not indulge an undue fondness for any study? It will tend to make us disrelish, or pervert others.

diffuse wide mischief, should draw along with it, most pernicious consequences, and perhaps extend to following generations.

These are some of the advantages, which arise from the eighth rule, namely, pursue every inquiry and study in proportion to its real value and importance.

IX. Have a care, lest some beloved notion, or some darling science so far prevail over your mind, as to give a sovereign tincture to all your other studies, and discolor all your ideas; like a person in the jaundice, who spreads a yellow scene with his eyes over all the objects which he meets. I have known a man of peculiar skill in music, and much devoted to that science, who found out a great resemblance of the Athanasian doctrine of the trinity in every single note; and he thought it carried something of argument in it to prove that doctrine. I have read of another, who accommodated the seven days of the first week of creation to the seven notes of music; and thus the whole creation became harmonious.*

Under this influence, derived from mathematical studies, some have been tempted to cast all their logical, their metaphysical, and their theological and moral learning into the method of mathematicians, and bring every thing relating to those abstracted or those practical sciences, under theorems, problems, postulates, scholiums, corollaries, &c. whereas the matter ought always to direct the method. For all subjects or matters of thought cannot be moulded or forced to one form. Neither the rules for the conduct of the understanding, nor the doctrines nor duties of religion and virtue, can be exhibited naturally in figures and diagrams. Things are to be considered as they are in themselves. Their nature is inflexible, and their natural relations unalterable. And therefore, in order to conceive them aright, we must bring our understandings to things, and not pretend to bend and strain things to comport with our fancies and forms.

X. Suffer not any beloved study to prejudice your mind so far in favor of it, as to despise all other learning. This is a fault of some little souls, who have got a smattering of astronomy, chemistry, metaphysics, history, &c. and for want of a due acquaintance with other sciences, make a scoff at them all, in comparison with their favorite science.

* Perhaps the author did not consider, that the "seven notes of music," if sounded together, will produce several discords; nor, that sounded separately, they will produce at best, only a melody.—Editor.

Their understandings are hereby cooped up in narrow bounds, so that they never look abroad into other provinces of the intellectual world, which are more beautiful perhaps, and more fruitful than their own. If they would search a little into other sciences, they might not only find treasures of new knowledge, but might be furnished also with rich hints of thought, and glorious assistances, to cultivate that very province, to which they have confined themselves.

Here I would always give some grains of allowance to the sacred science of theology, which is incomparably superior to all the rest, as it teaches us the knowledge of God, and the way to his eternal favor. This is that noble study, which is every man's duty; and every one who can be called a rational creature is capable of it. This is that science, which would truly enlarge the minds of men, were it studied with that freedom, that unbiassed love of truth, and that sacred charity, which it teaches; and if it were not made, contrary to its own nature, the occasion of strife, faction, malignity, a narrow spirit, and unreasonable impositions on the mind and practice. Let this, therefore, stand always chief.

XI. Let every particular study have due and proper time assigned it, and let not a favorite science prevail with you to lay out such hours upon it, as ought to be employed upon the more necessary and more important affairs or studies of your profession. When you have, according to the best of your discretion, and according to the circumstances of your life, fixed proper hours for particular studies, endeavor to keep those rules; not indeed with a superstitious preciseness, but with some good degrees of a regular constancy. Order and method in a course of study, save much time, and make large improvements. Such a fixation of certain hours will have a happy influence to secure you from trifling and wasting away your minutes in impertinence.

XII. Do not apply yourself to any one study at one time longer than the mind is capable of giving a close attention

---

Why is the science of theology superior to all the rest?

What effect would this science have upon mental improvement, if properly pursued?

What has theology occasioned, contrary to its own nature?

What shall we think of neglecting theology, for studies of little practical importance, in order to improve the mind? It seems to be a vast mistake, and doubly injurious.—How doubly?

Advantages of alloting particular times to particular studies? It saves much time, and is more likely to secure due proportion of time to each study.

Beyond what point, should we not apply ourselves, at one time?—Why?

to it, without weariness or wandering. Do not over-fatigue the spirits at any time, lest the mind be seized with a lassitude, and thereby be tempted to nauseate a particular subject, before you have finished it.

XIII. In the beginning of your application to any new subject, be not too uneasy under present difficulties, that occur, nor too importunate and impatient for answers and solutions to any questions that arise. Perhaps a little more study, a little further acquaintance with the subject, a little time and experience, will solve those difficulties, untie the knot, and make your doubts vanish. If you are under the instruction of a tutor, he can inform you, that your inquiries are perhaps too early, and that you have not yet learnt those principles, upon which the solution of such a difficulty depends.

XIV. Do not expect to arrive at certainty in every subject, which you pursue. There are a hundred things, wherein we mortals, in this dark and imperfect state, must be content with probability, where our best light and reasonings will reach no further. We must balance arguments, as justly as we can, and where we cannot find weight enough on either side to determine the scale with sovereign force and assurance, we must content ourselves perhaps with a small preponderation. This will give us a probable opinion; and those probabilities are sufficient for the daily determination of a thousand actions in human life, and many times even in matters of religion.

It is admirably well expressed by a late writer, "When there is great strength of argument set before us, if we will refuse to do what appears most fit for us, until every little objection is removed, we shall never take one wise resolution, as long as we live."

Suppose I had been honestly and long searching, what religion I should choose, and yet I could not find, that the arguments in defence of Christianity arose to complete certainty; but went only so far as to give me a probable evidence of the truth of it; though many difficulties still remained, yet I should think myself obliged to receive and practise that religion. For the God of nature and reason has bound us to assent and act according to the best evi-

---

Against what uncomfortable feelings, should we guard, at the commencement of a study?

With what, should we content ourselves, when we cannot gain certainty?

What may such probabilities determine?

What if we refuse to do what appears most fit, till every objection is removed?

dence we have, even though it be not absolute and complete; and as he is our supreme judge, his abounding goodness and equity will approve and acquit the man, whose conscience honestly and willingly seeks the best light, and obeys it, as far as he can discover it.

But in matters of great importance in religion, let him join all due diligence with earnest and humble prayer for divine aid in his inquiries; such prayer and such diligence as eternal concerns require, and such, as he may plead with courage before the Judge of all.

XV. Endeavor to apply every speculative study, as far as possible, to some practical use, that both yourself and others may be the better for it. Inquiries even in natural philosophy should not be mere amusements, and much less in the affairs of religion. Researches into the springs of natural bodies and their motions should lead men to invent happy methods for the ease and convenience of human life; or at least, they should be improved, to awaken us to admire the wondrous wisdom and contrivance of God our Creator in all the works of nature.

If we pursue mathematical speculations, they will inure us to attend closely to any subject, to seek and gain clear ideas, to distinguish truth from falsehood, to judge justly, and to argue strongly; and these studies do more directly furnish us with all the various rules of those useful arts of life, namely, measuring, building, sailing, &c.

Even our very inquiries and disputations about vacuum or space and atoms, about incommensurable quantities, and

---

To what, should we endeavor to apply every speculative study?

How should we treat studies, that are of little, or no practical use? With little, or no attention.

Why should we not attend to them, for the sake of improving the mind? Practical studies will probably improve the mind better.

What minds are likely to be peculiarly roused and invigorated, by practical studies? Those, that are ardently desirous of doing good.

To what, will mathematical studies inure us?

When is the best time to produce this effect? Probably in childhood.

Why? Because the mind is then very susceptible of impressions.

How young should children begin to study mathematics in books? In general, under six years old.

What branch of mathematics? Mental arithmetic.

Meaning of *mental arithmetic*? Arithmetic, in which all the operations are performed in the mind, without any mechanical exercise of the hand.

How early should the child be taught to answer questions in arithmetic? As early as possible.

First and fundamental idea of arithmetic? The idea of one.—Second? The idea of two.

What can you say with regard to changing our methods of study? They should rarely be changed, except in early life.

What important inference, may be deduced from this remark? That it is very important for youth to adopt the best methods of study.

the infinite divisibility of matter and eternal duration, which seem to be purely speculative, will shew us some good practical lessons, will lead us to see the weakness of our nature, and should teach us humility in arguing upon divine subjects, and matters of sacred revelation. This should guard us against rejecting any doctrine, which is expressly and evidently revealed, though we cannot fully understand it. It is good sometimes to lose and bewilder ourselves in such studies for this very reason, and to attain this practical advantage, this improvement in true modesty of spirit.

XVI. Though we should always be ready to change our sentiments of things upon just conviction of their falsehood, yet there is not the same necessity of changing our accustomed methods of reading, or study and practice, even though we have not been led at first into the happiest method. Our thoughts may be true, though we may have hit upon an improper order of thinking. Truth does not always depend upon the most convenient method. There may be a certain form and order, in which we have long accustomed ourselves to range our ideas and notions, which may be best for us now, though they were not originally best in themselves. The inconveniencies of changing may be much greater, than the conveniencies we could obtain by a new method.

As for instance; if a man in his younger days has ranged all his sentiments in theology in the method of Ames's Medulla Theologiæ, or Bishop Usher's Body of Divinity, it may be much more natural and easy for him to continue to dispose all his further acquirements in the same order, though perhaps neither of these treatises is in itself written in the most perfect method. So when we have long fixed our cases of shelves in a library, and ranged our books in any particular order, namely, according to their languages, or according to their subjects, or according to the alphabetical names of the authors, &c. we are perfectly well acquainted with the order, in which they now stand, and we can find any particular book, which we seek, or add a new book, which we have purchased, with much greater ease, than we do in finer cases of shelves, where the books are ranged in any different manner whatsoever. Any different position of the volumes would be new and strange and troublesome to us, and would not countervail the inconveniencies of a change.

So if a man of forty years old has been taught to hold his pen aukwardly in his youth, and yet writes sufficiently well for all the purposes of his station, it is not worth while to teach him now the most accurate methods of handling that instrument. For this would create him more trouble without equal advantage, and perhaps he might never attain to write better, after he had placed all his fingers perfectly right with this new accuracy.

CHAPTER XV.

OF FIXING THE ATTENTION.

A Student should labor by all proper methods, to acquire a steady fixation of thought. Attention is a very necessary thing, in order to improve our minds. The evidence of truth does not always appear immediately, nor strike the soul at first sight. It is by long attention and inspection, that we arrive at evidence; and it is for want of it, we judge falsely of many things. We make haste to determine upon a slight and a sudden view; we confirm our guesses, which arise from a glance; we pass a judgment, while we have but a confused or obscure perception, and thus plunge ourselves into mistakes. This is like a man, who walking in a mist, or being at a great distance from any visible object, (suppose a tree, a man, a horse or a church,) judges much amiss of the figure and situation and colors of it, and sometimes takes one for the other; whereas, if he would but withhold his judgment, till he came nearer to it, or stay, till clearer light came, and then would fix his eyes longer upon it, he would secure himself from those mistakes.

Now, in order to gain a greater facility of attention, we may observe these rules;

I. Cultivate a fondness for the study or knowledge you

What if a man holds his pen badly at 40 years old?

Fixing Attention.—What exercise is most important, in order to improve our minds?

If we determine a question upon a slight view, into what, shall we be likely to plunge?

What conduced more than any thing else to make Newton the prince of philosophers? Close attention, and patient thought.

Striking couplet, relating to Newton's discoveries?

Nature, and nature's laws were
sunk in night;
God said, *Let Newton be*, and all was
light.

First direction for fixing attention?

How can we cultivate a fondness

would pursue. We may observe, that there is not much difficulty in confining the mind to contemplate, what we have a great desire to know; and especially if they are matters of sense, or ideas which paint themselves upon the fancy. It is but acquiring a hearty good will and resolution to search out and survey the various properties and parts of such objects; and our attention will be engaged, if there be any delight or diversion in the study or contemplation of them. Therefore mathematical studies have a strange influence toward fixing the attention of the mind, and giving a steadiness to a wandering disposition; because they deal much in lines, figures and numbers, which affect and please the sense and imagination. Histories have a strong tendency the same way; for they engage the soul by a variety of sensible occurrences; when it has begun, it knows not, how to leave off. It longs to know the final event, through a natural curiosity. Voyages and travels, and accounts of strange countries and strange appearances, will assist in this work. This sort of study detains the mind by the perpetual occurrence and expectation of something new, and that which may gratefully strike the imagination.

II. Sometimes we may make use of sensible things and corporeal images for the illustration of those notions, which are more abstracted and intellectual. Therefore, diagrams greatly assist the mind in astronomy and philosophy; and the emblems of virtues and vices may happily teach children, and pleasingly impress those useful moral ideas on young minds, which perhaps might be conveyed to them with much more difficulty, by mere moral and abstracted discourses.

I confess, in this practice of representing moral subjects by pictures, we should be cautious, lest we so far immerse the mind in corporeal images, as to render it unfit to take in an abstracted and intellectual idea, or cause it to form wrong conceptions of immaterial things. This practice therefore is rather to be used, at first, in order to get a fixed habit of attention, and in some cases only; but it can never

---

for any study? By reading, thinking and conversing upon it, and by considering the pleasures and advantages of pursuing it.

What if it is a dry, useless study? God never required us to like such a study; and it is best to leave it off, before we meddle with it.

Second direction for fixing the attention? Represent intellectual objects by visible. Meaning of *visible*?

What caution should we use in following this rule? That we do not confound immaterial objects with material.

Meaning of *confound*?

Third direction? Study works, that are argumentative.—Meaning of the Latin phrase *Labor ipse voluptas*? Labor itself is pleasure..

be our constant way and method of pursuing all moral, abstracted and spiritual themes.

III. Apply yourself to those studies, and read those authors, who draw out their subjects into a perpetual chain of connected reasonings, wherein the following parts of the discourse are naturally and easily derived from those which go before. Several of the mathematical sciences, if not all, are happily useful for this purpose. This will render the labor of study delightful to a rational mind, and will fix the powers of the understanding with strong attention, to their proper operations, by the very pleasure of it. *Labor ipse voluptas*, is a happy proposition wheresoever it can be applied.

IV. Do not choose your constant place of study by the finery of the prospects, or the most various and entertaining scenes of sensible things. Too much light, or a variety of objects, which strike the eye or the ear, especially while they are ever in motion or often changing, have a natural and powerful tendency to steal away the mind too often from its steady pursuit of any subject, which we contemplate; and thereby the soul gets a habit of silly curiosity and impertinence, of trifling and wandering. Vagario thought himself furnished with the best closet for his study, among the beauties, gaieties and diversions of Kensington or Hampton-Court. But after seven years professing to pursue learning, he was a mere novice still.

V. Be not in too much haste to come to the determination of a difficult or important point. Think it worth your waiting, to find out truth. Do not give your assent to either side of a question too soon, merely on this account, that the study of it is long and difficult. Rather be contented with ignorance for a season, and continue in suspense, till your attention and meditation and due labor have found out sufficient evidence on one side. Some are so fond of knowing a great deal at once, and of talking of things with freedom and boldness, before they understand them, that they scarcely ever allow themselves attention enough to search the matter through and through.

VI. Have a care of indulging the more sensual passions and appetites of animal nature. They are great enemies to attention. Let not the mind of a student be under the

---

Is it desirable to have our study pleasantly situated?

What is recommended, with regard to deciding difficult and important points?

Effect of strongly desiring to know a great deal at once?

Effect of sensual indulgence upon the habit of attention?—of the indulgence of passions?

influence of any warm affection to things of sense, when he comes to engage in the search of truth, or the improvement of his understanding. A person under the power of love or fear or anger, great pain or deep sorrow, has so little government of his soul, that he cannot keep it attentive to the proper subject of his meditation. The passions call away the thoughts with incessant importunity toward the object, that excited them; and if we indulge the frequent rise and roving of passions, we shall thereby procure an unsteady and inattentive habit of mind.

Yet this one exception must be admitted, namely, If we can be so happy, as to engage any passion on the side of the study, which we are pursuing, it may have a great influence to fix the attention more strongly to it.

VII. It is, therefore, very useful to fix and engage the mind in the pursuit of any study, by a consideration of the divine pleasures of truth and knowledge, by a sense of our duty to God, by a delight in the exercise of our intellectual faculties, by the hope of future service to our fellow-creatures, and glorious advantage to ourselves, both in this world and that which is to come. These thoughts, though they may move our affections, yet they do it with a proper influence. These will rather promote our attention, than divert it from the subject of our meditations. A soul, inspired with the fondest love of truth, and the warmest aspirations after sincere celestial beatitude, will keep all its powers attentive to the incessant pursuit of them. Passion is then refined, and consecrated to its divinest purposes.

CHAPTER XVI.

OF ENLARGING THE CAPACITY OF THE MIND.

There are three things, which in an especial manner, go to make up that amplitude, or capacity of the mind, which is one of the noblest characters belonging to the understanding. 1. When the mind is ready to take in great and

---

When may a passion be conducive to fix attention?

Important inference from this remark? We should endeavor to engage our passions in favor of our studies.

Last direction for fixing attention?

How many of these seven directions can you now state?

What if the soul is inspired with the fondest love of truth, and warmest desires for heaven?

Enlarging the mind.—In what

sublime ideas, without pain or difficulty; 2. When the mind is free to receive new and strange ideas, upon just evidence, without great surprise or aversion; 3. When the mind is able to conceive or survey many ideas at once, without confusion, and to form a true judgment, derived from that extensive survey. The person, who wants either of these characters, may in that respect, be said to have a narrow genius. Let us diffuse our meditations a little upon this subject.

I. That is an ample and capacious mind, which is ready to take in vast and sublime ideas, without pain or difficulty. Persons, who have never been used to converse with any thing but the common, little and obvious affairs of life, have acquired a narrow or contracted habit of soul, that they are not able to stretch their intellects wide enough to admit large and noble thoughts. They are ready to make their domestic, daily and familiar images of things the measure of all that is, and all that can be. Talk to them of the vast dimensions of the planetary worlds; tell them, that our star called Jupiter is a solid globe, 1400 times larger than the earth; that the sun is a vast globe of fire, above a thousand times larger than Jupiter; that is, 1400,000 times larger than the earth; that the distance from the earth to the sun is 96 millions of miles; and that a cannon bullet, shot from the earth, would not arrive at the nearest of the fixed stars, in some hundreds of years; they cannot bear the belief, but hear all these glorious labors of astronomy, as a mere idle romance. Inform them of the amazing swiftness of the motion of some of the smallest or the largest bodies in nature. Assure them, according to the best philosophy, that the planet Venus, (that is, our morning or evening star, which is nearly as large as our earth,) though it seems to move from its place but a few yards in a month, does really fly 81,000 miles in an hour; tell them, that the rays of light shoot from the sun to our earth at the rate of 200,000 miles in the second of a minute, they stand aghast at such talk, and believe it no more, than the tales of giants fifty yards high, and the rabbinical fables of Leviathan, who every day swallows a fish, three miles long, and is thus preparing

---

three things, does amplitude of mind consist?

In what respect, is any person a narrow genius, who wants any of these?

What is that mind called, which can readily take in great and sublime ideas?

How are persons, who lack this quality, affected, when told of the wonders of astronomy?—of the wonders of the microscope?—Meaning of *astronomy*?—of *microscope*?

himself to be the food and entertainment of the blessed at the feast of Paradise.

NOTE VI, BY THE EDITOR.

[*Wonders of Astronomy.*—Since the days of Watts, vast improvements have been made in optical instruments, especially the telescope. This has enabled astronomers to cultivate a more intimate acquaintance with the starry heavens. Important corrections have been made in astronomical instruments; and the wonders of astronomy have appeared more wondrous still. Some of the statements of Watts, therefore, are far below the truth. There is no doubt now among philosophers, that Jupiter is 1400 times larger than the earth; that the sun is about 1000 times larger than Jupiter, that the earth is more than 95 millions of miles from the sun; that it moves 81,000 miles every hour; and that light moves about 200,000 miles every second. These corrections have accordingly been made in the statements of Watts.]

These unenlarged souls are in the same manner, disgusted with the wonders, which the microscope has discovered, concerning the shape, the limbs and motions of ten thousand little animals, whose united bulk would not equal a pepper corn. They are ready to give the lie to all the improvements of our senses, by the invention of a variety of glasses, and will scarcely believe any thing beyond the testimony of their naked eye, without the assistance of art. Now if we would attempt in a learned manner, to relieve the minds, that labor under this defect,

1. It is useful to begin with some first principles of Geometry, and lead them onward by degrees to the doctrine of quantities, which are incommensurable, or which will admit of no common measure, though it be ever so small. By this means, they will see the necessity of admitting the infinite divisibility of space or matter.

This same doctrine may also be proved to their understandings, and almost to their senses, by some easier argu-

---

Why are some of Watts's statements in astronomy, very different from those of the present day? See Note VI.

Meaning of *optics?*—of *telescope?*

What body moves 81,000 miles every hour?

With what first principles, should we begin, in order to cure the first kind of narrow-mindedness?

How many miles in circumference, is the earth? About 25,000.—Meaning of *circumference?*

ments in a more obvious manner. As the very opening and closing of a pair of compasses, will evidently prove, that if the smallest supposed part of matter be put between the points, there will be still less and less distance all the way between the legs, till you come to the head or joint. Wherefore, there is no such thing possible as the smallest quantity. But a little acquaintance with true philosophy and mathematical learning would soon teach them, that there are no limits either as to the extension of space, or to the division of body, and would lead them to believe, there are bodies amazingly great or small, beyond their present imagination.

2. It is proper also to acquaint them with the circumference of our earth, which may be proved by very easy principles of geometry, geography and astronomy, to be about 25,000 miles round; as it has been actually found to have this dimension by mariners who have sailed round it. Then let them be taught, that in every 24 hours, either the sun and stars must all move round this earth, or the earth must turn round upon its own axis. If the earth itself revolve thus, then each house or mountain near the equator, must move at the rate of a thousand miles in an hour. But if, as they generally suppose, the sun or stars move round the earth, then, the circumference of their several orbits or spheres being vastly greater than this earth, they must have a motion prodigiously swifter than a thousand miles an hour. Such a thought as this will by degrees, enlarge their minds, and they will be taught, even upon their own principle of the diurnal revolutions of the heavens, to take in some of the vast dimensions of the heavenly bodies, their spaces and motions.

3. To this, should be added the use of telescopes, to help them to see the distant wonders in the skies; and microscopes, which discover the minutest part of little animals, and reveal some of the finer and most curious works of nature. They should be acquainted also with some other noble inventions of modern philosophy, which have a great influence to enlarge the human understanding; of which I shall take occasion to speak more under the next head.

4. For the same purpose, they may be invited to read those parts of Milton's admirable Poem, entitled Paradise Lost, where he describes the armies and powers of angels, the wars and the senate of devils, the creation of this earth, together with the descriptions of heaven, hell and paradise,

It must be granted that poesy often deals in these vast and sublime ideas. And even if the subject or matter of the poem does not require such amazing and extensive thoughts, yet tropes and figures, which are some of the main powers and beauties of poesy, do so gloriously exalt the matter, as to give a sublime imagination, its proper relish and delight. So when a boar is chaffed in hunting,

................His nostrils flames expire,
And his red eye-balls roll with living fire.—*Dryden.*

When Ulysses withholds and suppresses his resentment,

................His wrath comprest
Recoiling, muttered thunder in his breast.—*Pope.*

But especially where the subject is grand, the poet fails not to represent it in all its grandeur. So when the supremacy of a God is described,

He sees with equal eye, as God of all,
A hero perish, or a sparrow fall;
Atoms or systems, into ruin hurl'd,
And now a bubble burst, and now a world.—*Pope.*

This sort of writings has a natural tendency to enlarge the capacity of the mind, and make sublime ideas familiar. But instead of running always to ancient Heathen poesy, with this design, we may with equal if not superior advantage, apply ourselves to converse with some of the best of our modern poets, as well as with the writings of the prophets, and the poetical parts of the Bible, namely, the book of Job and the Psalms, in which sacred authors, we shall find sometimes more sublime ideas, more glorious descriptions, more elevated language, than the fondest critics have ever found in any of the Heathen versifiers either of Greece or Rome; for the eastern writers use and allow much stronger figures and tropes than the western.

Now there are many and great and sacred advantages to be derived from this sort of enlargement of the mind.

It will lead us into more exalted apprehensions of the great God our Creator, than ever we had before. It will entertain our thoughts with holy wonder and amazement, while we contemplate that being who created these various

---

Effect of reading sublime poetry? Meaning of *sublime*?

Of whom, does this enlargement of mind help us to form exalted conceptions?

What feelings toward God, is the contemplation of his amazing works, suited to inspire?

Striking line, of Dr. Young, upon this subject? "An undevout astronomer, is mad."

works of surprising greatness, and surprising smallness; who has displayed most inconceivable wisdom in the contrivance of all the parts, powers and motions of these little animals invisible to the naked eye; who has manifested a most divine extent of knowledge, power and greatness, in forming and moving the vast bulk of the heavenly bodies, and in surveying and comprehending all those unmeasurable spaces, in which they move. Fancy, with all her images, is fatigued and overwhelmed in following the planetary worlds through such immense stages, such astonishing journies, as these are, and resigns its place to the pure intellect, which learns by degrees to take in such ideas as these, and to adore its Creator with new and sublime devotion.

And not only are we taught to form juster ideas of the great God by these methods, but this enlargement of the mind carries us on to nobler conceptions of his intelligent creatures. The mind, that deals only in vulgar and common ideas, is ready to imagine the nature and powers of man to come something too near to God his Maker; because we do not see or sensibly converse with any beings superior to ourselves. But when the soul has obtained a greater amplitude of thought, it will not then immediately pronounce every thing to be God, which is above man. It then learns to suppose, there may be as many various ranks of beings in the invisible world, in a constant gradation superior to us, as we ourselves are superior to all the ranks of being beneath us in this visible world; even though we descend downward far below the ant and the worm, the snail and the oyster, to the least and to the dullest animated atoms, which are discovered to us by microscopes.

By this means, we shall be able to suppose what powers angels, whether good or bad, must possess, as well as prodigious knowledge, in order to oversee the realms of Persia and Greece of old; or if any such superintend the affairs of Great Britain, France, Ireland, Germany, &c. in our days; what power and speed are necessary to destroy one hundred eighty-five thousand armed men in one night in the Assyrian camp of Sennacherib, and all the first-born in the land of Egypt in another, each of which is attributed to an angel.

By these steps, we shall ascend to form more just ideas of

Of whom, besides God, does this enlargement of mind help us to form nobler conceptions?

Sublime conjecture of Watts, concerning the various ranks of beings?

the knowledge and grandeur, the power and glory of the Man Jesus Christ, who is intimately united to God, and is one with him. Doubtless he is furnished with superior powers to all the angels in heaven, because he is employed in superior work, and appointed to be the sovereign Lord of all the visible and invisible worlds. It is his human nature, in which the Godhead dwells bodily, that is advanced to these honours and to this empire; and perhaps there is little or nothing in the government of the kingdoms of nature and grace, but what is transacted by the Man Jesus, inhabited by the divine power and wisdom, and employed as a medium or conscious instrument of this extensive gubernation.

II. I proceed now to consider the next thing, wherein the capacity or amplitude of the mind consists, and that is, when the mind is free to receive new and strange ideas and propositions upon just evidence, without any great surprise or aversion. Those, who confine themselves within the circle of their own hereditary ideas and opinions, and who never give themselves leave so much as to examine or believe any thing, beside the dictates of their own family or sect or party are justly charged with a narrowness of soul. Let us survey some instances of this imperfection, and then direct to the cure of it.

1. Persons who have been bred up all their days within the smoke of their father's chimney, or within the limits of their native town or village, are surprised at every new sight that appears, when they travel a few miles from home. The plowman stands amazed at the shops, the trade, the crouds of people, the magnificent buildings, the pomp and riches and equipage of the court and city, and would hardly believe what was told him, before he saw it. On the other hand, the cockney travelling into the country, is surprised at many actions of the quadruped and winged animals in the field, and at many common practices of rural affairs.

If either of these happens to hear an account of the familiar and daily customs of foreign countries, he pronounces them at once indecent and ridiculous. So narrow are their understandings, and their thoughts so confined, that they

---

Second narrowness of mind?

How is such narrowness cured? By travelling, reading, conversation, and philosophical experiments.

What amazes the plowman, when he visits the city?

What surprises the cockney, when he visits the country?

Meaning of *cockney*? An ignorant or contemptible Londoner.

know not how to believe any thing wise or proper, besides what they have been taught to practise.

This narrowness of mind should be cured by hearing and reading the accounts of different parts of the world, and the histories of past ages, and of nations and countries distant from our own, especially the more polite parts of mankind. Nothing tends in this respect so much to enlarge the mind, as travelling, that is, making a visit to other towns, cities or countries, besides those in which we were born and educated. Where our condition does not grant us this privilege, we must endeavor to supply the want by books.

2. It is the same narrowness of mind, that awakens the surprise and aversion of some persons, when they hear of doctrines and schemes in human affairs or in religion, quite different from what they have embraced. Perhaps they have been trained up from their infancy in one set of notions, and their thoughts have been confined to one single track both in the civil and religious life, without ever hearing or knowing, what other opinions are current among mankind; or at least, they have seen all other notions besides their own, represented in a false and malignant light; whereupon they judge and condemn at once, every sentiment but what their own party receives, and they think it a piece of justice and truth to lay heavy censures upon the practice of every different sect in Christianity or politics. They have so rooted themselves in the opinions of their party, that they cannot hear an objection with patience, nor can they hear a vindication, or so much as an apology for any set of principles beside their own. All the rest is nonsense or heresy, folly or blasphemy.

This defect also is to be relieved by free conversation with persons of different sentiments. This will teach us to bear with patience a defence of opinions contrary to our own. If we are scholars, we should also read the objections against our own tenets, and view the principles of other parties, as they are represented in their own authors, and not merely in the citations of those who would confute them. We should take an honest and unbiassed survey of the force of reasoning on all sides, and bring all to the test of unprejudiced reason and divine revelation.

Note, This is not to be done in a rash and self-sufficient

How do some very narrowminded persons regard all principles, but their own?

How can this be cured?

Meaning of *tenets*?

In what works, should we read the principles of other parties?

To what test, should we bring all our opinions, and all objections to them?

manner; but with a humble dependence on divine wisdom and grace, while we walk among snares and dangers.

By such a free converse with persons of different sects (especially those who differ only in particular forms of Christianity, but agree in the great and necessary doctrines) we shall find, that there are persons of good sense and virtue, persons of piety and worth, persons of much candor and goodness, who belong to different parties, and have imbibed sentiments opposite to each other. This will soften the roughness of an unpolished soul, and enlarge the avenues of our charity toward others, and incline us to receive them into all the degrees of unity and affection, which the word of God requires.

3. I may borrow further illustrations both of this freedom and this aversion to receive new truths, from modern astronomy and natural philosophy. How much is the vulgar part of the world surprised at the talk of the diurnal and annual revolutions of the earth? They have ever been taught by their senses and their neighbors, to imagine, the earth stands fixed in the centre of the universe, and that the sun, with all the planets and the fixed stars, is whirled round this little globe once in twenty-four hours; not considering, that such a diurnal motion, by reason of the distance of some of those heavenly bodies, must be almost infinitely swifter and more inconceivable, than any which the modern astronomers attribute to them. Tell these persons, that the sun is fixed in the centre, that the earth, and all the planets, roll round the sun in their several periods, and that the moon rolls round the earth in a lesser circle, while together with the earth, she is carried round the sun, they cannot admit a syllable of this new and strange doctrine, and they pronounce it utterly contrary to all sense and reason.

Acquaint them, that there are four moons also perpetually rolling round the planet Jupiter, and carried along with him in his periodical circuit round the sun, which little moons were never known till the year 1610, when Galileo discovered them by his telescope; inform them, that Saturn has seven moons of the same kind attending him; and that the body of that planet is encompassed with two broad, flat

---

What pleasing discoveries shall we make, by conversing kindly and freely, with persons of various religious denominations?

What effect will this have upon the unpolished mind?

To what, do many consider the wonders of astronomy, as being contrary?

How many moons has Saturn?

How many rings has Saturn?

circular rings, the nearest distant from the planet 34 thousand miles, they look upon these things as tales and fancies; and will tell you that the glasses do but delude your eyes with vain images; and even when they themselves consult their own eye-sight in the use of these tubes, the narrowness of their mind is such, that they will scarcely believe their senses, when they dictate ideas so new and strange.

And if you proceed further, and attempt to lead them into a belief, that all these planetary worlds are habitable, and it is probable, they are replenished with intellectual beings, dwelling in bodies, they will deride the folly of him that informs them; for they resolve to believe, there are no habitable worlds but this earth, and no spirits dwelling in bodies besides mankind; and it is well, if they do not fix the brand of heresy on the man, who is leading them out of their long imprisonment, and loosing the fetters of their souls.

There are many other things relating to mechanical experiments, and to the properties of the air, water, fire, iron, the loadstone, and other minerals and metals, as well as the doctrine of the sensible qualities, namely, colors, sounds, tastes, &c. which this class of men cannot believe, for want of a greater amplitude of mind.

The best way to convince them, is by giving them some acquaintance with the various experiments in philosophy, and proving by ocular demonstration the multiform and amazing operations of the air pump, the loadstone, the chemical furnace, optical glasses and mechanical engines. By this means, the understanding will stretch itself by degrees, and when they have found there are so many new and strange things, that are most evidently true, they will not be so forward to condemn every new proposition in any of the other sciences, or in the affairs of religion and civil life.

III. The capacity of the understanding includes yet another qualification, and that is, an ability to receive many ideas at once, without confusion. The ample mind takes a

---

What if these narrow-minded persons are told, that the planets are probably inhabited?

What experiments may be best suited to convince such persons of their errors?

Third thing, in which the amplitude of the mind consists?

Is it probable, that the mind can contemplate a great variety of objects, at the same moment? or may they be viewed in very rapid succession, and seem, as though they were viewed at the same moment?

Can any mind, contemplate more than one object, at the same moment? The divine Mind certainly can; and propably some human minds can at the same moment, contemplate several.

Why does such a view seem needful for a correct decision? Several

survey of several objects with one glance, keeps them all within sight, and present to the soul, that they may be compared together in their mutual respects. It forms just judgments, and it draws proper inferences from this comparison, even to a great length of argument, and a chain of demonstrations.

The narrowness, that belongs to minds in general, is a great imperfection and impediment to wisdom and happiness. There are but few persons, who can contemplate, or practise several things at once. Our faculties are very limited; and while we are intent upon one part or property of a subject, we have but a slight glimpse of the rest or we lose it out of sight. But it is a sign of a large and capacious mind, if we can with one single view take in a variety of objects; or at least, when the mind can apply itself to several objects with so swift a succession, and in so few moments, as attains almost the same ends, as if it were all done in the same instant.

This is a necessary qualification, in order to great knowledge and good judgment. For there are several things in human life, in religion and in the sciences, which have various circumstances, appendixes and relations attending them; and without a survey of all those ideas, which are mutually related and connected, we are often in danger of passing a false judgment on the subject proposed. It is for this reason, there are so many controversies among the learned and unlearned, in matters of religion, as well in the affairs of civil government. The notions of sin, and duty to God and our fellow-creatures; of law, justice, authority and power; of covenant, faith, justification, redemption and grace; of church, bishop, ordination, &c. contain in them such complicated ideas, that when we are to judge of any thing concerning them, it is hard to take into our view at once, all the attendants or consequents, that must and will be concerned in the determination of a single question. And yet without a due attention to many, or to most of these, we are in danger of determining the question amiss.

---

circumstances must be compared, in order for a correct conclusion.

How many ideas must be in the mind at a time, in order to form a comparison? At least two.

Why? A comparison always implies at least two things compared, and the mind cannot compare two ideas together, unless they are together.

How many ideas must the mind have at once, in order to form a clear conception of a triangle? At least three.

Why? Because a triangle has three sides.

It is owing to the narrowness of our minds, that we are exposed to the same peril in the matters of human duty and prudence. In many things, which we do, we ought not only to consider the mere naked action itself, but the persons who act, the persons toward whom, the time when, the place where, the manner how, the end for which, the action is done, together with the effects, that must, or that may follow, and all other surrounding circumstances. These things must necessarily to taken into our view, in order to determine whether the action, indifferent in itself, is either lawful or unlawful, good or evil, wise or foolish, decent or indecent, proper or improper.

Let me give a plain instance for the illustration of this matter. Mario kills a dog; which, considered merely in itself, seems to be an indifferent action. Now the dog was Timon's, and not his own. This makes it look unlawful. But Timon bid him do it. This gives it an appearance of lawfulness again. It was done at church, and in time of divine service. These circumstances added, cast on it an air of irreligion. But the dog flew at Mario, and put him in danger of his life. This relieves the seeming impiety of the action. But Mario might have escaped by flying thence. Therefore, the action appears to be improper. But the dog was known to be mad; this further circumstance makes it almost necessary, that the dog should be slain, lest he might attack the assembly, and do much mischief. Yet again, Mario killed him with a pistol, which he happened to have in his pocket, since yesterday's journey.—Now hereby the whole congregation was terrified and discomposed, and divine service was broken off. This carries in it an appearance of great indecency and impropriety. But after all, when we consider a further circumstance, that Mario, being thus violently assaulted by a mad dog, had no way of escape, and had no other weapon about him, it seems to take away all the color of impropriety, indecency or unlawfulness, and to allow, that the preservation of one or many lives may justify the act as wise and good. Now all these concurrent appendixes of the action ought to be surveyed, in order to pronounce with justice and truth, concerning it.

There are a multitude of human actions in private life, in domestic affairs, in traffic, in civil government, in courts of

---

Can you mention some of the circumstances, that must often be taken into view, in order to determine, whether an action is good or bad?

Did Mario do right, in the case mentioned?

What circumstances, taken by themselves, would seem to imply, that he did wrong?—that he did right?

justice, in schools of learning, &c. which have so many complicated circumstances, aspects and situations, with regard to time and place, persons and things, that it is impossible for any one to pass a right judgment concerning them, without entering into most of these circumstances, and surveying them extensively, and comparing and balancing them all aright.

Whence by the way, I may take occasion to say, how many thousands there are, who take it upon them to pass their censures on the personal and the domestic actions of others, who also, pronounce boldly on the affairs of the public, and determine the justice or madness, the wisdom or folly of national administrations, of peace and war, &c. whom neither God nor men ever qualified for such a post of judgment. They were not capable of entering into the numerous concurring springs of action; nor had they ever taken a survey of the twentieth part of the circumstances, which were necessary for such judgments or censures.

It is the narrowness of our minds, as well as the vices of the will, that often prevents us from taking a full view of all the complicated and concurring appendixes, that belong to human actions. Thence it comes to pass, that there is so little right judgment, so little justice, prudence or decency, practised among the bulk of mankind. Thence arise infinite reproaches and censures, alike foolish and unrighteous. You see, therefore, how needful and happy a thing it is, to be possest of some measure of this amplitude of soul, in order to make us very wise or knowing or just or prudent or happy.

I confess, this sort of amplitude or capacity of mind, is in a great measure, the gift of Nature; for some are born with much more capacious souls than others.

The genius of some persons is so poor and limited, that they can hardly take in the connection of two or three propositions, unless it be in matters of sense, and which they have learnt by experience. They are utterly unfit for

---

Why do many thousands often judge incorrectly of public and private actions?

What besides narrowness of mind, often prevents us from taking a full view of circumstances?

What is meant by the vices of the will? Bad passions or affections.

Can you mention some of them? Does this amplitude of mind depend upon native genius, or upon culture? — Upon which, most? — Meaning of *prolix*?

What should persons of dull genius never attempt to be?

What if these dull geniuses had been much better educated, from their very infancy? Probably, they would have been respectable scholars, perhaps enlighteners of mankind.

speculative studies. It is hard for them to discern the difference between right and wrong, in matters of reason, on any abstract subjects. These ought never to set up for scholars; but apply themselves to those arts and professions of life, which are to be learnt at an easier rate, by slow degrees and daily experience.

Others have a soul a little more capacious, and they can take in the connection of a few propositions pretty well; but if the chain of consequences be a little prolix, here they stick, and are confounded. If persons of this make ever devote themselves to science, they should be well assured of a solid and strong constitution of body, and well resolved to bear the fatigue of hard labor and diligence in study. If the iron be blunt, says Solomon, we must put to more strength.

But, in the third place, there are some of so bright and happy a genius, and so ample a mind, that they can take in a long train of propositions, if not at once, yet in a very few moments, and judge well concerning the dependence of them. They can survey a variety of complicated ideas without fatigue or disturbance; and a number of truths offering themselves, as it were in one view, to their understanding, does not perplex nor confound them. This makes a great man.

Now though there may be much owing to nature in this case, yet experience assures us, that even a lower degree of this capacity may be increased by diligence and application, by frequent exercise, and the observation of such rules as these.

I. Labor by all means, to gain an attentive and patient temper of mind, a power of confirming and fixing your thoughts on any subject, till you have surveyed it on every side, and in every situation, and run though the several powers, parts, properties and relations, effects and consequences of it. He, whose thoughts are very fluttering and wandering, and cannot be fixed attentively to a few ideas successively, will never be able to survey many and various objects distinctly at once, but will certainly be overwhelmed and confounded with the multiplicity of them. The rules for fixing the attention, in the former chapter, are proper to be consulted here.

II. Accustom yourself to clear and distinct ideas in every

What makes a great man?

How many rules does Watts give, for increasing the capacity and extent of thought?

What is the first of these rules?

To what kind of ideas, should we

thing you think. Be not satisfied with obscure and confused conceptions of things, especially where clearer may be obtained. For one obscure or confused idea, especially, if it be of great importance in the question, intermingled with many clear ones, and placed in its variety of aspects, will be in danger of spreading confusion over the whole; and thus may have an influence to overwhelm the understanding with darkness, and pervert the judgment. A little black paint will shamefully tincture and spoil twenty gay colors.

Consider yet further, that if you content yourself frequently with words instead of ideas, or with cloudy and confused notions of things, how impenetrable will that darkness be, and how vast and endless that confusion, which must surround and involve the understanding, when many of these obscure and confused ideas come to be set before the soul at once! and how impossible it will be, to form a clear and just judgment about them.

III. Use all diligence to acquire and treasure up a large store of ideas. Take every opportunity to add something to your stock; and by frequent recollection, fix them in your memory. Nothing tends to confirm and enlarge the memory, like a frequent review of its possessions. This will gradually give the mind a faculty of surveying many objects at once; as a room, that is richly adorned and hung round with a variety of pictures, strikes the eye almost at once, with all that variety, especially if they have been well surveyed one by one at first. This makes it habitual, and

---

accustom ourselves, for this purpose?

What may be the effect of one obscure idea, intermingled with many clear ones?

Of what, should we strive to treasure up a large store?

When should we add to our stock of ideas?

When should this treasure begin? In infancy.

Who should then endeavor to make this infantine store as rich as possible? Parents, teachers of infant schools, and all who can assist.

Why should this store of ideas begin in infancy? That the mind may be more improved, and more abundantly stored in the maturity of life.

May not persons learn enough, without this early effort? No one can learn half enough, even with it; and much less without it.

Why should not we spend our time upon trifles and fictions? Time is too short and too precious.

For what, will attention to fiction, be likely to destroy or diminish our regard? For truth and reality.

When may we attend to fiction? When a little instructive fiction is intimately connected with much useful truth, and when it is very manifest, that it is fiction.

What example of this is most striking? The parables of the Bible.

Why may we read Pilgrim's Progress, without injury? The spiritual meaning is so obvious and striking, that it should be regarded as a reality, rather than as a fiction.

How shall we retain the ideas, that we acquire?

more easy to the inhabitants to take in many of those painted scenes, with a single glance or two.

Here *note*, that by acquiring a rich treasure of notions, I do not mean single ideas only, but also propositions, observations and experiences, with reasonings and arguments upon the various subjects, that occur among natural or moral, common or sacred affairs; that when you are called to judge concerning any question, you will have some principles of truth, some useful axioms and observations always at hand, to direct and assist your judgment.

IV. It is necessary, that we should, as far as possible, lay up our daily new ideas, in a regular order, and arrange our mental acquisitions under proper heads, whether of divinity, law, physics, mathematics, morality, politics, trade, domestic life, civility, decency, &c. whether of cause, effect, substance, mode, power, property, body, spirit, &c. We should inure our minds to method and order continually. When we take in any fresh ideas, occurrences and observations, we should dispose of them in their proper places, and see how they stand and agree with the rest of our notions on the same subject; as a scholar would dispose of a new book on a proper shelf, among its kindred authors; or as an officer at the post-house in London disposes of every letter he takes in, placing it in the box, that belongs to the proper road or county.

In any of these cases, if things lay all in a heap, the addition of any new object would increase the confusion; but method gives a speedy and short survey of them with ease and pleasure. Method is of admirable advantage to keep our ideas from a confused mixture; and to preserve them ready for every use.

V. As method is necessary for the improvement of the mind, in order to make your treasure of ideas most useful; so in all your further pursuits of truth and acquirement of knowledge, observe a regular, progressive method. Begin with the most simple, easy and obvious ideas. Then by

---

When we acquire any new ideas, how shall we dispose of them?

What is meant by disposing of ideas in regular order? Associating them with other ideas, to which they are allied.

What is meant by the association of ideas? Uniting them, or having them so united in the mind, that when we think of one, it will have a tendency to make us think of the other.

How can we associate ideas together? By thinking of them at the same time, or in quick succession.

For what, is mental method of admirable advantage?

When should we inure our minds to method?

When should we observe a progressive method? As we advance in science.

degrees, join two and three and more of them together. Thus the complicated ideas, growing up under your observation, will not give the same confusion of thought, as they would, if they were all offered to the mind at once, without your observing the original and formation of them. An eminent example of this appears in the study of arithmetic. If a scholar, just admitted into the school, observes his master performing an operation in the rule of division, his head is at once disturbed and confounded with the manifold comparisons of the numbers of the divisor and dividend, and the mutiplication of the one, and subtraction of it from the other. But if he begins regularly at addition, and so proceeds by subtraction and multiplication, he will then in a few weeks, be able to take an intelligent survey of all those operations in division, and to practise them himself with ease and pleasure; each of which at first seemed all intricacy and confusion.

An illustration of the like nature may be borrowed from geometry and algebra, and other mathematical practices. How easily does an expert geometer, with one glance of his eye, take in a complicated diagram, made up of many lines and circles, angles and arcs! How readily does he judge of it, whether the demonstration designed by it be true or false! It was by degrees, he arrived at this stretch of understanding. He began with a single line or a point. He joined two lines in an angle. He advanced to triangles and squares, polygons and circles. Thus the powers of his understanding were stretched and augmented daily, till by diligence and regular application, he acquired this extensive faculty of mind.

But this advantage does not belong to mathematics only If we apply ourselves at first, in any science, to clear and single ideas, and never hurry ourselves on to the following and more complicated parts of knowledge, till we thoroughly understand the foregoing, we may practise the same method of enlarging the capacity of the soul with success in any one of the sciences, or in the affairs of life and religion.

Beginning with A, B, C, and making syllables out of letters, and words out of syllables, has been the foundation of all that glorious superstructure of arts and sciences, which have enriched the minds and libraries of the learned world

---

In what study, have we an eminent example of this?

In what other science, or thing mentioned, may we practise the same method?

in many ages. These are the first steps, by which the ample and capacious souls among mankind have arrived at that prodigious extent of knowledge, which renders them the wonder and glory of the nation, where they lived. Though Plato and Cicero, Descartes and Boyle, Locke and Newton, were doubtless favored by Nature, with a genius of uncommon amplitude; yet in their early years, and first attempts at science, this was but limited and narrow, in comparison of what they attained at last. But how vast and capacious were those powers, which they afterwards acquired by patient attention, and watchful observation, by the pursuit of clear ideas and regular method of thinking!

VI. Another means of acquiring this amplitude and capacity of mind, is a perusal of difficult, entangled questions, and of the solution of them in any science. Speculative and casuistical divinity will furnish us with many such cases and controversies. There are some such difficulties in reconciling several parts of the epistles of Paul, relating to the Jewish law, and the Christian gospel. A happy solution will require such an extensive view of things; and the reading of these happy solutions will enlarge this faculty in younger students. In morals and political subjects, Puffendorf's Law of Nature and Nations, and several determinations therein, will promote the same amplitude of mind. An attendance on public trials and arguments, in civil courts of justice, will be of advantage for this purpose; and after a man has studied the general principles of the law of nature and the laws of England, in proper books, the reading the reports of adjudged cases, collected by men of great sagacity and judgment, will richly improve his mind toward acquiring this desirable amplitude and extent of thought, and more especially in persons of that profession.

How did Locke, Newton, &c. vastly increase their powers of thought?

What is the last method, which Watts mentions, for acquiring amplitude and capacity of mind?

MISCELLANEOUS QUESTIONS, No. 5.

When should we learn to distinguish between names and things?

When we study words, of what should we endeavor to gain clear conceptions?

How far should delight be mingled with study?

What science is superior to all the rest?

Couplet respecting Newton's discoveries?

What are some of the things, in which amplitude of mind consists?

What planet has 7 moons?

When are words useless to us?

Why is it necessary to pay very particular attention to words in pursuing our studies?

In relation to what, may every study be rendered an amusement?

Relative importance of theology?

What conduced more than any thing else, to make Newton the prince of philosophers?

When may passion be useful in study?

Science, that treats of the heavenly bodies?

What mind can certainly contemplate many objects at the same time?

What is implied in knowing the meaning of words?

Why is it peculiarly desirable to have clear ideas upon theology?

How far are the circumstantials of religion to be regarded?

Who was the prince of philosophers?

In favor of what should we endeavor to engage our passions?

Instrument, that greatly magnifies very small objects?

Can a human mind contemplate more than one object at a time?

How are words formed, that we can see?

Why should we not begin to study a science in the middle?

In proportion to what, should we pursue every study?

Advantages of allotting particular times to particular studies?

What did close attention and patient thought conduce to make Newton?

Science, that treats of light and seeing?

What planet has 2 rings?

How are words formed, that we can hear?

If one study is much more important than another, which should we attend to most?

To what, shall we endeavor to apply every speculative study?

Instrument, that magnifies very distant objects?

What geometrical figure has three sides?

How many of the senses are employed in perceiving words?

How must we proceed, in order to learn very difficult truths?

Why are speculations sometimes useful?

How should we treat studies, that are of little or no practical use?

In what instruments, have there been very great improvements, since the days of Watts?

What may be the effect of one obscure idea, mingled with many clear ones?

What do written words immediately represent?

Effect of pursuing too many studies at once?

What speculations are most important?

How can we gain a fondness for any study?

What body is about 25,000 miles in circumference?

Property of things, which tends exceedingly to elevate the mind?

When should we add to our stock of ideas?

How shall we retain the ideas, that we acquire?

What do spoken words immediately represent?

How can dry studies be rendered agreeable?

To what doctrines of religion, should we pay most attention?

What caution should we use in representing intellectual objects by visible?

Who said "An undevout astronomer is mad?"

When should a person's treasure of ideas begin?

What is meant by the association of ideas?

Since whose days, have optical instruments been much improved?

CHAPTER XVII.

OF IMPROVING THE MEMORY.

MEMORY is a distinct faculty of the mind, very different from perception, judgment, reasoning, and its other powers. Then we are said to remember any thing, when the idea of it arises in the mind with a consciousness at the same time that we have had this idea before. Our memory is our natural power of retaining what we learn and of recalling it on every occasion. Therefore we can never be said to remember any thing, whether it be ideas or propositions, words or things, notions or arguments, of which we have not had some former idea or perception, either by sense or imagination, thought or reflection. Whatsoever we learn from observation, books, conversation, &c. it must all be laid up and preserved in the memory, if we would make it really useful.

NOTE VII, BY THE EDITOR.

[*Brown's Suggestion.*—Dr. Thomas Brown appears to have made an unhappy mistake in relation to this subject. He would substitute the term *suggestion* for *association.* But these words, acccording to established usage, signify very different things; as different, as any cause and effect. *Association* seems most happily to express that uniting or union or connecting of ideas, in consequence of which, one will suggest the other, or recall it to the view of the mind;

MEMORY.—What is memory?

How many faculties, seem to be expressed in this definition?

What are they often called? Retention and recollection.

How does it appear, that they are properly two faculties? One may be very perfect, and the other very imperfect, in the same person.

What other faculty is the memory sometimes considered as including? The faculty of storing up ideas in the mind.

What is the exercise of this latter faculty generally called? Committing to memory, or memorizing.

Which of these faculties does memory more especially signify?—Retention.

What other name is more generally given to the faculty of storing up ideas? Association, or association of ideas.

What name has Dr. Brown substituted, for association? See Note VII.

What might this word be more properly used to express?

What previous exercise prepares the way for one idea to suggest another?

or at least, tend to this effect. If the word *recollection* did not happily express the thing intended, suggestion might be substituted for this purpose. But with no shadow of propriety, can it be applied to that exercise, by which ideas are received into the mind, by being united with others, or for that union of ideas, which are said to be treasured up in the memory, in consequence of which union, one idea will suggest another; or in other words, may be recalled, or recollected, by means of its associate.]

So necessary and so excellent a faculty is the memory, that all other abilities of the mind borrow from it, their beauty and perfection. For other capacities of the soul are almost useless without this. To what purpose, are all our labors in knowledge and wisdom, if we want memory to preserve and use what we have acquired? What signify all other intellectual or spiritual improvements, if they are lost, as soon as they are obtained? It is memory alone, that enriches the mind, by preserving what our labor and industry daily collect. In a word, there can be neither knowledge nor arts nor sciences, without memory; nor can there be any improvement of mankind in virtue or morals, or the practice of religion, without the assistance and influence of this power. Without memory, the soul of man would be but a poor, destitute, naked being, with an everlasting blank spread over it, except the fleeting ideas of the present moment.

NOTE VIII, BY THE EDITOR.

[*Memory.*—These remarks of Watts upon memory, appear to be peculiarly excellent, and deserving of the most earnest attention. The youthful mind is now in great danger of erring exceedingly, respecting the relative importance of this faculty. Surely no faculty can be more important. What indeed could all the faculties do without memory? But how often do we now find writers and teachers speaking of memory almost in strains of contempt, as though it was a faculty, scarcely worth cultivating—scarcely worth

What do the other faculties borrow from memory?

When we remember any thing, are we always conscious, that it was in the mind before? Probably we are not.

What is the store house of knowledge?

What would the soul be, without memory?

Why is the youthful mind, in danger of erring, respecting the relative importance of memory? See Note VIII

possessing! There is no doubt, that in past ages, many have esteemed the memory too highly, in comparison with the judgment, the perception, &c. But perhaps their error was not greater, than that of many more modern declaimers upon these faculties. Watts appears to have been much more correct in considering all these faculties and their improvement of inestimable moment.]

Memory is very useful to those who speak, as well as to those who learn. It assists the teacher and the orator, as well as the scholar or the hearer. The best speeches and instructions are almost lost, if those who hear, immediately forget them. And those, who are called to speak in public, are much better heard and accepted, when they can deliver their discourse by the help of a lively genius and a ready memory, than when they are forced to read all they would communicate. Reading is certainly a heavier way of conveying our sentiments; and there are very few mere readers, who have the felicity of penetrating the soul, and awakening the passions of those who hear, by such a grace and power of oratory, as the man who seems to talk every word from his very heart, and pours out the riches of his own knowledge upon the people round about him, by the help of a free and copious memory. This gives life and spirit to every thing that is spoken, and has a natural tendency to make a deeper impression on the minds of men. It awakens the dullest spirits, causes them to receive a discourse with more affection and pleasure, and adds a singular grace and excellence both to the person and his oration.

A good judgment and a good memory are very different. A person may have a very strong, capacious and retentive memory, where the judgment is very weak; as sometimes it happens in those, who are but one degree above an idiot, who have manifested an amazing strength and extent

---

When was the memory too highly estimated, in comparison with the judgment, &c.?

What is likely to be the effect of preaching, if the preacher seems to speak every word, from his very heart?

Why are some preachers, who preach good sermons from memory, very lifeless and dull? Probably, because they make such an effort to recollect the words of their sermons.

Why are some, who read their sermons, very cold and uninteresting? Because they read badly.

Why are some extemporaneous preachers very unprofitable to their hearers? Either because they are not good workmen, or have not well studied their sermons.

What manner of preaching is best? One may be best for some preachers, and another for others.

Does a good judgment always attend a strong memory?

of memory, but have hardly been able to join or disjoin two or three ideas in a wise and happy manner to make a solid, rational proposition.

There have been instances of others, who have had but a very tolerable power of memory; yet their judgment has been of much superior degree, just and wise, solid and excellent.

Yet it must be acknowledged, that where a happy memory is found in any person, there is good foundation laid for a wise and just judgment of things, wherever the natural genius has any thing of sagacity to make a right use of it. A good judgment must always, in some measure, depend upon a survey and comparison of several things together in the mind, and determining the truth of some doubtful proposition, by that survey and comparison. When the mind has, as it were, set all those various objects present before it, which are necessary to form a true proposition or judgment concerning any thing, it then determines, that such and such ideas are to be joined or disjoined, to be affirmed or denied; and this in a consistency and correspondence with all those other ideas or propositions, which in any way, relate or belong to the same subject. Now there can be no such comprehensive survey of many things without a tolerable degree of memory. It is by reviewing things past, we learn to judge of the future. It happens sometimes, that if one needful or important object or idea be absent, the judgment concerning the thing considered, will thereby become false or mistaken.

You will inquire then, How comes it to pass, that there are some persons who appear in the world of business, as well as in the world of learning, to have a good judgment, and have acquired the just character of prudence and wisdom, and yet have neither a very bright genius nor sagacity of thought, nor a very happy memory, so that they cannot set before their minds at once, a large scene of ideas, in order to pass a judgment?

What does Watts here consider, as one foundation for a just judgment of things?

Upon what survey and comparison, must a good judgment always depend?

Of what, does this survey imply a tolerable degree?

Three grand obstacles to correct judgment? Hurry, perturbation and confusion.

How do we learn to judge of the future?

What science, then, is peculiarly important, for the direction of our conduct? History.

In applying the instructions of history, for what, should we be very cautious to make allowance? Difference of circumstances.

Now we may learn from Penseroso some account of this difficulty. You will scarcely ever find this man forward in judging and determining things proposed to him. He always takes time, and delays, and suspends, and ponders things maturely, before he passes his judgment. Then he practises a slow meditation, ruminates on the subject, and thus perhaps in two or three nights and days, rouses those several ideas, one after another, as he can, which are necessary, in order to judge right of the thing proposed, and make them pass before his review in succession. This he does to relieve the want both of a quick sagacity of thought, and of a ready memory and speedy recollection. This cautious practice lays the foundation of his just judgment and wise conduct. He surveys well, before he judges.

Whence, I cannot but take occasion to infer one good rule of advice to persons of higher as well as lower genius, and of large as well as narrow memories, namely, that they do not too hastily pronounce concerning matters of doubt or inquiry, where there is not an urgent necessity of present action. The bright genius is ready to be so forward, as often betrays itself into great errors in judgment, speech and conduct, without a continual guard upon itself, and using the bridle of the tongue. And it is by this delay and precaution, that many a person of much lower natural abilities, will often excel persons of the brightest genius in wisdom and prudence.

It is often found, that a fine genius has but feeble memory. For where the genius is bright, and the imagination vivid, the power of memory may be too much neglected, and lose its improvement. An active fancy readily wanders over a multitude of objects, and is continually entertaining itself with new flying images. It runs through a number of new scenes or new pages with pleasure, but without due attention, and seldom suffers itself to dwell long enough upon any one of them, to make a deep impression upon the mind, and commit it to lasting remembrance. This is one plain and obvious reason, why there are some persons of very

---

In what manner, does Penseroso judge?—Why?

Of what, does this slow and cautious practice lay the foundation?

Who may take courage and comfort from the example of Penseroso? Persons of ordinary powers of mind.

Into what, does bright genius often betray a person?

Why do bright geniuses so often mistake and err? From presumption and impatience.

Why has a fine genius often but a feeble memory?

How may a great memory cramp invention? By hindering a person from pursuing his own thoughts.

bright parts and active spirits, who have but short and narrow powers of remembrance; for having riches of their own, they are not solicitous to borrow.

As such a quick and various fancy and invention may be some hindrance to the attention and memory, so a mind of a good retentive ability, and which is ever crowding its memory with things, which it learns and reads continually, may prevent, restrain and cramp the invention itself. The memory of Lectorides is ever ready upon all occasions, to offer to his mind something out of other men's writings or conversations, and is presenting him with the thoughts of other persons perpetually. Thus the man, who had naturally a good flowing invention, does not suffer himself to pursue his own thoughts. Some persons, who have been blest by nature with sagacity and no contemptible genius, have too often forbid the exercise of it, by tying themselves down to the memory of the volumes they have read, and the sentiments of other men contained in them.

Where the memory has been almost constantly employing itself in gathering new acquirements, and where there has not been a judgment sufficient to distinguish, what things were fit to be recommended and treasured up in the memory, and what things were idle, useless or needless, the mind has been filled with a wretched heap and mixture of words or ideas; and the soul (may be said to have had large possessions, but no true riches.)

I have read in some of Mr. Milton's writings a very beautiful simile, whereby he represents the books of the fathers, as they are called in the Christian church. "Whatsoever," says he, "old Time, with his huge drag-net, has conveyed down to us along the stream of ages, whether it be shells or shell-fish, jewels or pebbles, sticks or straws, sea-weeds or mud, these are the ancients, these are the fathers." The case is much the same with the memorial possessions of the greatest part of mankind. A few useful things, perhaps, mixed and confounded with many trifles and all manner of rubbish, fill up their memories and compose their intellectual possessions. It is a great happiness,

When the memory has made vast collections, without judgment, or order, what may it be said to have gained?

With what are the memories of most people filled?

What should be the character of every thing, laid up in the memory?

Why should not some things be memorized, merely to strengthen the memory? There are more things of intrinsic value, than any one can possibly learn; and learning these will strengthen the memory quite as well.—Meaning of *memorize*?

therefore, to distinguish things aright, and to lay up nothing in the memory, but what has some just value in it, and is worthy to be numbered as a part of our treasure.

Whatever improvements are to the mind of man from the wise exercise of his own reasoning powers, these may be called his proper manufactures; and whatever he borrows from abroad, these may be termed his foreign treasures. Both together make a wealthy and happy mind.

How many excellent judgments and reasonings are framed in the mind of a man of wisdom and study in a length of years! How many worthy and admirable notions has he been possessed of in life, both by his own reasonings, and by his prudent and laborious collections in the course of his reading! But, alas! how many thousands of them vanish away, and are lost for want of a more retentive memory! When a young practitioner in the law was once said to contest a point in debate with that great lawyer in the last age, Serjeant Maynard, he is reported to have answered him, "Alas, young man, I have forgot much more law, than ever thou has learnt or read."

What an unknown and unspeakable happiness would it be to a man of judgment, and who is engaged in the pursuit of knowledge, if he had but a power of stamping all his own best sentiments upon his memory in some indelible characters; and if he could but imprint every valuable paragraph and sentiment of the most excellent authors he has read, upon his mind, with the same speed and facility, with which he read them! If a man of good genius and sagacity could but retain and survey all those numerous, those wise and beautiful ideas at once, which have ever passed through his mind upon one subject, how admirably would he be furnished to pass a just judgment about all present objects and occurrences! What a glorious entertainment and pleasure would fill and felicitate his spirit, if he could

---

What may we denominate those improvements, that are derived from our own reasoning powers?—what we borrow?

What do large amounts of both constitute?

For want of what, do a great part of a wise man's intellectual treasures vanish away?

What did Serjeant Maynard say to a young lawyer?

How may we avoid forgetting and losing so many of our most valuable acquisitions? By writing them down, and reviewing them; by conversing and meditating upon them; by putting them in practice; and by avoiding, as far as possible, vain company, vain reading, vain actions and vain thoughts.

Can you mention some of the happy consequences, that might result from a wise man's being able to retain all the excellent thoughts he ever acquired?

grasp all these in a single survey, as the skilful eye of a painter runs over a fine and complicate piece of history, wrought by the hand of a Titian or a Raphael, views the whole scene at once, and feeds himself with the extensive delight! But these are joys, which do not belong to mortality.

Thus far I have indulged some loose and unconnected thoughts and remarks with regard to the different powers of wit, memory and judgment. For it was very difficult to throw them into a regular form or method, without more room. Let us now with more regularity, treat of the memory alone.

Though the memory is a natural faculty of the mind of man, and belongs to spirits, which are not incarnate, yet it is greatly assisted or hindered, and much diversified by the brain, or the animal nature, to which the soul is united in this present state. But what part of the brain that is, wherein the images of things* lie treasured up, is very hard for us to determine with certainty. It is most probable, that those very fibres, pores or traces of the brain, which assist at the first idea or perception of any object, are the same, which assist also at the recollection of it; and then it will follow, that the memory has no special part of the brain devoted to its own service, but uses all those parts in general, which subserve our sensations, as well as our thinking and reasoning powers.

As the memory improves in young persons from their childhood, and decays in old age, so it may be increased by art and labor and proper exercise; or it may be injured and quite spoiled by sloth or by disease or a stroke on the head. There are some reasonings on this subject, which make it evident, that the goodness of a memory depends in a great degree upon the consistence and the temperament of that part

---

With what bodily organ, does the memory appear to be particularly connected?—Where is the brain?

Is it probable, that any particular part of the brain is exclusively devoted to the service of memory?

Meaning of *exclusively*?

At what period of life, does memory generally improve?—decay?

How may memory be injured and spoiled?

Are there any traces, forms or images, drawn on the brain? Probably there are not.

Is the brain affected in any way, when ideas are received or lost? It seems certain, that it is.

How? Probably, no person will ever know.

---

* It is hardly to be supposed that Watts really thought, that the "images of things" are in fact delineated upon the brain. It seems most rational to suppose that he used such expressions figuratively.

of the brain, which is appointed to assist the exercise of all our sensible and intellectual faculties. So for instance, in children; they perceive and forget a hundred things in an hour. The brain is so soft, that it receives immediately all impressions, like water or liquid mud, and retains scarcely any of them. All the traces, forms or images, which are drawn there, are immediately effaced or closed up again, as though you wrote with your finger on the surface of a river, or on a vessel of oil.

On the contrary, in old age, men have a very feeble remembrance of things, that were done of late, that is, the same day or week or year. The brain is grown so hard, that the present images or strokes make little or no impression; and therefore, they immediately vanish. Prisco, in his seventy-eighth year, will tell long stories of things done when he was in the battle of the Boyne, almost fifty years ago, and when he studied at Oxford seven years before. For those impressions were made, when the brain was more susceptive. They have been deeply engraven at the proper season, and therefore, they remain. But words or things, which he lately spoke or did, are immediately forgotten; because the brain is now grown more dry and solid in its consistence, and receives not much more impression, than if you wrote with your finger on a floor of clay, or a plastered wall.

But in the middle stage of life, or it may be, from fifteen to fifty years of age, the memory is generally in its happiest state; the brain easily receives and long retains the images and traces, which are impressed upon it; and the natural spirits are more active, to range these little infinite unknown figures of things in their proper cells or cavities, to preserve and recollect them.

Whatever, therefore, keeps the brain in its best consistence, may be a help to preserve the memory. But excess of wine, or luxury of any kind, as well as excess in study or business, may overwhelm the memory, by overstraining and weakening the fibres of the brain, wasting the spirits, injuring the consistence of that tender substance, and confounding the images, that are laid up there.

Why does Watts suppose children so soon gain and lose ideas?

Which are best remembered by the aged, ideas gained recently, or long ago?—Why?

Stage of life, when the memory is best?

Are there any natural spirits, that range through the brain, to preserve and recollect the images there? Probably not.

Why did Watts suppose their existence? It was agreeable to the notion of his day.

What excesses may impair the memory?

A good memory has these several qualifications; 1. It is ready to admit with great ease, the various ideas both of words and things, which are learned or taught. 2. It is large and copious, to treasure up these ideas in great number and variety. 3. It is strong and durable, to retain for a considerable time, those words or thoughts, which are committed to it. 4. It is faithful and active to suggest and recollect, upon every proper occasion, all those words or thoughts, which have been recommended to its care, or treasured up in it.

Now in every one of these qualifications, a memory may be injured, or improved. Yet I shall not insist distinctly on these particulars, but only in general, propose a few rules or directions, whereby this noble faculty, may be preserved or assisted, and shew, what are the practices, that both by reason and experience, have been found of happy influence to this purpose.

There is one great and general direction, which belongs to the improvement of other powers, as well as of the memory; and that is, to keep it always in due and proper exercise. Many acts by degrees form a habit; and thereby the ability or power is strengthened, and made more ready to be again in action. Our memories should be used and inured from childhood, to bear a moderate quantity of knowledge, let into them early; and they will thereby become strong for use and service. As any limb duly exercised, grows stronger, the nerves of the body are corroborated thereby. Milo took up a calf, and daily carried it on his shoulders. As the calf grew, his strength grew also; and he at last arrived at firmness enough to bear the ox.

Our memories will be, in a great measure, moulded and formed, improved or injured, according to the exercise of them. If we never use them, they will be almost lost. Those, who are wont to converse or read about a few things only, will retain but a few in their memory. Those who are used to remember things but for an hour, and charge their memories with it no longer, will retain them but an

---

Four properties of a good memory?

By what adjectives, may these properties be expressed? *Susceptive*, *capacious*, *retentive* and *ready*.

In which of these, may memory be injured or improved?

Grand direction for improving every faculty?

To what, should memory be inured from childhood?

According to what, will our memories be in a great measure moulded, injured or improved?

What if we scarcely ever use our memories?

What if we charge our memories to remember things but for an hour?

hour. Let words be remembered, as well as things, that so you may acquire a copiousness of language, as well as of thought, and be more ready to express your mind on all occasions.

Yet there should be a caution given in some cases. The memory of a child, or any infirm person, should not be overburthened; for a joint or a limb may be overstrained by being too much loaded, and its natural power never be recovered. Teachers should wisely judge of the power and constitution of youth, and impose no more on them, than they are able to bear with cheerfulness and improvement.

And particularly they should take care, that the memory of the learner be not too much crowded with a tumultuous heap or overbearing multitude of documents or ideas at one time. This is the way to remember nothing. One idea effaces another. An over-greedy grasp does not retain the largest handful. But it is the exercise of memory with a due moderation, that is one general method toward its improvement.

The particular rules are such as these;

1. Due attention and diligence to understand things, which we would commit to memory, is a rule of great necessity in this case. When the attention is strongly fixed to any particular subject, all that is said concerning it, makes a deeper impression upon the mind. There are some persons, who complain, they cannot remember divine

---

Why should we remember words, as well as things?

What other advantage will result from learning words in connection with things? It will assist us to retain a knowledge of the things.

How does this furnish an argument in favor of having printed questions, adapted to school books? They will induce the pupil to commit to memory most important words and phrases.

Which should we learn first, things or their names? It seems of little importance, which we learn first, provided we learn them very nearly together.

Why should both be learned nearly at the same time? The name and thing may often help to explain each other. The knowledge of both is much more useful, and may be more easily remembered, than of one alone.

What kind of a school-book seems to be most needed? A book to teach the young child reading, spelling, pronunciation and signification at the same time.

For what literary object might 10,000 dollars be most usefully bestowed? To reward the person who should write the best book for this purpose.

What caution does the author give with regard to tasking the memory of a child, or any infirm person?

What is the utmost task that a teacher should impose upon his pupils?

What if the memory be too much crowded?

What is the first first rule for committing to memory?

Why cannot some remember discourses, that they hear?

or human discourses, which they hear; when in truth, their thoughts are wandering half the time; or they hear with such coldness and indifference, and a trifling temper of spirit, that it is no wonder, the things, which are read or spoken, make but a slight impression on the brain, and get no firm footing in the memory; but soon vanish and are lost.

It is needful, therefore, if we would maintain a long remembrance of the things, which we read or hear; that we should engage our delight in those subjects, and use the methods, which are already prescribed, in order to fix the attention. Sloth and idleness will no more bless the mind with intellectual riches, than it will fill the hand with grain, the field with corn, or the purse with treasure.

Let it be added also, that not only the slothful and the negligent deprive themselves of proper knowledge for the furniture of their memory, but such as appear to have active spirits, who are ever skimming over the surface of things with a volatile temper, will fix nothing in their mind. Vario will spend whole mornings in running over loose and unconnected pages, and with fresh curiosity, is ever glancing over new words and ideas, that strike his present fancy. He is fluttering over a thousand objects of art and science; and yet treasures up but little knowledge. There must be the labor and the diligence of close attention to particular subjects of thought and inquiry, which only can impress what we read or think of upon the remembering faculty in man.

2. Clear and distinct apprehension of the things, which we commit to memory, is necessary, in order to make them dwell there. If we would remember words, or learn the names of persons or things, we should have them recommended to our memory, by clear and distinct pronunciation, spelling or writing. If we would treasure up the ideas of things, notions, propositions, arguments and sciences, these should be recommended also to our memory by a clear and distinct perception of them. Faint, glimmering and confused ideas will vanish, like images seen in twilight. Every thing, which we learn, should be conveyed to the mind in the plainest expressions, without any ambiguity, that we may not mistake, what we desire to remember. This is a general rule, whether we would employ the memory about words or things; though it must be confest, that mere

---

Second rule?
Effect of pronouncing or writing words, that we would learn?

sounds and words are much harder to fix in the mind, than the knowledge of things.

For this reason, take heed, as I have often before warned you, that you do not take up with words instead of things, nor mere sounds, instead of sentiments and ideas. Many a lad forgets what has been taught him, merely because he never well understood it. He never clearly and distinctly took in the meaning of those sounds and syllables, which he was required to get by heart.

This is one reason, why boys make so poor a proficiency in learning the Latin tongue, under masters, who teach them by grammars and rules written in Latin. And this is a common case with children, when they learn their catechisms in their early days. The language and the sentiments, conveyed in those catechisms, are far above the understanding of creatures of that age; and they have no clear ideas from the words. This makes the answers much harder to be remembered, and in truth, they learn nothing but words without ideas; and if they are ever so perfect in repeating the words, yet they know nothing of divinity.

For this reason, it is necessary in teaching children the principles of religion, that they should be expressed in very plain, easy and familiar words, brought as low as possible, down to their understandings, according to their different ages and capacities; and thereby they will obtain some useful knowledge, when the words are treasured up in their memory; because at the same time, they will treasure up those divine ideas too.

3. Method in the things we commit to memory, is necessary, in order to make them take more effectual possession of the mind, and abide there long. As much as systematical learning is decried by some vain and humorous triflers of the age, it is certainly the happiest way to furnish the mind with a variety of knowledge.

Whatever you would trust to your memory, let it be disposed in a proper method, connected well together, and referred to distinct and particular heads or classes, both general and particular. An apothecary's boy will much

---

Why has many a lad soon forgotten what he had been taught?

Greatest improvement in schools, since the days of Watts? Children are better taught to understand what they learn.

Two improvements, that now seem most desirable to be introduced into our schools? That children should be better instructed in religion, and made more fully to understand what they learn.

In what kind of language, should children be taught religion?

What does he recommend in the third rule?

sooner learn all the medicines in his master's shop, when they are ranged in boxes or on shelves, according to their distinct natures, whether herbs, drugs or minerals, whether leaves or roots, whether chemical or galenical preparations, whether simple or compound, &c. and when they are placed in some order according to their nature, their fluidity, or their consistence, &c. in vials, bottles, gallipots, cases, drawers, &c. So the genealogy of a family is more easily learnt, when you begin at some great grandfather as the root, and distinguish the stock, the large boughs, the lesser branches, the twigs and the buds, till you come down to the present infants of the house. And indeed all sorts of arts and sciences, taught in a method, are more easily committed to the mind or memory.

I might give another plain simile, to confirm the truth of this. What horse or carriage can take up and bear away all the various, rude and unwieldy loppings of a branchy tree at once? but if they are divided yet further, so as to be laid close, and bound up in a more uniform manner into several faggots, perhaps those loppings may be all carried as one single load or burden.

The mutual dependance of things on each other, helps the memory of both. A wise connection of the parts of a discourse in a rational method, gives great advantage to the reader or hearer, in order to his remembrance of it. Therefore, many mathematical demonstrations in a long train, may be remembered much better, than a heap of sentences, which have no connection. The book of Proverbs, at least, from the tenth chapter and onward, is much harder to remember, than the book of Psalms, for this reason; and some Christians have told me, that they remember what is written in the epistle to the Romans, and that to the Hebrews, much better than many others of the sacred epistles; because there is more exact method and connection observed in them.

He, that would learn to remember a sermon, which he hears, should acquaint himself by degrees with the method, in which the several important parts of it are delivered. It is a certain fault in a multitude of preachers, that they utterly neglect method; or at least, they refuse to render their method visible and sensible to the hearers. One

---

What effect upon the memory, has the mutual dependence of things?

Why is the greater part of the book of Proverbs, hard to be remembered?

What hint does he give for remembering a sermon?

What does he mention as a fault in a multitude of preachers?

would be tempted to think, it was for fear their auditors should remember too much of their sermons, and prevent their preaching them three or four times over. But I have candor enough to persuade myself, that the true reason is, they imagine it to be a more modish way of preaching without particulars. I am sure it is a much more useless one. And it would be of great advantage both to the speaker and hearer, to have discourses for the pulpit cast into a plain and easy method, and the reasons or inferences ranged in proper order, and that under the words, *first*, *secondly* and *thirdly*, however they may be now fancied to sound unpolite or unfashionable. But archbishop Tillotson did not think so in his days.

4. A frequent review and careful repetition of the things we would learn, and an abridgment of them in a narrow compass, has a great influence to fix them in the memory. Therefore, it is, that the rules of grammar and useful examples of the variation of words, and the peculiar forms of speech in any language, are so often appointed by the masters, as lessons for the scholars, to be repeated; and they are contracted into tables for frequent review, that what is not fixed in the mind at first, may be stamped upon the memory, by a perpetual survey and rehearsal.

Repetition is so very useful a practice, that Mnemon, even from his youth to his old age, never read a book without making some small points, dashes or hooks in the margin, to mark, what parts of the discourse were proper for a review; and when he came to the end of a section or chapter, he always shut his book, and recollected all the sentiments or expressions, he had marked, so that he could give a tolerable analysis and abstract of every treatise he had read, just after he had finished it. Thence he became so well furnished with a rich variety of knowledge.

Even when a person is hearing a sermon or a lecture, he may give his thoughts leave now and then to step back so far, as to recollect the several heads of it from the begin-

---

Why does he suppose, they neglect method?

Is it desirable, that a sermon should contain numerical divisions, expressed by *first*, *second*, *third*, &c.?—Why?

What does he recommend in the fourth rule?

Mnemon's method of reading?

Effect of this method?

What liberty may we take to look back, in hearing a discourse?

How may a preacher greatly assist his hearers, to remember what he says? By making a long pause before naming a new head; by mentioning each head twice; and by sometimes repeating the preceding heads.

Is it best to take notes, while we are hearing a sermon? For some very ready writers, it may be best.

ning, two or three times, before it is finished. The omission or loss of a sentence or two among the amplifications, is richly compensated by preserving in the mind the method and order of the whole discourse, in the most important branches of it.

If we would fix in the memory the discourses we hear, or what we design to speak, let us abstract them into brief compends and review them often. Lawyers and divines have need of such assistances. They write down short notes or hints of the principal heads of what they desire to commit to memory, in order to preach or plead. For such abstracts and epitomes may be reviewed much sooner, and the several amplifying sentiments or sentences will be more easily invented or recollected in their proper places. The art of *short hand* is of excellent use for this, as well as other purposes. It must be acknowledged, that those who scarcely ever take a pen in their hands to write short notes or hints of what they are to speak or learn, who never try to cast things into method, or to contract the survey of them, in order to commit them to memory, need a double degree of power to retain and recollect what they read or hear or intend to speak.

Do not plunge yourself into other businesses or studies, amusements or recreations, immediately after you have attended upon instruction, if you can avoid it. Get time, if possible, to recollect the things you have heard, that they may not be washed all away from the mind by a torrent of other occurrences or engagements, nor lost in the croud or clamor of other loud and importunate affairs.

Talking over the things, which you have read, with your

Best method of taking such notes? Write enough of the doctrine or leading proposition, to be able to remember it; and a word or two of each head; and sometimes, perhaps, note a very striking thought besides.

Why not write as much as possible at the time? The effort of writing will be likely to prevent all good impression of the truths delivered.

What should we do immediately after attending on a sermon? Think over the heads and substance of it, and endeavor to make it as profitable to ourselves as possible, by self application, prayer, and perhaps by writing the most striking parts.

Most important duty in relation to hearing a sermon? Most devoutly to apply it to our own consciences, to reprove and correct us.

What does he say of forming brief compends of what we would remember?

Meaning of *compend*?—of *brief*?

Is it best to learn the art of short hand? Probably not one person among ten thousand will find it worth so much to him, as it will cost.

Why should we not plunge into business or amusements, immediately after attending upon instruction?

What does he say of conversing upon what we learn?

companions, on the first proper opportunity, is a most useful manner of review or repetition, in order to fix them upon the mind. Teach them to your younger friends, in order to establish your own knowledge, while you communicate it to them. The animal powers of your tongue and of your ear, as well as your intellectual faculties, will all join to help the memory. Hermetas studied hard in a remote corner of the land, and in solitude; yet he became a very learned man. He seldom was so happy, as to enjoy suitable society at home, and therefore he talked over to the fields and the woods, in the evening, what he had been reading in the day, and found so considerable advantage by this practice, that he recommended it to all his friends, since he could set his approbation to it from 17 years' trial.

5. Delight in the things we learn, gives great assistance toward the remembrance of them. Whatever, therefore, we desire, a child should commit to memory, make it as pleasant to him, as possible; endeavor to search his genius and his temper; and let him take in the instructions you give him, or the lesssons you appoint him, as far as may be, in a way suited to his natural inclinations. Fabellus would never learn any moral lesson, till they were moulded into the form of some fable, like those of Esop, or till they put on the appearance of a parable, like those, wherein our blessed Savior taught the ignorant. Then he remembered well the emblematical instructions, that were given him, and learnt to practise the moral sense and meaning. Young Spectorius was taught virtue, by setting before him, a variety of examples of the various good qualities in human life; and he was appointed daily to repeat some story of this kind out of Valerius Maximus. The same lad was early instructed to avoid the common vices and follies of youth in the same manner. This is akin to the method, whereby the Lacedemonians trained up their children to hate drunk-

---

To what, did Hermetas talk over what he had learned?

Why is it much better to talk to a living audience? For their instruction and our own.

Meaning of *audience*?

What does he say of the pleasure of learning, as it affects the memory?

To what, should we endeavor to suit the instructions we give to a child?

What was the only form, in which Fabellus would learn moral lessons?

Why should the fabulous humor of Fabellus be renounced? That we may study the rest of the Bible, as well as the parables; that we may become a patient, thorough scholar.

How was Spectorius taught virtue?

What book contains the best stories, to teach children virtue? The Bible.

How did the Lacedemonians train up their children, to hate drunkenness?—Was this right? [See Rom. 3: 8.]

enness and intemperance, namely, by bringing a drunken man into their company, and showing them, what a beast he had made of himself. Such visible and sensible forms of instruction, will make long and useful impressions upon the memory.

Children may be taught to remember many things in a way of sport and play. Some young creatures have learnt their letters and syllables, and the pronouncing and spelling of words, by having them pasted or written upon many little flat tablets or dies. Some have been taught vocabularies of different languages, having a word in one tongue written on one side of these tablets, and the same word in another tongue on the other side of them.

There might be also many entertaining contrivances for the instruction of children in several things relating to geometry, geography and astronomy, in such alluring methods, which would make a most agreeable and lasting impression on their minds.

6. The memory of useful things may receive considerable aid, if they are thrown into verse. For the numbers and measures and rhyme, according to the poesy of different languages, have a considerable influence upon mankind, both to make them receive with more ease, the things proposed to their observation, and preserve them longer in their remembrance. How many are there of the common affairs of life, which have been taught in early years by the help of rhyme, and have been like nails, fastened in a sure place, and rivetted, by daily use?

So the number of the days of each month is engraven on the memory of thousands, by these four lines;

> Thirty days hath September,
> April, June, and November;
> February, twenty-eight alone;
> And all the rest have thirty-one.

Who may be taught to remember many things, by way of sport and play?

Why should not children be taught every thing in this way? They should be taught to feel, that God did not make them to spend their lives in play, but to endure hardness, as good soldiers of Jesus Christ.

Why should they be trained up, thus to endure hardness? This is the way, in which they should go, that they may fight the good fight of faith. Prov. 22: 8. 1 Tim. 6: 12.

What danger is thought to attend many infant schools? That the children will consider their exercises play and sport.

Present state of infant schools? They seem to be yet in their infancy.

What may we hope from infant schools? That they will be among the chief means of so raising mankind, as to make them appear like another race of beings.

What does Watts say of verse, in relation to memory?

Repeat the lines that may enable you to remember the number of days in each month.

So have rules of health been prescribed in the book called Schola Salernitana: and many a person has preserved himself doubtless from evening gluttony, and the pains and diseases consequent upon it, by these two lines

> *Ex magna cæna, stomacho fit maxima pæna;*
> *Ut sis nocte levis, fit tibi cæna brevis.*

Englished;

> To be easy all night,
> Let your supper be light;
> Or else you'll complain
> Of a stomach in pain.

And a hundred proverbial sentences in various languages, are formed into rhyme or verse, whereby they are made to remain in the memory of old and young.

It is from this principle, that moral rules have been cast into a poetic mould, from all antiquity. So the golden verses of the Pythagoreans, in Greek; Cato's distichs *De Moribus*, in Latin; Lilly's precepts to scholars, called *Qui mihi*, with many others; and this has been done with very good success. A line or two of this kind recurring to the memory, has often guarded youth from a temptation to vice and folly, as well as put them in mind of their present duty.

7. When you would remember new things or words, endeavor to associate them with some words or things, which you have well known before, and which are established in your memory. This association of ideas is of great importance, and may be of excellent use in many instances of human life. One idea, which is familiar to the mind, connected with others which are new and strange, will bring those new ideas into easy remembrance. Maronides had got the first hundred lines of Virgil's Enead printed upon his memory so perfectly, that he knew not only the order and number of every verse from one to a hundred, but the order and number of every word in each verse also; and by this means, he would remember two or three hundred names of persons or things by some rational or fantastic connection between some word in the verse, and some letter, syllable, property or accident of the name or thing to be remembered, even though they had been repeated but once or twice in his hearing. Animato practised much the same art of memory, by getting the Latin

---

If we would remember new words or things, with what, should we associate them?

names of twenty-two animals into his head, according to the alphabet, namely, asinus, basilicus, canis, draco, elephas, felis, gryphus, hircus, juvencus, leo, mulus, noctua, ovis, panthera, quadrupes, rhinoceros, simia, taurus, ursus, xiphias, hyena or yena, zibetta. Most of these he divided also into four parts, namely, head and body, feet fins, or wings, and tail; and by some arbitary or chimerical attachment of each of these to a word or thing, which he desired to remember, he committed them to the care of his memory, and that with good success.

It is also by this association of ideas, that we may better imprint any new idea upon the memory, by joining with it, some circumstance of the time, place, company, &c. wherein we first observed, heard or learnt it. If we would recover an absent idea, it is useful to recollect those circumstances of time, place, &c. The substance will many times be recovered, and brought to the thoughts by recollecting the shadow. A man recurs to our fancy by remembering his garment, his size or stature, his office or employment, &c. A beast, bird or fish by its color, figure, or motion, by the cage or court-yard or cistern, wherein it was kept.

To this head, also we may refer that remembrance of names and things, which may be derived from our recollection of their likeness to other things, which we know; either their resemblance in the name, character, form, accident or any thing that belongs to them. An idea or word, which has been lost or forgotten, has been often recovered by hitting upon some other kindred word or idea, which has the nearest resemblance to it, and that in the letters, syllables or sound of the name, as well as properties of the thing.

If we would remember Hippocrates or Galen or Paracelsus, think of a physician's name, beginning with H. G. or P. If we would remember Ovidius Naso, we may represent a man with a great nose; if Plato, we may think upon a person with large shoulders; if Crispus, we may fancy another with curled hair; and so of other things.

And sometimes a new or strange idea may be fixed in the memory, by considering its contrary or opposite. So if we cannot hit on the word Goliath, the remembrance of David may recover it; or the name of a Trojan may be recovered by thinking of a Greek, &c.

8. In such cases, wherein it may be done, seek after a

How may we often recover an absent idea? What does he say of resemblances and contraries, in relation to memory? What is meant by a local memory?

local memory, or a remembrance of what you had read by the side or page, where it is written or printed; whether the right or the left, whether at the top, the middle or the bottom; whether at the beginning of a chapter or a paragraph, or the end of it. It has been some advantage for this reason to accustom ourselves to books of the same edition; and it has been of constant and special use to divines and private Christians, to be furnished with several Bibles of the same edition; that wherever they are, whether in their chamber, parlor or study, in the younger or elder years of life, they may find the chapters and verses standing in the same parts of the page.

This is also a great convenience to be observed by printers in the new editions of Grammars, Psalms, Testaments, &c. to print every chapter, paragraph or verse in the same part of the page, as the former, that so it may yield a happy assistance to those young learners, who find, and even feel the advantage of a local memory.

9. Let every thing we desire to remember be fairly and distinctly written, and divided into periods, with large characters; for by this means, we shall the more readily imprint the matter and words on our minds, and recollect them with a glance, the more remarkable the writing appears to the eye. This sense conveys the ideas to the fancy better than any other; and what we have seen is not so soon forgotten, as what we have only heard.

For the assistance of weak memories, the first letters or words of every period, in every page, may be written in distinct colors, yellow, green, red, black, &c. and if you observe the same order of colors in the following sentences, it may be still the better. This will make a greater impression, and may much aid the memory.

Under this head, we may take notice of the advantage, which the memory gains, by having the several objects of our learning drawn out into schemes and tables. Matters

---

Meaning of *local*?

What advantage may arise from always reading the same Bible, or same edition?

What disadvantage? We shall be more likely to make the same mistakes in successive readings.

Is it best on the whole, as far as may be convenient, always to use the same copy of the Scripture?

Do you think of any other method, to aid remembrance?

What is thought to be the best method, to aid us in remembering dates? Grey's Memoria Technica, or Artificial Memory.*

---

* An account of this method with improvements, may be found in recent editions of Whelpley's Compend of History, and in Worcester's Elements of History.

of mathematical science and natural philosophy are not only let into the understanding, but preserved in the memory by figures and diagrams. The situation of the several parts of the earth are better learnt by one day's conversing with a map, or sea-chart, than by merely reading the description of their situation a hundred times over in books of geography. So the constellations in astronomy, and their position in the heavens, are more easily remembered by hemispheres of the stars well drawn. It is by having such memorials, figures and tablets hung round our studies or places of resort, that our memory of these things will be greatly assisted and improved, as I have shewn at large in the twentieth chapter of the Use of the Sciences.

I might add here also, that once writing over what we design to remember, and giving due attention to what we write, will fix it more in the mind, than reading it five times. And in the same manner, if we had a plan of the naked lines of longitude and latitude, projected on the meridian printed for this use, a learner might much more speedily advance himself in the knowledge of geography by his own drawing the figures of all the parts of the world upon it by imitation, than by many days survey of a map of the world so printed. The same also may be said concerning the constellations of the heavens, drawn by the learner, on a naked projection of the circles of the spheres upon the plane of the equator.

10. It has sometimes been the practice of men to imprint names or sentences on their memory, by taking the first letters of every word of that sentence or of those names, and making a new word out of them. So the name *Maccabees* is borrowed from the first letters of the Hebrew words which make that sentence *Mi Camoka Bealim Jehovah*, that is, *Who is like thee among the gods, O Jehovah?* which was written on their banners. So the word *vibgyor* teaches us to remember the order of the seven original colors, as they appear by the sun-beams, cast through a prism on a white paper, or formed by the sun in a rainbow, according to the different refrangibility of the rays, namely, violet, indigo, blue, green, yellow, orange, red.

Other artificial helps to memory may be just mentioned here.

Dr. Grey in his book call Memoria Technica, has exchanged the figures 1, 2, 3, 4, 5, 6, 7, 8, 9, for some consonants, *b*, *d*, *t*, *f*, *l*, *y*, *p*, *k*, *n*, and some vowels, *a*, *e*, *i*, *o* *u*, and several diphthongs, and thereby formed words, that denote numbers, which may be more easily remembered. Mr. Lowe has improved his scheme in a small pamphlet called Mnemonics Delineated, whereby in seven leaves, he has comprized almost an infinity of things in science and in common life, and reduced them to a sort of measure, like Latin verse; though the words may be supposed to be very barbarous, being such a mixture of vowels and consonants, as are very unfit for harmony.

But after all, the very writers on this subject have confessed, that several of these artificial helps of memory are so cumbersome, as not to be suitable to every temper or person; nor are they of any use for the delivery of a discourse by memory, nor of much service in learning the sciences; but they may be sometimes practised for assisting our remembrance of certain sentences, numbers or names.

CHAPTER XVIII.

OF DETERMINING A QUESTION.

I. When a subject is proposed to your thoughts, consider, whether it be knowable at all, or not, and then, whether it be not above the reach of your inquiry and knowledge in the present state; and remember, that it is a great waste of time to busy yourselves too much among unsearchables. The chief object of these studies is to keep the mind humble, by finding its own ignorance and weakness.

II. Consider again, whether the matter be worthy of your inquiry at all; and then, how far it may be worthy of your present search and labor, according to your age, your time of life, your station in the world, your capacity, your profession, your chief design and end. There are many things, worthy inquiry to one man, which are not so to another; and there are things, that may deserve the study of the same person in one part of life, which would be improper or impertinent at another. To read books on the art

---

When a question is proposed for determination, what should we first consider?

Meaning of *knowable*?

What may be the use of paying a little attention to unsearchables?—Meaning of *unsearchable*?

If we find we can probably determine the point, what farther inquires should we then make?

of preaching, or disputes about church discipline, are proper for a theological student, in the end of his academical studies, but not at the beginning. To pursue mathematical studies very largely may be useful for a professor of philosophy, but not for a divine.

III. Consider, whether the subject of your inquiry be easy or difficult; whether you have sufficient foundation or skill, furniture and advantages for pursuing it. It would be madness for a young statuary to attempt at first, to carve a Venus or a Mercury, and especially without proper tools. And it is equal folly for a man to pretend to make great improvements in natural philosophy, without due experiments.

IV. Consider, whether the subject be in any way, useful or not, before you engage in the study of it. Often put this question to yourselves, *Cui bono? To what purpose?* What end will it attain? Is it for the glory of God? for the good of men? for your own advantage? for the removal of any natural or moral evil? for the attainment of any natural or moral good? Will the profit be equal to the labor? There are many subtle impertinencies learnt in the schools, many painful trifles even among the mathematical theorems and problems, many laborious follies of various kinds, which some ingenious men have been engaged in. A due reflection upon these, will call the mind away from vain amusements, and save much time.

V. Consider, what tendency it has to make you wiser and better, as well as to make you more learned. Those questions, which tend to wisdom and prudence in our conduct among men, as well as piety toward God, are doubtless more important, than all those inquiries, which only improve our knowledge in mere speculations.

VI. If the question appears to be well worth your diligent application, and you are furnished with the necessary requisites to pursue it, then consider, whether it be drest up and entangled in more words, than are needful, and contain or include more complicated ideas, than are necessary. If so, endeavor to reduce it to a greater simplicity and plainness; which will make the inquiry and argument easier and plainer all the way.

VII. If it be stated in an improper, obscure or irregular

If the subject appears worthy of our attention, what should we next inquire?

Next inquiry?

What if the question contains needless words and ideas?

What if it is obscure?

form, it may be meliorated by changing the phrase, or transposing the parts. But be careful always to keep the grand and important point of inquiry the same in your new stating of the question. Little tricks and deceits of sophistry, by sliding in, or leaving out, such words as entirely change the question, should be abandoned.

Stating a question with clearness and correctness, often goes a great way toward answering it. The greatest part of true knowledge lies in a distinct perception of things, which are in themselves distinct; and some men give more light and knowledge by the bare stating of the question, than others do, by talking of it in gross confusion, for whole hours together. To state a question is but to separate and disentangle the parts from one another, as well as from every thing, which does not concern the question, and then to lay the disentangled parts of the question in due order and method. Oftentimes without more ado, this fully resolves the doubt, and shews the mind, where the truth lies, without argument or dispute.

VIII. If the question relate to an axiom or first principle of truth, remember, that a long train of consequences may depend upon it. It should therefore, not be suddenly admitted.

It is not enough to determine the truth of a proposition, much less to raise it to the honor of an axiom or first principle, to say, that it has been believed through many ages, that it has been received by many nations, that it is almost universally acknowledged, or nobody denies it, that it is established by human laws, or that temporal penalties or reproaches will attend the disbelief of it.

IX. Nor is it enough to forbid any proposition the title of an axiom, because it has been denied by some persons, and doubted by others; for some persons have been unreasonably sceptical. Then only should a proposition be called an axiom, or a self-evident truth, when by a moderate attention to the subject and predicate, their connection appears in so plain a light, and so clear an evidence, as needs no third idea or middle term, to prove them to be connected.

X. While you are in search after truth in questions of a doubtful nature, or such as you have not yet thoroughly

---

To what, does the clear statement of the question very much conduce?

What if the question relates to an axiom?—Meaning of *axiom*?

What is mentioned as insufficient to entitle a proposition to be regarded as an axiom?

To exclude it?

What should we most ardently desire in our investigations?

examined, keep up a just indifference to each side of the question, if you would be led honestly into the truth; for a desire or inclination leaning to either side, biasses the judgment strangely. Whereas by this indifference for every thing but truth, you will be excited to examine fairly, instead of presuming; and your assent will be secured from going beyond your evidence.

XI. For the most part, people are born to their opinions, and never question the truth of what their family or their party profess. They clothe their minds, as they do their bodies, after the fashion; not one of a hundred ever examines his principles. We shall be suspected of lukewarmness, if we suppose examination necessary; and be charged as tending to apostacy, if we attempt to examine them. Persons are applauded for presuming, they are/in the right; and, as Mr. Locke says, he that considers and inquires into the reasons of things, is counted a foe to orthodoxy; because possibly he may deviate from some of the received doctrines. And thus men without any industry or acquisition of their own, lazy and idle as they are, inherit local truths, that is, the truths of that place, where they live, and are inured to assent without evidence.

This has a long and unhappy influence; for if a man bring his mind once to be positive and fierce for propositions, whose evidence he has never examined, and that in matters of the greatest concernment, he will naturally follow this short and easy way of judging and believing in cases of less moment, and build all his opinions upon insufficient grounds.

XII. In determining a question, especially when it is a matter of difficulty and importance, do not take up with partial examination; but turn your thoughts on all sides to gather in all the light you can, toward the solution. Take time, and use all the helps that are to be obtained, before you fully determine, except only where present necessity of action calls for speedy determination.

If you would know what may be called a partial examination, take these instances, namely,

When you examine an object of sense, or inquire into

How do most people come by their opinions?

If a person considers and inquires into the reason of things, to what is he sometimes considered as a foe?

In determining a difficult and important question, how should we generally proceed?

When must we proceed otherwise?

Can you mention some instances of imperfect examination?

some matter of sensation at too great a distance from the object, or in an inconvenient situation of it, or under any indisposition of the organs, or any disguise whatsoever relating to the medium or the organ of the object itself; or when you examine it by one sense only, where others might be employed; or when you inquire into it by sense only, without the use of the understanding and judgment and reason.

If it be a question which is to be determined by reason and argument, than your examination is partial, when you turn the question only in one light, and do not turn it on all sides; when you look upon it only in its relations and aspects to one sort of object and not to another; when you consider only the advantages of it and the reasons for it, and neglect to think of the reasons against it, and never survey its inconveniencies too; when you determine on a sudden, before you have given yourself a due time for weighing all circumstances, &c.

Again, If it be a question of fact, depending up the report or testimony of men, your examination is but partial, when you inquire only, what one man or a few say, and avoid the testimony of others; when you only ask, what those report, who were not eye or ear-witnesses, and neglect those, who saw and heard it; when you content yourself with mere loose and general talk about it, and never enter into particulars; or when there are many who deny the fact, and you never concern yourself about their reasons for denying it, but resolve to believe only those who affirm it.

There is yet a further fault in your partial examination of any question, when you resolve to determine it by natural reason only, where you might be assisted by revelation; or when you decide the point by some word or sentence, or by some part of revelation, without comparing it with other parts, which might give further light, and better help to determine the meaning.

It is also a culpable partiality, if you examine some doubtful or pretended vision or revelation, without the use of reason; or without the use of that revelation, which is undoubted, and sufficiently proved to be divine. These are all instances of imperfect examination; and we should never determine a question by one or two lights, when we may have the advantage of three or four.

What caution does he give, respecting favorite hypotheses?

Meaning of *hypotheses*?

XIII. Take heed lest some darling notion, some favorite hypothesis, some beloved doctrine, or some common but unexamined opinion, be made a test of the truth or falsehood of all other propositions about the same subject. Dare not build much upon such a notion or doctrine, till it be very fully examined, accurately adjusted, and sufficiently confirmed. Some persons, by indulging such a practice, have been led into long ranks of errors; they have found themselves involved in a train of mistakes, by taking up some petty hypothesis or principle, either in philosophy, politics or religion, upon slight and insufficient grounds, and establishing that as a test and rule, by which to judge of all other things.

XIV. For the same reason, have a care of suddenly determining any one question, on which, the determination of any kindred or parallel cases will easily or naturally follow. Take heed of receiving any wrong turn in your early judgment of things; be watchful, as far as possible, against any false bias, which may be given to the understanding, especially in younger years. The indulgence of some one silly opinion, or the giving credit to one foolish fable, lays the mind open to be imposed upon by many. The ancient Romans were taught to believe that Romulus and Remus, the founders of their state and empire, were exposed in the woods, and nursed by a wolf. This story prepared their minds for the reception of any tales of the like nature relating to other countries. Trogus Pompeius would enforce the belief, that one of the ancient kings of Spain was also nursed and suckled by a hart, from the fable of Romulus and Remus. It was by the same influence, they learned to give up their hopes and fears to omens and sooth-saying, when they were once persuaded, that the greatness of their empire and the glory of Romulus their founder, were predicted by the happy omen of twelve vultures appearing to him, when he sought where to build the city. They readily received all the following legends of prodigies, auguries and prognostics, for many ages together, with which Livy has furnished his huge history.

Into what, have some been led by indulging such a practice?

What questions should we be particularly cautious in determining?

In what stage of life, should persons be especially cautious of wrong biasses?

What fabulous account did the Romans believe respecting Romulus and Remus?

For what, did this story prepare their minds?

How did the Romans learn to give up their hopes and fears to omens?—Meaning of *omen*

So the child, who is once taught to believe any one occurrence to be a good or evil omen, or any day of the month or week to be lucky or unlucky, has a wide inroad made on the soundness of his understanding in the following judgments of his life. He lies ever open to all the silly impressions and idle tales of nurses; and imbibes many a foolish story with greediness, which he must unlearn, if ever he become acquainted with truth and wisdom.

XV. Have a care of interesting your warm and religious zeal in those matters, which are not sufficiently evident in themselves, or which are not fully proved; for this zeal, whether right or wrong, when it is once engaged, will have a powerful influence to establish your own minds in those doctrines which are really doubtful, and to stop up all the avenues of further light. This will bring upon the soul a sort of sacred awe and dread of heresy; with a concern to maintain whatever you have espoused as divine, though perhaps you have espoused it, without any just evidence, and ought to have renounced it, as false and pernicious.

We ought to be zealous for the most important points of our religion, and to contend earnestly for the faith once delivered to the saints; but we ought not to employ this sacred fervor of spirit in the service of any article, till we have seen it made out with plain and strong conviction,

---

If a child has been taught to believe in omens, or in lucky or unlucky days, on what has this made a wide inroad?—Meaning of *inroad*?—of *luck*?—of *lucky*?

Of the words *luck* and *lucky*, which is the primitive word?—the derivative?

Meaning of *primitive*?—of *derivative*?

What important idea is implied in *lucky*, that is not implied in *luck*?

Can you think of any other derivative, essentially different in meaning, from its English primitive?*

First inference contained in the note?—Second?

If a child believes in lucky days, &c. what must he do, in order to become truly wise?

How can he unlearn them? By learning, that they are mere fictions.

For what points, does he say, we should not indulge religious zeal?

What will such zeal tend to prevent?

What sacred awe and dread will it be likely to bring upon the soul?

For what points, should we be zealous?

For what, should we earnestly contend?

Meaning of *faith* here? The doctrines of the bible, believed by faith.

What caution does he give, with regard to this sacred fervor?

---

* English words generally differ, and often very greatly, from their primitives of other languages. Hence, we can scarcely ever know the exact meaning of an English word, by knowing its derivation from another language. Hence too, persons sometimes use English words improperly, by adhering too closely to their etymological signification; as the phrase *averse from*, instead of *averse to*.

that it is a necessary or important point of faith or practice, and is either an evident dictate of the light of nature, or an assured article of revelation. Zeal must not reign over the powers of our understanding, but obey them. God is the God of light and truth, a God of reason and order, and he never requires mankind to use their natural faculties amiss for the support of his cause. Even the most mysterious and sublime doctrines of revelation, are not to be believed without just reason; nor should our pious affections be engaged in the defence of them, till we have plain and convincing proof, that they are certainly revealed, though perhaps we may never in this world attain to such clear and distinct ideas of them, as we desire.

XVI. As a warm zeal ought never to be employed in the defence of any revealed truth, till our reason be well convinced of the revelation; so neither should wit and banter, jest and ridicule, ever be indulged to oppose or assault any doctrines of professed revelation, till reason has proved, they are not really revealed. And even then, these methods should be used very seldom, and with the utmost caution and prudence. Raillery and wit were never made to answer our inquiries after truth, nor to determine a question of rational controversy; though they may sometimes be serviceable to expose to contempt, those inconsistent follies, which have been first abundantly refuted by argument. They serve indeed only to cover nonsense with shame, when reason has first proved it to be mere nonsense

It is therefore a silly and most unreasonable test, which some of our Deists have introduced, to judge of divine revelation, namely, to try, if it will bear ridicule and laughter. They are effectually beaten in all their combats at the weapons of men, that is, reason and argument; and it would not be unjust, though it is a little uncourtly, to say, that they would now attack our religion with the talents of a vile animal, that is, grin and grimace.

I cannot think that a jester or a monkey, a droll or a puppet, can be a proper judge or decider of controversy. That which dresses up all things in disguise, is not likely to lead us into any just sentiments about them. Plato or Socrates Cesar or Alexander, might have a fool's coat clapt upon

---

Should zeal govern or obey the understanding?

From what discussions, should wit and banter be excluded?

What have some infidels most unreasonably considered as the test of truth?—Meaning of *test*?

Who, does he say, are not proper deciders of controversy?

him; and perhaps in this disguise, neither the wisdom of the one, nor the majesty of the other, would secure him from a sneer. This treatment would never inform us, whether they were kings or slaves, whether they were fools or philosophers. The strongest reasoning, the best sense and the politest thoughts may be set in a most ridiculous light by this grinning faculty. The most obvious axioms of eternal truth may be drest in a very foolish form, and wrapt up in artful absurdities by this talent; but they are truth and reason and good sense still. Euclid, with all his demonstrations, might be so covered and overwhelmed with banter, that a beginner in the mathematics might be tempted to doubt, whether his theorems were true or not, and to imagine, they could never be useful. So weaker minds might be easily prejudiced against the noblest principle of truth and goodness; and the younger part of mankind might be beat off from the belief of the most serious, the most rational and important points even of natural religion, by the impudent jests of a profane wit. The moral duties of the civil life, as well as the articles of Christianity, may be painted over with the colors of folly, and exposed upon a stage, so as to ruin all social and personal virtue among the gay and thoughtless part of the world.

XVII. It should be observed also, that these very men cry out loudly against the use of all severe railing and reproach in debates, and all penalties and persecutions of the state, in order to convince the minds and consciences of men, and determine points of truth and error. Now I renounce these penal and smarting methods of conviction, as much as they do; and yet I think still, these are every whit as wise, as just and as good for this purpose, as banter and ridicule. Why should public mockery in print, or a merry joke upon a stage, be a better test of truth, than severe railing, sarcasms, and public persecutions and penalties? Why should more light be derived to the understanding, by a song of scurrilous mirth or a witty ballad, than there is by a rude cudgel? When a professor of any religion is set up to be laughed at, I cannot see, how this should help

---

By what faculty, may the strongest reasoning and most excellent thoughts be set in a most ridiculous light?

Should ridicule ever be used in discussions? Rarely, and never in opposition to argument.

What scripture seems to imply, that ridicule may sometimes be used in such cases? Answer a fool according to his folly.

Against what method of conviction, do infidels loudly exclaim?

What method of theirs appears to be no better?

us to judge of the truth of his faith any better, than if he were scourged. The jeers of a theatre, the pillory and the whipping-post, are very near akin. When the person or his opinion is made the jest of the mob, or his back the shambles of the executioner, I think, there is no more conviction in the one, that in the other.

XVIII. Besides, supposing it is but barely possible, that the great God should reveal his mind and will to men by miracle, vision or inspiration, it is a piece of contempt and profane insolence, to treat any tolerable or rational appearance of such a revelation with jest and laughter, in order to find, whether it be divine or not. And yet, if this be a proper test of revelation, it may be properly applied to the true, as well as the false, in order to distinguish it. Suppose, a royal proclamation were sent to a distant part of the kingdom, and some of the subjects should doubt whether it came from the king or not. Is it possible, that wit and ridicule should ever decide the point? or would the prince ever think himself treated with just honor, to have his proclamation canvassed in this manner, on a public stage, and become the sport of buffoons, in order to determine the question, Whether it is the word of a king or not?

Let such sort of writers go on at their peril, and sport themselves in their own deceivings; let them at their peril, make a jest of the Bible, and treat the sacred articles of Christianity with scoff and merriment. But then let them lay aside all their pretences to reason, as well as to religion; and as they expose themselves by such writings, to the neglect and contempt of men, so let them prepare to meet the majesty and indignation of God.

XIX. In reading philosophical, moral or religious controversies, never raise your esteem of any opinion, by the assurance and zeal, wherewith the author asserts it, nor by the highest praises, he bestows upon it. Nor on the other hand, let your esteem of an opinion be abated, nor your aversion to it raised, by the supercillious contempt, cast upon it by a warm writer, nor by the sovereign airs, with which he condemns it. Let the force of argument alone influence your assent or dissent. Take care, that your soul be not warped or biassed on one side or the other, by any strains of flattering or abusive language; for there is

---

To what, should scoffers at the Bible, lay aside all pretence?

How should our opinion of any work be affected by the very high praise or blame cast upon it?

Only thing, that should influence our assent or dissent?

no question whatsoever, but has some defenders or opposers. Leave those writers to their own follies, who practise thus upon the weakness of their readers, without argument. Leave them to triumph in their own fancied possessions and victories. It is oftentimes found, that their possessions are but a heap of errors, and their boasted victories are but overbearing noise and clamor, to silence the voice of truth.

In philosophy and religion, the bigots of all parties are generally the most positive, and deal much in this sort of arguments. Sometimes these are the weapons of pride; for a haughty man supposes all his opinions to be infallible, and imagines, the contrary sentiments are very ridiculous, and not worthy of notice. Sometimes these ways of talking are the mere arms of ignorance. The men, who use them, know little of the opposite side of the question, and therefore, they exult in their own vain pretences to knowledge, as though no man of sense could oppose their opinion. They rail at an objection against their own sentiments; because they can find no other answer to it but railing. And men of learning, by their excessive vanity, have been sometimes tempted into the same insolent practice, as well as the ignorant.

Yet let it be remembered too, that there are some truths so plain and evident, that the opposition to them is strange, unaccountable, and almost monstrous. In vindication of such truths, a writer of good sense may sometimes be allowed to use a degree of assurance, and pronounce them strongly with an air of confidence, while he defends them with reasons of convincing force.

XX. Sometimes a question may be proposed, which is of so large and extensive a nature, and refers to such a multitude of subjects, as ought not in justice to be determined at once by a single argument or answer; as if one should ask me, Are you a professed disciple of the Stoics or the Platonists? Do you give an assent to the principles

---

What characters are generally most positive in matters of philosophy and religion?

Meaning of *bigot*?

Why do many rail at an objection to their sentiments?

When may a writer of good sense be allowed to use some degree of assurance?

What shall we say, if asked whether we are Calvinists, Arminians, &c.?

What if we have not time to enter into a detail of particulars? We may say, that in general, we agree with Calvin or Arminius, or other writers, but not in all particulars, according as truth may allow us to state.

of Gassendi, Descartes or Sir Isaac Newton? Have you chosen the hypothesis of Tycho or Copernicus? Have you devoted yourself to the sentiments of Arminius or Calvin? Are your notions Episcopal, Presbyterian or Independent? I think it may be very proper in such cases, not to give an answer in the gross, but rather to enter into a detail of particulars, and explain one's own sentiments. Perhaps there is no man, nor set of men upon earth, whose sentiments I entirely follow. God has given me reason, to judge for myself; and though I may see sufficient ground to agree with the greatest part of the opinions of one person or party, yet it does by no means follow, that I should receive them all. Truth does not always go in the gross; nor does error tincture and spoil all the articles of belief, that some one party professes.

Since there are difficulties attending every scheme of human knowledge, it is enough for me in the main, to incline to that side, which has the fewest difficulties; and I would endeavor, as far as possible, to correct the mistakes or the harsh expressions of one party, by softening and reconciling methods, by reducing the extremes, and by borrowing some of the best principles or phrases from another. Cicero was one of the greatest men of antiquity, and gives us an account of the various opinions of philosophers in his age; but he himself was of the Eclectic sect, and chose out of each of them such positions, as in his judgment came nearest to the truth.

XXI. When you are called in the course of life or religion, to judge and determine concerning any question, and to affirm or deny it, take a full survey, of the objections against it, as well as of the arguments for it, as far as your time and circumstances admit, and see, on which side, the preponderation falls. If either the objections against any proposition, or the arguments for the defence of it, carry in them most undoubted evidence, and are plainly unanswerable, they will and ought to constrain the assent, though there may be many seeming probabilities on the other side, which at first sight, would flatter the judgment to favor it. But where the reasons on both sides, are very nearly of equal weight, there suspension or doubt is our duty, unless

---

What does Watts say respecting his own sentiments?

For what, had God given him reason?

As there are difficulties in every scheme, to which side, should we incline?

When we are called to decide a question, what should we consider, besides the arguments in favor?

What if the reasons appear equal on both sides?

in cases wherein present determination or practice, is required; and there we must act according to the present appearing preponderation of reasons.

XXII. In matters of importance, it is our duty indeed to seek after certain and conclusive arguments, if they can be found, in order to determine a question. But where the matter is of little consequence, it is not worth our labor, to spend much time in seeking after certainties. Is it sufficient here, if probable reasons offer themselves. And even in matters of greater importance, especially where daily practice is necessary, and where we cannot attain any sufficient or certain grounds, to determine a question, we must then take up with such probable arguments, as we can arrive at. But this general rule should be observed, namely, to take heed, that our assent be no stronger, than the probable argument will support.

XXIII. There are many things even in religion, as well as in philosophy and the civil life, which we believe with very different degrees of assent; and this should be always regulated according to the different degrees of evidence, which we enjoy. Perhaps there are a thousand gradations in our assent to the things we believe; because there are thousands of circumstances relating to different questions, which increase or diminish the evidence we have concerning them, and that in matters both of reason and revelation.

I believe, there is a God, and that obedience is due to him from every reasonable creature. Of this, I am most fully assured, because I have the strongest evidence, since it is the plain dictate both of reason and revelation.

Again, I believe, there will be a future resurrection of the dead; because scripture tells us so in the plainest terms, though reason says nothing of it. I believe also, that the same matter of our bodies, which died, in part at least, will rise. But I am not so fully assured of this circumstance; because the revelation of it is not so clear and express. Yet further, I believe, that good men, who were acquainted here on earth, will know each other in heaven. But my persuasion of it is not absolutely certain; because my assent to it arises only from circumstantial reasonings of men upon what God has told us; and therefore, my evidences are not strong, beyond a possibility of mistake.

What if we must act immediately?

In proportion to what, should always be our assent?

Why may there be a great many degrees of assent?

What does reason say respecting the resurrection of the body?

This direction cannot be too often repeated, that our assent ought always to keep pace with our evidence; and our belief of any proposition, should never rise higher, than the proof or evidence we have, to support it; nor should our faith run faster, than right reason can encourage it.

XXIV. Perhaps it will be objected here, "Why then does our Savior, in the histories of the gospel, so much commend a strong faith, and lay out both his miraculous benefits and his praises upon some of those poor creatures of little reasoning, who profest an assured belief of his commission and power to heal them?"

I answer, the God of nature has given every man his own reason, to judge of evidence to himself in particular, and to direct his assent in all things, about which he is called to judge; and even the matters of revelation are to be believed by us, because our reason pronounces the revelation to be true. Therefore, the great God will not, or cannot in any instance, require us to assent to any thing, without reasonable or sufficient evidence; nor to believe any proposition more strongly, than our evidence for it will support. We have, therefore, abundant ground to believe, that those persons, of whom our Savior requires such a strong faith, or whom he commends for their strong faith, had as strong and certain evidence of his power and commission, from the credible and incontestable reports they had heard of his miracles; which were wrought, on purpose to give evidence to his commission. When our Savior gently reproves Thomas for his unbelief, in John 20: 29, he does it in these words; "Because thou hast seen me, Thomas, thou hast believed; blessed are they, who have not seen, and yet have believed;" that is, blessed are they, who, though they have not been favored with the evidence of their senses, as thou hast been, yet have been convinced by the reasonable and sufficient moral evidence of the well-grounded report of others, and have believed in me upon that evidence. Of this moral evidence, Mr. Ditton writes exceedingly well, in his book on the Resurrection of Christ. Now in such a case, both this strong faith and the open profession of it were very worthy of public en-

---

What direction concerning assent can hardly be too often repeated?

Of whom, did our Savior require strong faith? Those whom he would heal.

What reason was there for such requirement? There was the fullest evidence, that Christ was able to heal.

For what purpose, has God given reason to every man?

Why are matters of revelation to be believed?

couragement and praise from our Saviour, because of the great and public opposition, which the magistrates and the priests and the doctors of the age made against Jesus, the man of Nazareth, when he appeared as the Messiah.

And besides all this, it may be reasonably supposed, with regard to some of those strong exercises of faith, which are required and commended, that these believers had some further hints of inward evidence and immediate revelation from God himself; as when Peter confesses Christ to be the Son of God, Matth. 16: 17, our blessed Savior commends him, saying, "Blessed art thou Simon Bar-jona;" but he adds, "flesh and blood hath not revealed it unto thee, but my Father, who is in heaven."

And the same may be said concerning the faith of miracles, the exercise whereof was sometimes required of the disciples and others, that is, when by inward and divine influences, God assured them, such miracles should be wrought, their obedience to and compliance with these divine illuminations was expected and commended. Now this supernatural inspiration, carried sufficient evidence with it to them, as well as to the ancient prophets, though we who never felt it are not so capable to judge and distinguish it.

XXV. What is said above concerning truth or doctrines, may be also affirmed concerning duties. The reason of both is the same. As the first are truths for our speculation, the others are truths for our practice. Duties, which are expressly required in the plain language of scripture, or dictated by the most evident reasoning upon first principles, ought to bind our consciences more than those, which are but dubiously inferred, and that only from occasional occurrences, and circumstances; as for instance, I am certain, that I ought to pray to God. My conscience is bound to this, because there are most evident commands for it to be found in scripture, as well as to be derived from reason. I believe also, that I may pray to God, either by a written form, or without one; because neither reason nor revelation expressly requires either of these modes of prayer at all times, nor forbids the other. I cannot, therefore, bind my conscience to practise the one, so as utterly to renounce the other; but I would practise either of them, as my reason and other circumstances direct me.

What does Watts say of written forms of prayer, and of extemporaneous prayer?

Again, I believe, that Christians ought to remember the death of Christ, by the symbols of bread and wine; and I believe, there ought to be pastors in a Christian church, some way ordained or set apart to lead the worship, and to bless and distribute the elements. But the last of these practices is not so expressly directed, prescribed and required in scripture, as the former; and therefore, I feel my conscience evidently bound to remember the death of Christ with some society of Christians or other, since it is a most plain command, though their method of ordaining a pastor be very different from other men's, or from my own opinion; or whether the person, who distributes these elements, be only an occasional or a settled administrator; since none of these things are plainly determined in scripture. I must not omit or neglect an express command, because some unnecessary circumstances are dubious. And I trust, I shall receive approbation from the God of nature, and from Jesus my judge at the last day, if I have endeavored in this manner to believe and practise every thing, in proportion to the degree of evidence, which God has given me about it, or which he has put me into a capacity to seek and obtain.

Query. Whether the obstinate Deists and Fatalists of Great Britain will find sufficient apology from this principle? But I leave them to venture the awful experiment.

XXVI. We may observe these three rules in judging of probabilities, which are to be determined by reason, relating either to things past, or things to come.

1. That, which agrees most with the constitution of nature, carries the greatest probability in it, where no other circumstance appears to counterpoise it; as, if I let loose a greyhound within sight of a hare upon a large plain, there is great probability the greyhound will seize her; and that a thousand sparrows will fly away at the sight of a hawk among them.

2. That, which is most conformable to the constant observations of men, or to experiments frequently repeated, is most likely to be true; as that a winter will not pass away in England without some frost and snow; that if you deal out great quantities of strong liquor to the mob, there will be many drunk; that a large assembly of men will be of different opinions on any doubtful point; that a thief will make his escape out of prison, if the doors of it are unguarded at midnight.

First rule for judging of probabilities? Second rule?

3. In matters of fact, which are past or present, where neither nature nor observation nor custom gives us any sufficient information on either side of the question, there we may derive a probability from the attestation of wise and honest men by word or writing, or the concurring witness of multitudes, who have seen and known what they relate, &c. This testimony in many cases will arise to the degree of moral certainty. So we believe, that the tea plant grows in China; and that the emperor of the Turks lives at Constantinople; that Julius Cesar conquered France, and that Jesus our Savior lived and died in Judea; that thousands were converted to the Christian faith in a century after the death of Christ; and that the books, which contain the Christian religion, are certain histories and epistles, which were written nearly two thousand years ago. There is an infinite variety of such propositions, which can admit of no reasonable doubt, though they are not matters, which are directly evident to our own senses, or our mere reasoning powers.

XXVII. When a point has been well examined, and our own judgment settled upon just arguments in our manly age, and after a large survey of the merits of the cause, it would be a weakness for us always to continue flattering in suspense. We ought, therefore, to stand firm in such well established principles, and not be tempted to change for the sake of every difficulty, or every occasional objection. We are not to be carried about with every flying doctrine, like children tossed to and fro, and wavering with the wind. It is a good thing to have the heart established with grace, not with meats; that is, in the great doctrines of the gospel of grace and in Jesus Christ, who is the same yesterday, to day and forever. But it is not so necessary in the more minute matters of religion, such as meats and drinks, forms and ceremonies, which are of less importance, and for which, scripture has not given such express directions. This is the advice of the great apostle, Eph. 4: 14. Heb. 13: 8, 9.

In short, those truths, which are the springs of daily practice, should be settled, as soon as we can with the exercise of our best powers, after the state of manhood. But those things, wherein we may possibly mistake, should

---

Third rule, when neither nature nor observation gives us any sufficient information?

To what, does probability from testimony often rise?

When would it be a weakness in us, to feel in suspense respecting our opinion?

What of truths, relating to daily practice?

never be so absolutely and finally established, as though we were infallible. If the Papists of Great Britain had maintained such a resolute establishment and assurance in the days of king Henry VIII, or queen Elizabeth, there never had been a reformation; nor would any Heathen have been converted even under the ministry of Paul, if their obstinate settlement in their idolatries had kept their eyes shut against all further light. Yet this should not hinder us from settling our most important principles of faith and practice, where reason shines with its clearest evidence; and the word of God plainly determines truth and duty.

XXVII. But let us remember also, that though the gospel is an infallible revelation, we are but fallible interpreters, when we determine the sense even of some important propositions written there; and therefore, though we seem to be established in the belief of any particular sense of scripture, and though there may be just calls of providence to profess and subscribe it, yet there is no need, that we should resolve or promise, subscribe or swear never to change our mind; since it is possible in the nature and course of things, we may meet with such a solid and substantial objection, as may give us a quite different view of things from what we once imagined, and may lay before us sufficient evidence of the contrary. We may happen to find a fairer light cast over the same scriptures, and see reason to alter our sentiments even in some points of moment. *Sic sentio, sentiam*, that is, *So I believe, and so I will believe*, is the prison of the soul for life, and a bar against all the improvements of the mind. To impose such a profession on other men in matters not absolutely necessary, and not absolutely certain, is a criminal usurpation and tyranny over faith and conscience, and which none has power to require but an infallible dictator.

CHAPTER XIX.

OF INQUIRING INTO CAUSES AND EFFECTS.

Some effects are found out by their causes; and some causes, by their effects. Let us consider both these.

I. When we are inquiring into the causes of any par-

Why should we not promise never to change our opinion?

What does he say of the declaration, *So I believe, and so I will believe?*

What is it to impose such a profession on others?

ticular effect or appearance, either in the world of nature, in the civil or moral concerns of men, we may follow this method;

1. Consider, what effects or appearances you have known of a kindred nature, and what have been the certain and real causes of them. For like effects have generally like causes, especially, when they are found in the same sort of subjects.

2. Consider, what are the several possible causes, which may produce such an effect; and find out by some circumstances, how many of those possible causes are excluded in this particular cause. Thence proceed by degrees, to the probable causes, till a more close attention and inspection shall exclude some of them also, and lead you gradually to the real and certain cause.

3. Consider, what things preceded such an event or appearance, which might have any influence upon it; and though we cannot certainly determine the cause of any thing merely from its going before the effect, yet among the many forerunners, we may probably light upon the true cause, by further and more particular inquiry.

4. Consider, whether one cause be sufficient to produce the effect, or whether it does not require a concurrence of several causes; and then endeavor, as far as possible, to adjust the degrees of influence, that each cause might have in producing the effect, and the proper agency and influence of each.

So in natural philosophy, if I would find, what are the principles or causes of that sensation, which we call heat, when I stand near the fire; here I shall find it is necessary, that there be an agency of the particles of fire on my flesh, either mediately by themselves, or at least by the intermediate air; there must be a particular sort of motion and vellication imprest upon my nerves; there must be a communication of that motion to the brain; and there must be an attention of my soul to this motion. If either of these is wanting, the sensation of heat will not be produced.

So in the moral world, if I inquire into the revolution of a state or kingdom, perhaps I find it brought about by the tyranny or folly of a prince, or by the disaffection of his

---

In ascertaining the causes of effects, what is the first thing to be considered?

Second thing to be considered?

Third thing to be considered?

Fourth thing to be considered?

Can you mention some of the causes, that may produce the revolution of a kingdom?

own subjects; and this disaffection and opposition may arise, either on account of impositions in religion, or injuries relating to their civil rights; or the revolution may be effected by the invasion of a foreign army, or by the opposition of some person at home or abroad, that lays claim to the government, &c. or a hero, who would guard the liberties of the people; or by many of these concurring together. Then we must adjust the influences of each, as wisely as we can, and not ascribe the whole event to one alone.

II. When we are inquiring into the effects of any particular cause or causes, we may follow this method;

1. Consider diligently the nature of every cause apart, and observe, what effect every part or property of it will tend to produce.

2. Consider the causes united together in their several natures, and ways of operation; inquire how far the powers or properties of one will hinder or promote the effects of the other, and wisely balance the proportions of the influence.

3. Consider, what the subject is, upon which the cause is to operate; for the same cause on different subjects will often produce different effects, as the sun, which softens wax, will harden clay.

4. Be frequent and diligent in making all proper experiments, in setting such causes at work, whose effects you desire to know, and putting together in an orderly manner, such things, as are most likely to produce some useful effects, according to the best survey you can take of all the concurring causes and circumstances.

5. Observe carefully all the events, which happen either by an occasional concurrence of various causes, or by the industrious application of knowing men; and when you see any happy effect certainly produced and often repeated, treasure it up, together with its known causes, among your improvements.

6. Take a just survey of all the circumstances, which attend the operation of any cause or causes, whereby any special effect is produced, and find out, as far as possible, how far any of those circumstances had a tendency either to obstruct or promote or change those operations, and consequently, how far the effect might be influenced by them.

When we are inquiring into the effects of causes, what is the first thing to be considered?—the second?—the third?

What does he recommend in the fourth place?

Do you recollect any other particulars under this general head?

In this manner, physicians practise, and improve their skill. They consider the various known effects of particular herbs or drugs; they consider, what will be the effect of their composition, and whether the virtues of the one will exalt or diminish the force of the other, or correct any of its noxious qualities. Then they observe the native constitution, and the present temper or circumstances of the patient, and what is likely to be the effect of such a medicine on such a patient. And in all uncommon cases, they make wise and cautious experiments, and nicely observe the effects of particular compound medicines on different constitutions, and in different diseases; and by these treasures of just observation, they grow up to an honorable degree of skill in the art of healing.

So the preacher considers the doctrines and reasons, the precepts, the promises and threatenings of the word of God, and what are the natural effects of them upon the mind; he considers, what is the natural tendency of such a virtue or vice; he is well apprised, that the representation of some of these things may convince the understanding, some may terrify the conscience, some may allure the slothful, and some encourage the desponding. He observes the temper of his hearers, or of any particular person that converses with him about things sacred, and he judges, what will be the effects of each representation on such persons. He reviews and recollects, what have been the effects of some special parts and methods of his ministry; and by a careful survey of all these, he attains greater degrees of skill in his sacred employment.

Note, In all these cases, we must distinguish those causes and effects, which are naturally and necessarily connected with each other, from those, which have only an accidental or contingent connection. Even in those causes, where the effect is but contingent, we may sometimes arrive at a very high degree of probability; yet we cannot arrive at such certainty, as where the causes operate by an evident and natural necessity, and the effects necessarily follow the operation.

See more on this subject, Logic Part II. Chap. V. Sect. 7. "Of the principles and rules of judging concerning things past, present and to come, by the mere use of reason."

In what manner, do physicians reason in relation to their patients?

Meaning of *patients*, as here used?

What do physicians sometimes do in uncommon cases?

Can you mention some things, that a preacher should consider, when he would produce an effect upon his hearers?

What, does Watts say, we must distinguish in all these cases?

CHAPTER XX.

OF THE SCIENCES, AND THEIR USE IN PARTICULAR PROFESSIONS.

I. The best way to learn any science, is to begin with a regular system, or a short and plain scheme of that science, well drawn up into a narrow compass, omitting the deeper and more abstruse parts, and that also under the conduct and instruction of some skilful teacher. Systems are necessary to give an entire and comprehensive view of the several parts of any science, which may have a mutual influence toward the explication or proof of each other; whereas if a man deals always and only in essays and discourses on particular parts of a science, he will never obtain a distinct and just idea of the whole, and may perhaps omit some important part of it, after seven years reading of such occasional discourses.

For this reason, young students should apply themselves to their systems much more than to pamphlets. That man is never so fit to judge of particular subjects relating to any science, who has never taken a survey of the whole.

It is a remark of an ingenious writer, "Should a barbarous Indian, who had never seen a palace or a ship, view their separate and disjointed parts, and observe the pillars, doors, windows, cornices and turrets of the one, or the prow and stern, the ribs and masts, the ropes and shrouds, the sails and tackle of the other, he would be able to form but a very lame and dark idea of either of those excellent and useful inventions. In like manner, those, who contemplate only the fragments or pieces broken off from any science, dispersed in short unconnected discourses, and do not discern their relation to each other, and how they may be adapted, and by their union, procure the delightful sym-

---

With what, should we begin, if we would learn any science?

What parts should we at first, omit?

Why are systems necessary?

What if a person attends only to essays upon particular parts of a science?

Of what, must we take a survey, in order to judge of any part of a science?

metry of a regular scheme, can never survey an entire body of truth, but must always view it as deformed and dismembered; while their ideas, which must be ever indistinct, and often repugnant, will lie in the brain unsorted, and thrown together without order or coherence. Such is the knowledge of those men, who live upon the scraps of the sciences.

A youth of genius and lively imagination, of an active and forward spirit, may form within himself, some alluring scenes and pleasing schemes in the beginning of a science, which are utterly inconsistent with some of the necessary and substantial parts of it, which appear in the middle or end. And if he never read and pass through the whole, he takes up and is satisfied with his own hasty, pleasing schemes, and treasures up those errors among his solid acquisitions; whereas his own labor and study farther pursued would have shewn him his early mistakes, and cured him of his self-flattering delusions.

Hence it comes to pass, that we have so many half scholars, and there is so much confusion and inconsistency in the notions and opinions of some persons. It is because they devote their hours of study entirely to short essays and pamphlets, and cast contempt upon systems under a pretence of greater politeness; whereas the true reason of this contempt of systematical learning, is mere laziness and want of judgment.

II. After we have become well acquainted with a short system or compendium of a science, which is written in the plainest and most simple manner, it is then proper to read a larger, regular treatise on that subject, if we design a complete knowledge and cultivation of it; and either while we are reading this larger system, or after we have done it, then occasional discourses and essays upon the particular subjects and parts of that science may be read with the greatest profit; for in these essays we may often find very considerable corrections and improvements of what these compends, or even the larger systems may have taught us, mingled with some mistakes.

These corrections or improvements should be as re-

Why have we so many half scholars?

Why do they despise systematic learning?

What shall we next do, after learning a short compendium?

When should we read occasional essays?

What may we expect to find in these essays?

What social exercise is peculiarly useful in learning a science? Much conversation with superiors, inferiors and equals.

marks, adjoined by way of note or commentary in their proper places, and superadded to the regular treatise we have read. Then a studious and judicious review of the whole, will give us a tolerable acquaintance with that science.

III. It is a great happiness to have such a tutor, or such friends and companions at hand, who are able to inform us, what are the best books, written on any science, or any part of it. For want of this advantage, many a man has wasted his time in reading over perhaps some whole volumes, and learnt little more by it, than to know, that those volumes were not worth his reading.

IV. As for the languages, they are certainly best learned in the younger years of life. The memory is then most empty and unfurnished, and ready to receive new ideas continually. We find that children in two year's time after they are born, learn to speak their native tongue.

V. The more abstract sciences, which depend more upon the understanding and judgment, and which deal much in abstract ideas, should not be imposed upon children too soon. Such are logic, metaphysics, ethics, politics, or the

---

Grand advantage of conversing with superiors?—with equals? It allows us the most favorable opportunity for discussion, and free conversation.

Advantage of such discussion? It is an exercise, most invigorating to the mind, and peculiarly calculated to increase and familiarize our acquaintance with the subject.

Advantage of conversing with inferiors? It is peculiarly fitted to give us a clear, distinct and familiar view of the first principles; and must always gives us new ideas upon the subject.

When does Watts think the best time for learning languages?—Why?

What seems much more important for children, than loading their memories with languages? To teach them their own language, to teach them the Bible, the history of their own country, and of others, most intimately connected, &c. &c.

Why is it very important for children to attend to these things? Deeply to impress them upon their tender minds, to improve their faculties, and to prepare them for usefulness and for heaven.

When should they attend to other languages? At a later period, if they have a prospect of finding them particularly useful.

Why do many wish to learn, or to have their children learn, other languages? More perhaps for the name of it, than for any thing else?

What is often the effect of trying to learn languages and a multitude of other branches? Nothing is learnt well.

Caution respecting the study of the deep sciences?

When may children learn something of the rudiments of these sciences? Very young.

How soon does a child begin to reason, or to practise logic? As soon as he can speak.

How soon does he know something about mathematics? As soon as he knows the meaning of the word *one*.

How soon does he know something about metaphysics? As soon as he knows the meaning of any such words, as *pain*, *ache*, *glad*, *sorry*, *can*, &c.

What is the way to make a child very great in these sciences? To

depth and difficulties of grammar and criticism. Yet it must be confessed, the first rudiments of grammar are necessary, and very convenient to be known, when a youth learns a new language; and some general easy principles and rules of morality and divinity are needful, in order to teach a child his duty to God and man. But to enter far into abstract reasonings on these subjects, is beyond the capacity of children.

VI. There are several of the sciences, that will more agreeably employ our younger years, and the general parts of them may be easily known by boys; as the first principles and easier practices of arithmetic, geometry, plain trigonometry, measuring heights, depths, lengths, distances, &c. The rudiments of geometry and astronomy, together with something of mechanics, may be easily conveyed into the minds of acute young persons, nine or ten years old. These studies may be entertaining and useful to young ladies, as well as to gentlemen, and to all those, who are bred up to the learned professions. The fair sex may intermingle those with the operations of the needle, and the knowledge of domestic life. Boys may be taught to join them with their rudiments of grammar, and their labor in the languages. And even those, who never learn any language, but their mother-tongue, may be taught these sciences, with lasting benefit in early days.

That this may be done with ease and advantage, take these three reasons;

1. Because they depend so much upon schemes and numbers, images, lines and figures and sensible things, that the imagination or fancy will greatly assist the understanding, and render the knowledge of them much more easy.

2. These studies are so pleasant, that they will make the dry labor of learning words, phrases and languages more tolerable to boys in a Latin school, by this most agreeable mixture. The employment of youth in these studies will tempt them to neglect many of the foolish plays of childhood; and they will find sweeter entertainment for themselves and their leisure hours by a cultivation of these pretty pieces of alluring knowledge.

3. The knowledge of these parts of science is both easy

---

begin with him very young, to teach him such parts, as he can clearly understand, and let him gradually advance to the more difficult parts.

Mention some of the studies, that Watts thinks, may be pursued by children 9 or 10 years old.

With what other pursuits, may females unite these studies?

What useless operations may these studies induce children to neglect?

and worthy to be retained in memory, by all children, when they come to manly years; for they are useful through all the parts of human life. They tend to enlarge the understanding early, and to give a various acquaintance with useful subjects betimes. And surely it is best, as far as possible, to train up children in the knowledge of those things, which they should never forget, rather than to let them waste years of life on trifles, or hard words, which are not worth remembering.

And here by the way, I cannot but wonder, that any author in our age should attempt to teach any of the exploded physics of Descartes, or the nobler inventions of Sir Isaac Newton in his hypothesis of the heavenly bodies and their motions, in his doctrine of light and colors, and other parts of his physiology, or to instruct children in the knowledge of the theory of the heavens, earth and planets, without any figures or diagrams. Is it possible to give a boy or a young lady, the clear, distinct and proper apprehensions of these things, without lines and figures to describe them? Does not their understanding want the aid of fancy and images, to convey stronger and juster ideas of them to the inmost soul? Or do they imagine, that youth can penetrate into all these beauties and artifices of nature, without those helps, which persons of maturer age find necessary for that purpose? I would not willingly name the books; because some of the writers are said to be gentlemen of excellent acquirements.

VII. After we have first learnt any of those arts or sciences, which are to be explained by diagrams, figures and schemes, such as geometry, geography, astronomy, optics, mechanics, &c. we may best preserve them in memory, by having those schemes and figures in large sheets of paper, hanging always before the eye in closets, parlors, halls, chambers, entries, staircases, &c. Thus the learned images will be perpetually imprest on the brain, and will keep the learning, that depends upon them alive and fresh in the mind, through the growing years of life. The mere diagrams and figures will ever recall to our thoughts those theorems, problems and corollaries, which have been demonstrated by them.

When is a knowledge of these branches useful?

In the knowledge of what things, should children be trained up?

In what studies, are diagrams and other visible representations very useful? In studies relating to visible objects.

Meaning of *diagram*?—of *visible*?

Easiest method of preserving a knowledge of those branches?

It is incredible, how much geography may be learnt in this way, by the two terrestrial hemispheres, and by particular maps and charts of the coasts and countries of the earth, happily disposed round about us. Thus we may learn also the constellations by just projections of the celestial sphere, hung up in the same manner. And I must confess, for the bulk of learners of astronomy, I like that projection of the stars best, which includes all the stars in our horizon, and therefore it reaches to the 38 1-2 degree of southern latitude, though its center is the north-pole. This gives us a better view of the heavenly bodies, as they appear every night to us, and it may be made use of with a little instruction, and with ease, to serve for a nocturnal, and shew the true hour of the night.

But remember, that if there be any coloring upon these maps or projections, it should be laid on so thin, as not to obscure or conceal any part of the lines, figures or letters; whereas most times they are daubed so thick with gay and glaring colors, and hung up so high above the reach of the eye, that should survey and read them, as though their only design were to make a gaudy show upon the wall, and they hung there merely to cover the naked plaster or wainscot.

Those sciences, which may be drawn out into tables may also be hung up, and disposed in proper places, such as brief abstracts of history, chronology, &c. and indeed, the schemes of any of the arts or sciences may be analysed in a sort of skeleton, and represented upon tables, with the various dependences and connections of their several parts and subjects, that belong to them. Mr. Solomon Lowe has happily thrown the grammar of several languages into such tables; and a frequent review of those abstracts would tend much to imprint them on the brain, when they have been once well learned; this would keep those learned traces always open, and assist the weakness of a laboring memory. In this manner, may a scheme of scripture history be drawn out, and perpetuate those ideas in the mind, with which our daily reading furnishes us.

VIII. Every man, who pretends to the character of a scholar, should attain some general idea of most or all the sciences; for there is a certain connection among the various parts of human knowledge, so that some notions borrowed from any one science, may assist our acquaintance with any other, either by way of explication, illustration or

---

What direction does he give for coloring maps, &c.?

Who should gain some idea of most of the sciences?—Why?

proof; though there are some sciences conjoined by a much nearer affinity than others.

IX. Let those parts of every science be chiefly studied at first, and reviewed afterwards, which have a more direct tendency to assist our profession as men, or our general profession as Christians. always observing what we ourselves have found most necessary and useful to us in the course of our lives. Age and experience will teach us to judge, which of the sciences, and which parts of them, have been of greatest use, and most valuable; but in younger years, we are not sufficient judges of this matter, and therefore should seek advice from others.

X. There are three learned professions among us, namely, divinity, law and medicine. Though every man, who pretends to be a scholar or a gentleman, should so far acquaint himself with all the sciences, as not to stand amazed, like a mere stranger, at the mention of the common subjects, that belong to them; yet there is no necessity for every man of learning to enter into their difficulties, and deep recesses, nor to climb the heights, to which some others have risen. The knowledge of them in a proper measure, may be happily useful to every profession, not only because all arts and sciences have a sort of communion and connection with each other, but it is an angelic pleasure to grow in knowledge; it is a matter of honor and esteem, and renders a man more agreeable and acceptable in every company.

But let us survey several of them more particularly, with regard to the learned professions; and first, of the mathematics.

XI. Though I have so often commended mathematical studies, and particularly the speculations of arithmetic and geometry, as a means to fix a wavering mind, to produce a habit of attention, and to improve the faculty of reason; yet I would by no means, be understood to recommend to all, a pursuit of these sciences to those extensive lengths, to which the moderns have advanced them. This is neither necessary nor proper for any students but those few who

---

What parts of each science should we more particularly study and review?

What will teach us to know these parts?

How shall young persons know?

What are the three learned professions?

Who should have some general acquaintance with each of these?

Whom would Watts advise to study mathematics deeply?

Why should not persons in general study mathematics deeply? They have not time; and if they had, it

shall make these studies their chief profession and business of life, or those gentlemen whose capacities and turn of mind are suited to these studies, and have all manner of advantage to improve in them.

The general principles of arithmetic, algebra, geometry and trigonometry, of geography, of modern astronomy, mechanics, statics and optics, have their valuable and excellent uses, not only for the exercise and improvement of the faculties of the mind; but the subjects themselves are very well worth our knowledge in a moderate degree, and are often made of admirable service in life. So much of these subjects, as Dr. Wells has given us in his three volumes, entitled, 'The Young Gentleman's Mathematics,' is richly sufficient for the greatest part of scholars or gentlemen; though perhaps there may be some single treatises, at least, on some of these subjects, which may be better written, and more useful to be perused, than those of that learned author.

But a penetration into the abstruse difficulties and depths of modern algebra and fluxions, the various methods of quadratures, the mensuration of all kinds of curves, and their mutual transformation, and twenty other things, that some modern mathematicians deal in, are not worth the labor of those, who design either of the three learned professions, as the business of life. This is the sentence of a considerable man, namely, Dr. George Cheyne, who was a very good proficient and writer on these subjects. He affirms, that they are but barren and airy studies for a man entirely to live upon, and that for a man to indulge and riot in these exquisitely bewitching contemplations, is only proper for public professors, or for gentlemen of estates, who have a strong propensity this way, and a genius fit to cultivate them. "But," says he, "to own a great but grievous truth, though they may quicken and sharpen the invention, strengthen and extend the imagination, improve and refine the reasoning faculty, and are of use both in the necessary and the luxurious refinement of mechanical arts; yet having no tendency to rectify the will, to sweeten the temper, or mend the heart, they often leave a stiffness, a positiveness, and sufficiency on weak minds, which is much more pernicious to society, and to the interests of the great end

---

would probably be more injurious than useful.

How? By diverting their meditations from more useful studies.

Would it not very much strengthen and improve their minds? Probably very little, as it relates to other pursuits.

of our being, than all their advantages can recompense." He adds further concerning launching into the depth of the studies, that they are apt to beget a secret and refined pride, an over-weening and overbearing vanity, the most opposite temper to the true spirit of the gospel. This tempts them to presume on a kind of omniscience in respect to their fellow-creatures, who have not risen to their elevation. Nor are they fit to be trusted in the hands of any but those, who have acquired a humble heart, a lowly spirit, and a sober and teachable temper. See Dr. Cheyne's preface to his Essay on Health and long Life.

XII. Some of the practical parts of geometry, astronomy, dialing, optics, statics, mechanics, &c. may be agreeable entertainments and amusements to students in every profession at leisure hours, if they enjoy such circumstances of life, as to furnish them with conveniences for this sort of improvement. But let them take great care, lest they encroach upon more necessary employments, and so fall under the charge and censure of wasting time.

Yet I cannot help making this observation, that where students, or indeed any young gentlemen, have in their early years, made themselves masters of a variety of elegant problems in the mathematic circle of knowledge, and gained the most easy, neat and entertaining experiments in natural philosophy, with some short and agreeable speculations or practices in any other of the arts or sciences, they have hereby laid a foundation for the esteem and love of those, with whom they converse; they have been often guarded by this means, from the temptation of pleasures, and have secured both their own hours and the hours of their companions, from running to waste in sauntering and trifles, and from a thousand silly dialogues. Gaming and drinking, and many criminal and foolish scenes of talk and action, have been prevented, by these innocent and improving elegancies of knowledge.

XIII. History is a necessary study in the supreme place for gentlemen who deal in politics. The government of nations, and distressful and desolating events which have in all ages attended the mistakes of politicians, should be ever present to their minds, to warn them to avoid the like conduct. (Geography and chronology) which precisely inform us of the place and time where such transactions or

---

What caution does he give to those, who pursue various sciences? Study, peculiarly needful for politicians? What are the eyes of history?—Meaning of *chronology*?

events happened, are the eyes of history, and of absolute necessity in some measure to attend it.

But history, so far as it relates to the Bible, is as necessary to divines, as to gentlemen of any profession. It helps to reconcile many difficulties in scripture, and demonstates a divine providence. Dr. Prideaux's Connection of the Old and New Testament, is an excellent treatise of this kind.

XIV. Among the smaller histories, biography, or the memoirs of the lives of great and good men, has a high rank, as worthy of the perusal of every person, who devotes himself to the study of divinity. Therein we frequently find our holy religion reduced to practice, and many parts of Christianity shining with a transcendant and exemplary light. We learn there, how deeply sensible great and good men have been of the ruin of human nature, by the first apostasy from God, and how they have toiled and labored, and turned themselves on all sides, to seek a recovery in vain, till they have found the gospel of Christ an all-sufficient relief. We are there furnished with effectual and unanswerable evidences, that the religion of Jesus, with all its self-denials, virtues and devotions, is a very practicable thing; since it has been carried to such a degree of honor by some wise and holy men. We have been there assured, that the pleasures and satisfactions of the Christian life, in its present practice and its future hopes, are not the mere raptures of fancy and enthusiasm, when some of the strictest professors of reason have added the sanction of their testimony.

In short, the lives or memoirs of persons of piety, well written, have been of infinite and unspeakable advantage to the disciples and professors of Christianity, and have given us admirable instances and rules, how to resist every temptation of a soothing or a frowning world, how to practise important and difficult duties, how to love God above all, and to love our neighbors as ourselves; to live by the faith of the Son of God, and to die in the same faith, in sure and certain hope of a resurrection to eternal life.

XV. Remember, that logic and metaphysics are neces-

To whom else, is history equally necessary, as far as it relates to scripture?

What excellent work upon this subject, does Watts recommend?

What does he say of biography?—Meaning of *biography*?—of *memoirs*?

What are some of the advantages of attending to the memoirs of the eminently pious?

sary sciences, though they have been greatly abused by the scholastic writers, who have professed to teach them in former ages. Not only all students, whether they design the profession of theology, law or physic, but all gentlemen should at least acquire a superficial knowledge of them. The introduction of so many subtleties, nice distinctions and insignificant terms, without clear ideas, has brought a great part of the logic or metaphysics of the schools into just contempt. Their logic has appeared the mere art of wrangling; and their metaphysics, the skill of splitting a hair, of distinguishing without a difference, and of putting long hard names upon common things, and sometimes upon a confused jumble of things, which have no clear ideas belonging to them.

It is certain, that an unknown heap of trifles and impertinences have been intermingled with these useful parts of learning, upon which account, many persons in this polite age have made it a part of their business to throw a jest upon them; and to rally them has been esteemed a more valuable talent, than to understand them.

But this is running into a wide extreme; nor ought these parts of science to be abandoned by the wise, because some writers of former ages have played the fool with them. True logic teaches us to use our reason well, and brings light into the understanding. True metaphysics, casts a light upon all the objects of thought, by ranging every being with all the absolute and relative perfections and properties, modes and attendants of it, in proper ranks or classes, and thereby it discovers the various relations of things to each other, and what are their general or special differences, wherein a great part of human knowledge consists. And by this means, it greatly conduces to instruct us in method, or the disposition of every thing into its proper rank and class of beings, attributes or actions.

XVI. If I were to say any thing of natural philosophy, I would venture to lay down my sentiments thus;

I think, it must needs be very useful to a divine to understand something of natural science. The mere natural

---

What has conduced to bring logic and metaphysics into contempt?

What have been mingled with these useful parts of learning?

What have some considered a more valuable talent, than to understand them?—Meaning of *rally*?

Into what, does logic bring light?

What objects receive light from metaphysics?

What natural history does Watts include in natural philosophy, or natural science?

To what, is natural philosophy generally confined? To inanimate and unorganized matter.

history of birds, beasts and fishes, of insects, trees and plants, as well as of meteors, such as clouds, thunders, lightnings, snow, hail, frost, &c. in all their common or uncommon appearances, may be of considerable use to one who studies divinity, to give him a wider and more delightful view of the works of God, and to furnish him with lively and happy images and metaphors, drawn from the large volume of nature, to display and represent the things of God and religion in the most beautiful and affecting colors.

And if the mere history of these things is useful for this purpose, surely it will be of further advantage to be led into the reasons, causes and effects of these natural objects and appearances, and to know the established laws of nature, matter and motion, whereby the great God has carried on his extensive works of providence from the creation to this day.

I confess, the old Aristotelean scheme of this science, will teach us very little, that is worth knowing; but the later writers, who have explained nature and its operations in a more sensible and geometrical manner, are well worth the moderate study of a divine; especially of those, who have followed the principles of that wonder of our age and nation, Sir Isaac Newton. There is much pleasure and entertainment, as well as real profit, to be derived from those admirable improvements, which have been advanced in natural philosophy of late years, by the assistance of mathematical learning as well as from the multitude of experiments, which have been made, and are still making, in natural subjects.

XVII. This is a science, which indeed eminently belongs to the physician. He ought to know all the parts of human nature, what are the sound and healthy functions of an animal body, and what are the distempers and dangers which attend it; he should also be furnished with a large knowledge of plants and minerals, and every thing, which makes up the materia medica, or the ingredients of which medicines are made; and many other things in natural philosophy are subservient to his profession, as well as to the kindred art of surgery.

Meaning of *inanimate*?—of *unorganized*?

What science treats of beasts? Zo-ology.—Of birds? Ornithology. —Of insects? Entomology. —Of fishes? Ichthyology.—Of vegetables? Botany.

Meaning of *insect*?—of *vegetable*?

More extensive sense of the word *Zo-ology*? The science, that treats of all irrational animals.

What advantage may divines and persons in general, derive from some acquaintance with natural history?

What science eminently belongs to the physician?

XVIII. Questions about the powers and operations of nature, may also sometimes come into the lawyer's cognizance, especially such, as relate to assaults, wounds, murders, &c. I remember, I have read a trial of a man for murder by drowning, wherein the judge on the bench heard several arguments concerning the lungs being filled or not filled with water, by inspiration or expiration, &c. to all which, he professed himself so much a stranger, as did not do him any great honor in public.

XIX. But I think, no divine, who can obtain it, should be utterly destitute of this knowledge. By the assistance of this study, he will be better able to survey the various monuments of creating wisdom in the heavens, the earth and the seas, with wonder and worship; and by the use of a moderate skill in this science, he may communicate so much information of the astonishing works of God in the formation and government of this visible world, and so far instruct many of his hearers, as may assist the transfusion of the same ideas into their minds, and raise them to the same delightful exercises of devotion. "O Lord, how manifold are thy works! In wisdom, hast thou made them all! They are sought out by all that have pleasure in them."

Besides, it is worthy of the notice of every student in theology, that he ought to have some acquaintance with the principles of nature, that he may judge, how far they will go; so that he may not be imposed upon, to take every strange appearance in nature for a miracle; that he may reason the clearer upon this subject, that he may better confirm the miracles of Moses and of Christ, nor yield up his faith to any pretences to prodigies and wonders, which are either the occasional and uncommon operations of the elements, or the crafty sleights of men, well skilled in philosophy and mechanical operations, to delude the simple.

XX. The knowledge also of animal nature and of the rational soul of man, and the mutual influence of these two

---

Why should divines know something of the animal and rational nature of man?

What is that science called, which treats of the rational part of man? Mental philosophy, or intellectual philosophy.

Most famous writers upon mental philosophy? Locke, Reid, Stewart and Brown.

Best writer upon mental philosophy? Probably Watts.

Why? His writings upon this subject appear to be more correct, more practical, more useful, and much more intelligible.

What literary work seems now to be needed, more than almost any other? A treatise upon mental philosophy, much greater and better,

ingredients of our composition, upon each other, is worthy the study of a divine. It is of great importance to persons of this character and office, to judge, how far the animal powers have influence upon such and such particular appearances and practices of mankind; how far the appetites or passions of human nature are owing to flesh and blood, or to the mind; how far they may be moderated, and how far they ought to be subdued; and what are the happiest means of obtaining these ends. By this science also, we may be better informed, how far these passions or appetites are lawful, and how far they are criminal, by considering how far they are subject to the power of the will, and how far they may be changed and corrected by our watchfulness, care and diligence.

It comes also very properly under the cognizance of this profession, to be able in some measure, to determine questions, which may arise relating to real inspiration or prophecy, to wild enthusiasm, to fits of convulsion, to melancholy or phrenzy, &c. and what directions are proper to be given, concerning any appearances of this nature.

XXI. Next to the knowledge of natural things, and acquaintance with the human nature and constitution, which is made up of soul and body, I think natural religion properly takes its place. This consists of these two parts, namely, 1. The speculative or contemplative; which is the knowledge of God in his various perfections, and in his relations to his rational creatures, so far, as may be known by the light of nature. It includes also, 2. That which is practical or active, which is the knowledge of the several duties, that arise from our relation to God, and our relation to our fellow-creatures, and our proper conduct and government of ourselves. This has been called ethics or moral philosophy.

XXII. The knowledge of these things is proper for all men of learning; not only, because it teaches them to obtain juster views of the several parts of revealed religion, and of Christianity, which are built upon them, but because every branch of natural religion and of moral duty is con-

---

than any we have.

Grand sources of light upon this subject? The Bible, consciousness, observation, history and the writings of others.

Grand defect of writers upon this subject? Neglect of the Bible.

Why is the Bible the best source of information, respecting the human mind? It was inspired by Him, who knows perfectly what is in man, and relates very much to the human mind.

First part of natural religion?

Second part of natural religion?

In what, is every branch of natural religion and moral duty contained and implied?

tained, and necessarily implied in revealed religion. We may well suspect, that religion does not come from God, which renounces any part of natural duty.

Whether mankind live under the dispensation of the patriarchs or of Moses or the prophets or of our Lord Jesus Christ, still we are bound to know the one true God, and to practise all that adoration and reverence, all that love to him, that faith in his perfections, with that obedience and submission to his will, which natural religion requires. We are still bound to exercise that justice, truth and goodness towards our neighbors, that restraint and moderation of our own appetites and passions, and that regular behavior toward ourselves and all our fellow-creatures around us, which moral philosophy teaches. There is no sort of revealed religion, that will dispense with these natural obligations; and a happy acquaintance with the several appetites, inclinations and passions of human nature, and the best methods to rule and restrain, to direct and govern them, are our constant business, and ought to be our everlasting study.

Yet I would lay down this caution, namely, that since students are instructed in the knowledge of the true God, in their lectures on Christianity, and since among the Christian duties, they are also taught all the moral dictates of the light of nature, or a complete scheme of ethics, there is no absolute necessity of learning these two parts of natural religion, as distinct sciences, separate and by themselves; but still, it is of great importance for a tutor, while he is reading to his pupils these parts of the Christian religion, to give them notice, how far the light of nature or mere reason will instruct us in these doctrines and duties, and how far we are obliged to divine revelation and scripture, for clearing up and establishing the firm foundation of the one, for affording us superior motives and powers to practise the other, for raising them to more exalted degrees, and building so glorious a superstructure upon them.

XXIII. The study of natural religion, namely, the knowledge of God, and the rules of virtue and piety, as far as they are discovered by the light of nature, is needful indeed to prove the truth of divine revelation or scripture, in the most effectual manner. But after the divine authority of scripture is established, that will be a very sufficient spring,

---

Why is it not absolutely necessary to study natural religion, as a distinct science?

What study is previously necessary, in order to prove the truth of Scripture most effectually.

from whence the bulk of mankind may derive their knowledge of divinity or the Christian religion, in order to their own present faith and practice, and their future and eternal happiness. In this sense, theology is a science, necessary for every one, that hopes for the favor of God, and the felicity of another world; and it is of infinitely more importance, than any of the arts and sciences, which belong to any of the learned professions here on earth.

XXIV. Perhaps it will be thought necessary, I should say something concerning the study of the civil law, or the law of nature and nations.

If we would speak with great justness and propriety, the civil law signifies the peculiar law of each state, country or city; but what we now usually mean by the civil law, is a body of laws, composed out of the best of the Roman and Grecian laws, and which was in the main, received and observed through all the Roman dominions for about twelve hundred years.

The Romans took the first grounds of this law from what they call *the twelve tables*, which were the abridgments of the laws of Solon at Athens, and of other cities in Greece, famous for knowledge and wisdom; to which, they added their own ancient customs of the city of Rome, and the laws, which were made there. These written laws were subject to various interpretations; whence controversies daily arising, they were determined by the judgment of the learned; and these determinations were what they first called *jus civile, civil law.* All this by degrees, grew to a vast number of volumes; and therefore, the emperor Justinian commanded his chancellor Tribonian to reduce them to a perfect body; and this is called the body of the civil law.

XXV. But that, which is of most importance for all learned men to be acquainted with, is the law of nature, or the knowledge of right and wrong among mankind, whether it be transacted between single persons or communities, so far as common reason and the light of nature dictate and direct. This is what Puffendorf calls the law of nature and nations, as will appear if you consult Sect. 3. chap. III. of

---

What is the most important of all sciences?

To whom, is theology important?

What is the civil law, strictly so called?

What is it usually considered?

From what, did the Romans take the first grounds of their law?

Meaning of *jus civile*?

What law is it more important, that all should know, than the civil law?

What does Puffendorf call this law?

that most valuable folio, he has written on the subject; which is well worthy the study of every man of learning, particularly lawyers and divines, together with other treatises on the same theme.

If any question proposed relate to right and property, and justice between man and man, in any polite and civilized country, though it must be adjudged chiefly according to the particular statutes and laws of that country, yet the knowledge of the law of nature will very considerably assist the lawyer and the civil judge in determination. And this knowledge will be of great use to divines, not only in deciding cases of conscience among men, and answering any difficult enquiries, which may be proposed to them on this subject, but it will greatly assist them also in their studies relating to the law of God, and the performance or violation of it, the nature of duty and sin, reward and punishment.

XXVI. I have spoken something of the languages before; but let me here resume the subject, and put in a few thoughts about those studies, which are wont to be called philological; such as history, languages, grammar, rhetoric, poesy and criticism.

An acquaintance with some of the learned languages at least, is necessary for all the three learned professions.

XXVII. The lawyers, who have the least need of foreign tongues, ought to understand Latin. During many ages, very important matters in the law were always written and managed in that language by the lawyers, as prescriptions in medicine by the physicians, and citations of the scriptures in divinity were always made in Latin by the divines. Prayers also were ordained to be said publicly and privately in the Roman tongue. Pater-nosters and Ave-marias were half the devotion of those ages. These cruel impositions upon the people, would not suffer them to read in their own mother tongue, what was done, either to or for their own souls, their bodies or their estates. I am ready to suspect, this was all owing to the craft and policy of the priesthood and church of Rome, who endeavored to aggrandize themselves, and exalt their own profession into a sovereign tyranny, and to make mere slaves of the laity, by

---

How will a knowledge of this law assist divines?

Literal meaning of *pater-noster*? Our father.

What is the phrase used to signify? The Lord's prayer.

Meaning of *ave-Maria*? Hail, Mary.—Used to signify? An address to the virgin Mary.

keeping them in utter ignorance, darkness and dependence. And they were willing to compound the matter with the physicians and the laywers, and allow them a small share in this tyranny over the populace, to maintain their own supreme dominion over all.

But, we thank God, the world has grown somewhat wiser; and of late years, the British Parliament has been pleased to give relief from that bondage in matters relating to the law also, as in the age of the Reformation, we were delivered from saying our prayers in Latin, from being bound to read the word of God in a tongue unknown to the people, and from living in an everlasting subjection to the clergy in matters of this life and the life to come.

But to return. There are still so many forms of proceedings in judicature, and things called by Latin names in the profession of the law, and so many barbarous words with Latin terminations, that it is necessary, lawyers should understand this language. Some acquaintance also with the old French tongue, is needful for the same persons and profession, since the tenures of Lyttleton, which are a sort of Bible to the gentlemen of the long robe, were written in that language; and this tongue has been interwoven in some forms of the English law, from the days of William the Conqueror, who came from Normandy in France.

XXVIII. Physicians should be skilled in the Greek, as well as in the Latin; because their great master Hippocrates wrote in that tongue, and his writings are still of good value and use. A multitude of the names, both of the parts of the body, of diseases, and of medicines, are derived from the Greek language; and there are many excellent books of physic both in the theoretical and practical parts of it, which are delivered to the world in the Roman tongue, and of which that profession should not be ignorant.

XXIX. Such, as intend the study of theology, should be well acquainted also with the Latin, because it has been for many hundred years the language of the schools of learning. Their disputations are generally limited to that language, and many excellent books of divinity must be entirely concealed from the students, unless they are acquainted with Latin authors.

But those, that design the sacred profession of theology, should make it their labor of chief importance to be conversant with their Bibles, both in the Old and New Testa-

---

With what book, should ministers be best acquainted?

ment; and this requires some knowledge of those original languages, Greek and Hebrew, in which the scriptures were written. All that will pursue these studies with honor, should be able to read the Old Testament tolerably in the Hebrew tongue; at least, they should be so far acquainted with it, as to find out the sense of a text, by the help of a lexicon. But scarcely any man should be thought worthy of the name of a solid divine or a skilful teacher of the gospel in these days of light and liberty, unless he has pretty good knowledge of the Greek; since all the important points of the Christian religion are derived from the New Testament, which was first written in that language.

XXX. As for the Syriac and Arabic tongues, if one divine in thirty or in three hundred, travel far into these regions, it is enough. A few learned men skilled in these languages, will make sufficient remarks upon them for the service of the whole Christian world; which remarks may sometimes happen to be of use to those divines, who are unacquainted with them in reading the Bible. But the advantage of these tongues is not of so great importance, as it has been too often represented. My reader will agree with me, when he considers, that the chief uses of them are these.

The Arabic is a language which has some kindred and affinity to the Hebrew, and perhaps we may now and then guess at the sense of some uncommon and doubtful Hebrew word, which is found but once or twice in the Bible, by its supposed affinity to the Arabic. But whatsoever conjectures may be made by some kindred of a Hebrew word to an Arabic root, yet there is no certainty to be gathered from it; for even words of the same language, which are undoubtedly derived from the same theme or primitive, will give us but very doubtful and sorry information concerning the true sense of kindred words, which spring from the same root.

Let me give a plain instance or two of this uncertainty. The word *strages* signifies slaughter; *stratum* is Latin for a bed; *stramen* is straw; and *stragulum* is a quilt or coverlet. They are all drawn and derived from *sterno*, which signifies to throw down, to kill, or to spread abroad. Let the critics say, what certain sense they could put upon either of those four words by their mere cognation with

---

Foreign languages, most important for ministers to know?—Why? Why should a minister know Greek, better than Hebrew? What proportion of ministers should know Syriac and Arabic?

each other, or their derivation from one common verb. Again, who could tell me the certain meaning and precise idea of the word *honest* in English, and assure me, that it signifies a man of integrity, justice and probity, though it is evidently derived from *honestus* in Latin? whereas *honestus* has a very different idea, and signifies a man of some figure in the world, or a man of honor. Let any man judge, then, how little service toward explaining the Hebrew tongue can be furnished from all the language of Arabia. Surely a great part of the long, learned fatigues and tiresome travels of men through this country, is almost vain and useless, to make the Hebrew Bible better understood.

As for the Syriac language, it is granted, there may be some small advantage drawn from the knowledge of it; because there is a very ancient translation of the New Testament in that tongue; and perhaps this may sometimes give a proper and apposite meaning to a difficult and doubtful text, and offer a fair hint for recovering the true meaning of the scripture from the perverse glosses of other writers. But there are several commentators and lexicographers, who have been acquainted with the Syriac language, and have given us the chief of these hints in their writings.

And after all, since none of these assistances can yield us a sufficient proof of a true interpretation, and give us the certain sense of a text, who would be persuaded to waste any great number of his better hours in such dry studies, and in labors of so little profit?

XXXI. The Chaldean language indeed is much nearer to the Hebrew; and it is proper for a divine to have some acquaintance with it, because there are several verses or chapters of Ezra and Daniel, which are written in that language; and the old Jewish targums or commentaries, which are written in the Chaldean tongue, may sometimes happen to cast a little light upon a doubtful scripture of the Old Testament.

But it must still be owned, that the knowledge of the Eastern tongues does not deserve to be magnified to such a degree, as some of the proficients in them have indulged; wherein they have carried matters beyond all reason and justice, since scarcely any of the most important subjects of the gospel of Christ and the way of salvation, can gain any advantage from them.

XXXII. The art of grammar comes now to be men-

From what languages, does Watts say that the doctrines of the gospel derive scarcely any advantage?

tioned. It is a distinct thing from the mere knowledge of the languages; for all mankind are taught from their infancy to speak their mother tongue, by a natural imitation of their mothers and nurses, and those who are round about them, without any knowledge of the art of grammar, and the various observations and rules that relate to it. Grammar, indeed, is nothing else but rules and observations drawn from the common speech of mankind in their several languages; and it teaches us to speak and pronounce, to spell and write, with propriety and exactness, according to the custom of those in every nation, who are or were supposed to speak and write their own language best. Now it is a shame for a man to pretend to science and study in any of the three learned professions, who is not in some measure acquainted with the propriety of those languages, with which, he ought to be conversant in his daily studies, and more especially in such, as he may sometimes be called upon to write, as well as read.

XXXIII. Next to grammar, we proceed to consider rhetoric. Now rhetoric in general is the art of persuading, which may be distinguished into these three parts, namely, 1. Conveying the sense of the speaker to the understanding of the hearers in the clearest and most intelligent manner, by the plainest expressions and the most lively and striking representations, so that the mind may be thoroughly convinced of the thing proposed. 2. Persuading the will effectually to choose or refuse the thing suggested and represented. 3. Raising the passions in the most vivid and forcible manner, so as to set all the soul and every power of nature at work, to pursue or avoid the thing in debate.

To attain this end, there is not only a great deal of art necessary in the representation of matters to the auditory, but also in the disposition or method of introducing these particular representations, together with the reasons, which might convince, and the various methods, which might persuade and prevail upon the hearers. There are certain seasons, wherein a violent torrent of oration in a disguised and concealed method, may be more effectual, than all the nice forms of logic and reasoning. The figures of interrogation and exclamation, have sometimes a large place and happy effect in this sort of discourse; and no figure of

---

How does he define Grammar? General definition of rhetoric? Three principal things, to be accomplished by rhetoric? To instruct, persuade and inflame.

speech should be wanting here, where the speaker has art enough happily to introduce it.

There are many remarks and rules laid down by the teachers of this art, to improve a young genius in those glorious talents whereby Tully and Demosthenes acquired that amazing influence and success in their own respective ages and nations, and that immortal fame through all nations and ages. And it is with great advantage, these rules may be perused and learned. But a happy genius, a lively imagination and warm passions, together with a due degree of knowledge and skill in the subject to be debated, and a perpetual perusal of the writings of the best orators, and hearing the best speakers: will do more to make an orator, than all the rules of art in the world, without these natural talents and this careful imitation of the most approved and happiest orators.

XXXIV. Now you will presently suppose, that pleaders at the bar have great need of this art of rhetoric; but it has been a just doubt, whether pleading in our British courts of justice, before a skilful judge, should admit of any other aid from rhetoric, than that which teaches to open a cause clearly, and spread it in the most perspicuous, complete and impartial manner, before the eyes of him that judges; for impartial justice being the thing which is sought, there should be no artifices used, no eloquence or powers of language employed, to persuade the will, or work upon the passions, lest the decisive sentence of the judge should be biassed or warped into injustice. For this reason, Mr. Locke would banish all pleaders in the law for fees, out of his government of Carolina, in his posthumous works; though perhaps that great man might possibly be too severe, in so universal a censure of the profession.

XXXV. But the case is very different with regard to divines. The eloquence of the pulpit, beyond all controversy, has a much larger extent. Their business is not to plead a cause of right and wrong before a wise and skilful

---

What orators have acquired immortal fame though all nations and ages?

Advantage of rules in rhetoric? To avoid what is bad, to select what is good, and to express and arrange it in the best manner.

What will do more to make an orator, than all the rules of art?

To which, is eloquence most needful, a minister or a lawyer?

Why is eloquence very desirable in a minister?

Why should a lawyer have some eloquence? To keep the attention fixed upon the subject.

Why is it not desirable, that a lawyer should be very eloquent? Judge and jury are not so likely to see the truth by the glare of great eloquence, as by more calm and steady light.

judge, but to address all the ranks of mankind, the high and low, the wise and the unwise, the sober and the vicious, and persuade them all to persevere in virtue with regard to themselves, in justice and goodness with regard to their neighbors, and piety towards God. These are affairs of everlasting importance; and most of the persons, to whom these addresses are made, are not wise and skilful judges; but are influenced and drawn strongly to the contrary side, by their own sinful appetites and passions, and bribed or biassed by the corrupt customs of the world.

There is, therefore, a necessity not only of a clear and faithful representation of things to men, in order to convince their judgment, but of all the skill and force of persuasion, addressed to the will and the passions. So Tully addressed the whole senate of Rome; and Demosthenes, the Athenian people, among whom, were capacities and inclinations of infinite variety; and therefore, these orators made use of all the lightning and thunder, all the entreaties and terrors, all the soothing elegances and the flowery beauties of language, which their art could furnish. Divines in the pulpit have much the same sort of hearers; and therefore, they should imitate those ancient examples. The understanding indeed ought to be first convinced, by the plainest and strongest force of reasoning. But when this is done, all the powerful motives should be used, which have any just influence upon human nature; all the springs of passion should be touched, to awaken the stupid and the thoughtless into consideration, to penetrate and melt the hardest heart, to persuade the unwilling, to excite the lazy, to reclaim the obstinate, and reform the vicious part of mankind, as well as to encourage those, who are humble and pious, and to support their practice and their hope. The tribes of men are sunk into so fatal a degeneracy, and dreadful distance from God, and from all that is holy and happy, that all the eloquence which a preacher is master of, should be employed, in order to recover the world from its shameful ruin and wretchedness, by the gospel of our blessed Savior, and restore it to virtue and piety, to God and happiness, by the divine power of this gospel. O may such glorious masters of sacred oratory never be wanting in the pulpits of Great Britain!

When should ministers exert their utmost eloquence? When they would persuade others to act according to acknowledged truth.

When should they be more cool and deliberate? When they would instruct and convince.

XXXVI. Shall I now speak something of my sentiments concerning poesy?

As for books of poesy, whether in the learned or in the modern languages, they are of great use to be read at hours of leisure, by all persons, that make any pretence to good education or learning; and that for several reasons.

1. There are many couplets or stanzas written in poetic measures, which contain a variety of morals or rules of practice. relating to the common prudentials of mankind, as well as to matters of religion; and the poetic numbers, or rhyme, if there be any, add very considerable force to the memory.

Besides, many elegant and admirable sentiments or descriptions of things, which are found among the poets, are well worth committing to memory; and the particular measures of verse greatly assist us in recollecting such excellent passages, which might sometimes raise our conversation from low and groveling subjects.

2. In heroic verse, but especially in the grander lyrics, there are sometimes such noble elevations of thought and passion, as illuminate all things around us, and convey to the soul most exalted and magnificent images and sublime sentiments. These furnish us with glorious springs and mediums, to raise and aggrandize our conceptions, to warm our souls, to awaken the better passions, and to elevate them even to a divine pitch, and that for devotional purposes. It is the lyric ode, which has shown to the world some of the happiest examples of this kind; and I cannot say but this part of poesy has been my favorite amusement above all others.

And for this reason it is, that I have never thought the heroic poems, Greek, Latin or English, which have obtained the highest fame in the world, are sufficiently diversified, exalted or animated. for want of the interspersion of now and then an elegiac or a lyric ode. This might have been done with great and beautiful propriety, where the poet has introduced a song at a feast, or the joys of a victory, or the soliloquies of a divine satisfaction, or the pensive and despairing agonies of distressing sorrow. Why should that, which is called the most glorious form of poesy, be

---

Who should read poetry?

First reason for reading poetry?—second?—third?—fourth?

What objection does Watts make to the most famous heroic poems?

Meaning of *heroic poem*? A poem that celebrates the achievements of heroes?

Meaning of *achievement*?

bound down and confined to such a long and endless uniformity of measures, when it should kindle or melt the soul, swell or sink it into all the various and transporting changes, of which human nature is capable?

Cowley, in his unfinished fragment of the Davideis, has shown us this way to improvement; and whatever blemishes may be found in other parts of that heroic essay, this beauty and glory of it ought to be preserved for imitation. I am well assured, that if Homer and Virgil had happened to practise it, it would have been renowned and glorified by every critic. I greatly mistake, if this wise mixture of numbers would not be a further reach of perfection, than they have ever attained. Let it be remembered, that it is not nature and strict reason, but a weak and awful reverence for antiquity and of the vogue of fallible men, that has established those Greek and Roman writings as absolute and complete patterns. In several ages, there have been some men of learning, who have very justly disputed this glory, and have pointed to many of their mistakes.

3. But still there is another end of reading poesy, and perhaps the most considerable advantage to be obtained from it by the bulk of mankind; and that is, to furnish our tongues with the richest and the most polite variety of phrases and words upon all occasions of life and religion. He, that writes well in verse, will often find a necessity to send his thoughts in search through all the treasure of words, that express any one idea in the same language, that so he may comport with the measures or the rhyme of the verse which he writes, or with his own most beautiful and vivid sentiments of the thing he describes. Now by much reading of this kind, we shall insensibly acquire the habit and skill of diversifying our phrases upon all occasions, and of expressing our ideas in the most proper and beautiful language, whether we write or speak of the things of God or men.

It is a pity, that some of these harmonious writers have ever indulged in any thing impure, to defile their paper, and abuse the ears of their readers, or to offend against the rules of the nicest virtue and politeness. But still, among the writings of Mr. Dryden and Mr. Pope and Dr. Young, as well as others, there is a sufficient choice in our own language, wherein we shall not find any indecency to shock the most modest tongue or ear.

What does Watts lament, as a fault of some of our harmonious writers?

Perhaps there has hardly been a writer in any nation, and I may dare to affirm, there is none in ours, who has a richer and happier talent of painting to the life, or has ever discovered such a large and inexhausted variety of description, as the celebrated Mr. Pope. If you read his translation of Homer's Iliad, you will find almost all the terms or phrases in our tongue, that are needful to express any thing that is grand or magnificent. But if you peruse his Odyssey, which descends much more into common life, there is scarcely any usual subject of discourse or thought, or any ordinary occurrence, which he has not cultivated and dressed in the most proper language; and yet still he has ennobled and enlivened even the lower subjects, with the brightest and most agreeable ornaments.

I should add here also, that if the same author had more frequently employed his pen on divine themes, his short poem on the Messiah, and some parts of his letters between Abelard and Eloisa, with that ode of the dying Christian, &c. sufficiently assure us, that his pen would have honorably imitated some of the tender scenes of penitential sorrow, as well as the sublimer odes of the Hebrew psalmist; and perhaps discovered to us, in a better manner, than any other translation has done, how great a poet sat upon the throne of Israel.

4. After all that I have said, there is yet a further use of reading poesy, and that is, when the mind has been fatigued with studies of a more laborious kind, or when it is in any way unfit for the pursuit of more difficult subjects, it may be as it were unbent, and repose itself a while on the flowery meadows, where the muses dwell. It is a very sensible relief to the soul, when it is over-tired, to amuse itself with the numbers and the beautiful sentiments of the poets; and in a little time, this agreeable amusement may recover the languid spirits to activity, and more important service.

XXXVII. All this I propose to the world, as my best observations about reading of verse. But if the question were offered to me, "Shall a student of a bright genius never divert himself with writing poesy?" I would answer, "Yes, when he cannot possibly help it." A lower genius

---

What English poet does Watts consider as having the happiest talent for painting and description?

When would Watts have a student write poetry?

What may be the advantage of a student's writing poetry, even when he can help it? It may conduce to fire his genius, to wing his imagination, to improve his taste, and give him a better command of language.

Grand advantage of improving his

in mature years, would heartily wish, that he had spent much more time in reading the best authors of this kind, and employed much fewer hours in writing. But it must be confessed, or supposed at least, that there may be seasons, when it is hardly possible for a poetic soul to restrain the fancy, or quench the flame, when it is hard to suppress the exuberant flow of lofty sentiments, and prevent the imagination from this sort of style or language. That is the only season, I think, wherein this inclination should be indulged; especially by persons, who have devoted themselves to professions of a different kind; and one reason is, because what they write in that hour, is more likely to carry in it some appearances above nature, some happy imitation of the dictates of the muse.*

XXXVIII. There are other things besides history, grammar and languages, rhetoric and poesy, which have been included under the name of philological knowledge; such as, an acquaintance with the notions, customs, manners, tempers, polity, &c. of the various nations of the earth, or the distinct sects and tribes of mankind. This is necessary, in order to understand history the better; and every man who is a lawyer or a gentlemen, ought to obtain some acquaintance with these things, without which, he can never read history to any great advantage; nor can he maintain his own station and character in life with honor and dignity, without some insight into them.

XXXIX. Students in divinity ought to seek a larger acquaintance with the Jewish laws, polity, customs, &c. in order to understand many passages of the Old Testament and the New, and to vindicate the sacred writers from the reproaches of infidels. An acquaintance also with many

---

poetic taste? It will enable him to read with more pleasure and profit, the best poems in our language, especially the poetic parts of the Bible.

What passages of poetry are most worthy of being committed to memory? Those that are best suited to direct the conduct, and fit the soul for heaven.

What poem in our language, has probably more such passages than any other? Young's Night Thoughts.

Heathen sense of the noun *muse*?—philosopic *sense*?

Meaning of *polity*?

Literal meaning of *critic*? A judge.

What is criticism? The art of judging.

To what, is the word more generally applied? To judging literary productions, and to the fine arts.

What are the fine arts? Those arts, which relate in a great measure, to ornament and eloquence.

What are the other arts called?

---

* The muse in the ancient heathen sense is supposed to be a goddess but in the philosophic sense it can mean no more than a bright genius with a warm and strong imagination, elevated to an uncommon degree.

of the Roman and Grecian affairs is needful, to explain several texts of scripture in the New Testament, to lead sincere inquirers into the true and genuine sense of the evangelists and apostles, and to guard their writings from the unreasonable cavils of men.

XL. The art of criticism is reckoned by some as a distinct part of philology; but it is in truth nothing else, but a more exact and accurate knowledge or skill in the other parts of it, and a readiness to apply that knowledge upon all occasions, in order to judge well of what relates to these subjects, to explain what is obscure in the authors which we read, to supply what is defective, and amend what is erroneous in manuscripts or ancient copies, to correct the mistakes of authors and editors in the sense or the words, to reconcile the controversies of the learned, and by this means, to spread a juster knowledge of these things among the inquisitive part of mankind.

Every man, who pretends to a learned profession, if he does not rise to be a critic himself in philological matters, should be frequently conversing with those books, whether dictionaries, paraphrases, commentaries or other critical works, which may relieve any difficulties he meets with, and give him a more exact acquaintance with those studies, which he pursues.

And whenever any person has arrived at such a degree of knowledge in these things, as to furnish him well for the practice of criticism, let him take great care, that pride and vanity, contempt of others, with inward wrath and insolence, do not mingle with his remarks and censures. Let him remember the common frailties of human nature, and the mistakes, to which the wisest man is sometimes liable, that he may practise this art with due modesty and candor.

The useful arts, mechanical arts or trades.

Which are most important?

What caution does Watts give to critics?

Proper business of a critic? To point out and explain the excellences and imperfections of what he examines.

Into what capital faults are critics in danger of falling? Flattery or severity.

Miscellaneous Questions, No. VI.

What effect upon the judgment, have hurry, pertubation and confusion?

What if the memory be too much crowded?

For what points, should we not indulge religious zeal?

Greatest improvement in schools, since the days of Watts?

To what, should scoffers at the Bible, lay aside all pretence?

Grand advantage of conversing with equals?

Meaning of *mental philosophy*?

Grand advantage of improving poetic taste ?

Into what, does bright genius often betray its possessor ?

Why is the greater part of Proverbs hard to be remembered ?

In proportion to what, should always be our assent ?

Most distinguished writers upon mental philosophy ?

Advantages of a student's sometimes writing poetry ?

With what, are the memories of most persons filled ?

Why may there be a great many degrees of assent ?

Advantage of conversing with inferiors ?

What passages of poetry are most worthy of being committed to memory ?

What word is often used to signify the faculties of retention, recollection and storing up ideas in the mind ?

What word signifies the art of persuasion ?

How should we proceed in studying a science, when we have learnt a short compendium ?

Meaning of *memorize* ?

How may we avoid forgetting and losing the greater part of our most valuable mental acquisitions ?

What direction concerning assent can hardly be too often repeated ?

In what studies, are diagrams and other visible representations peculiarly useful ?

To what extent, have Demosthenes and Cicero acquired immortal fame ?

What word signifies committing to memory ?

What bodily organ seems always to be affected, when ideas are acquired ?

Into what, should we not plunge, immediately after attending upon instruction ?

For what purpose, has God given reason to every man ?

Of what does Zoology treat ?

To which, is eloquence most needful, a minister or a lawyer ?

Why did Watts suppose the existence of animal spirits ?

Why should not children be taught wholly by way of sport and play ?

Why should we not promise never to change our opinion ?

Of what, does ornithology treat ?

Why is eloquence very desirable in a preacher ?

Grand direction for improving every faculty ?

Present state of infant schools, 1832 ?

What are some of the things to be considered in ascertaining the causes of effects ?

Meaning of *entomology* ?

Why is some eloquence desirable in a lawyer ?

Proper business of a critic ?

From what faculty of the mind, does Watts say, that all the others draw all their beauty and perfection ?

What if we scarcely ever use our memories ?

If we would remember new words or things, with what, should we associate them ?

What are to be considered, when we would ascertain what are the causes of certain effects ?

Meaning of *ichthyology* ?

Why is it not desirable that a lawyer should be very eloquent ?

Of what, is memory the storehouse ?

Why should not some things be memorized, merely to strengthen the memory ?

Which should be learnt first, things, or their names ?

How may we often recover an absent idea ?

What parts should we omit, when we begin to learn a science ?

Meaning of *botany* ?

Mention some reasons for attending to poetry ?

What is the consequence of a preacher's reading his sermons badly ?

Why should things and their names be learnt nearly at the same time ?

How do most people come by their opinions ?

Of what, must we take a survey, in order to judge of any part of a science ?

END.

Published by

Facsimile Publisher
Ashok Vihar, Delhi-110052 (India)
Website: www.facsimilepublishers.com

Distributed by

Gyan Books Pvt. Ltd.
5, Ansari Road, Daryaganj, New Delhi-110002 (India)
E-mail: books@gyanbooks.com, Website: www.gyanbooks.com

9 789333 140300